The Way, the Truth and the Light

The Way, the Truth and the Light

By Hua-Ching Ni

SevenStar Communications
SANTA MONICA. CALIFORNIA

Thanks and appreciation to Suta Cahill and Janet DeCourtney for typing, editing and desktop publishing this book.

SevenStar Communications Group, Inc.
1314 Second Street
Santa Monica, California 90401

The paper used in this publication meets the minimum requirements of the American National Standard for Information Sciences Permanence of Paper for Printed Library Materials, ANSI 239.48-1984.

First Printing July 1993

Library of Congress Cataloging-in-Publication Data

Ni, Hua-Ching.
    The way, the truth, and the light / by Hua-Ching Ni.
        p.   cm.
        Includes index.
    ISBN 0-937064-56-4 (pbk. : alk. paper) : $14.95
    ISBN 0-937064-67-X (hardcover : alk. paper) : $22.95
    1. Spiritual life --Taoism   I. Title
    BL1923.N573 1993   92-50543
    299'.51444--dc20   CIP

*Dedicated to those who value
nurturing their own inner light
and also know to use this inner light
to light up the world.*

To female readers,

According to natural spiritual teaching, male and female are equally important in the natural sphere. This is seen in the diagram of Tai Chi. Thus, discrimination is not practiced in our tradition. All my work is dedicated to both genders of human people.

Wherever possible, constructions using masculine pronouns to represent both sexes are avoided; where they occur, we ask your tolerance and spiritual understanding. I hope that you will take the essence of the teaching and overlook the superficiality of language. Gender discrimination is inherent in English; ancient Chinese pronouns do not have differences of gender. I wish that all of you achieve above the level of language or gender.

Thank you, H. C. Ni

Contents

Prelude   i
The Teaching of the Integral Way   ii
Preface   iii

1. The Light Was Born 1

2. Informal Teaching is of Greater Service Than Formal 6

3. Through Spiritual Learning One Becomes Less, Not More 11

4. Truth is for the Developed Ones 15

5. The Highest Magic is Being Spiritually Self-Centered 21

6. The Power that Comes from Patience is Greater than the Power that Comes from Magic - the Sudden Gathered Faith 29

7. Option and Choice Offer Humans the Freedom to be Unchained from their Animal Nature 36

8. It is Not a Matter of Giving Life to Truth But Embracing the Truth of Eternal Life 47

9. The Most Worthwhile Learning is How to Cross the Torrent of Life 60

10. Spiritual Achievement Overcomes the Power of Yin and Yang 67

11. A Successful Future Lies in Preparation 74

12. Love of People 82

13. Spiritual Teaching is Undoing the Student 87

14. Do You Have a Godly Government Within Yourself? 92

15. The Opportunity for Survival is Found from Death 98

16. Spiritual Essence Needs to Live With Form 105

17. The Basic Spiritual Unity of an Individual 110

18. The Interpretation of the Precious, Wordless Teaching is Found Within Your Developed Spirit 114

19.	The Yin and Yang Pattern of Internal and External Nature 118

20.	From the Dualistic World, Know the One Truth 127

21.	Being the One-Headed Nature of Life 133

22.	New Hope 139

23.	The Childlike Heart is the Pass to Enter Heaven 143

24.	It is the Nature of Life to Love Life 151

25.	The Wild Man 155

26.	Reaching the Universal, Infinite Source of Life 166

27.	A Thousand Mile Trip Within One Step 171

28.	Harmony With the Subtle Law 175

29.	Higher Achievement is Known to the One Who is Close to It 180

30.	All Life is One Life Spirit 188

31.	Conclusion: The Evergreen Life 195

Afterword 205

The Integral Way 206

Prelude

The Subtle Essence conveyed by the teaching of the Integral Way is the deep truth of all religions, yet it transcends all religions, leaving them behind like clothing worn in different seasons or places. The teaching of the Subtle Essence includes everything of religious importance, yet it goes beyond the level of religion. It directly serves your life, surpassing the boundary of all religions and extracting the essence of them all.

The Subtle Essence as conveyed by the teaching of the Integral Way is also the goal of all sciences, but it surpasses all sciences, leaving them behind like partial and temporal descriptions of this universal Integral Truth. Unlike any partial science, the Way goes beyond the level of any single scientific search.

The Subtle Essence is the master teaching. It does not rely on any authority. It is like a master key which can unlock all doors directly leading you to the inner room of the ultimate truth. It is not frozen at the emotional surface of life. It does not remain locked at the level of thought or belief with the struggling which extends to skepticism and endless searching.

The teaching of the One Great Path of the Subtle Essence presents the core of the Integral Truth and helps you reach it yourself.

The Teaching of the Integral Way

as presented by Hua-Ching Ni

T   *stands for Truth*

A   *stands for Above*

O   *stands for Oneself*

Thus, Tao stands for
TRUTH ABOVE ONESELF.

Also,

T   *stands for Truth*

A   *stands for Among*

O   *stands for Ourselves*

Thus, at the same time, Tao stands for
TRUTH AMONG OURSELVES.

Preface

When I finished writing the *Esoteric Tao Teh Ching*, I considered that work to be the conclusion of my teaching. That was last year. In the early part of this year, I made a trip to South America in response to the search and trust of those beloved young people. I saw that I had not accomplished my work, thus I have added this book to the list of titles I offer. This book contains a story which I have cherished for many years, a story which I heard from my parents.

In this story, I did not deliberately try to associate with someone, nor try to avoid the connection, because it is unnecessary to me. My connection in spiritual teaching can be told by the following story:

Once an older man had a vineyard. He was quite well off because of his lifetime of diligent work tending the grapes. He had also raised a big family, having a number of sons who had married and had children of their own. His sons, however, did nothing but enjoy the prosperity of the old father.

When the time came of the last days of the old one, each son and daughter-in-law was hoping to receive a special favor from the old man. They believed that he had a secret treasure hidden somewhere and might tell them where it was. On the day of his passing, all the family members were gathered at the side of his death bed. The old man whispered into the ears of each lazy son, "I have hidden my treasure under the ground of the vineyard."

As soon as the funeral was over, each son went with his own family over to the vineyard, carrying their picks, plows and shovels, etc. They all began to dig the ground of the large vineyard. By doing so, almost every inch of the land was loosened. At the end of this, no one found any buried treasure, yet the digging improved the soil and brought about the greatest harvest that the vineyard had had for many years.

This story is not a hint that I am going away. Because I have not come, so neither do I go. I did not teach anything to anyone, so I do not need to stop teaching. I am just advising you that spiritual learning which leads you to work on your own well-being is more useful than a treasure which has never existed. The real treasure is your well-balanced life. Quit indulging in fantasies and stop quarreling over differences of ideology, etc. Instead, work on yourself by learning from the truth given by the wise ones.

Ni, Hua-Ching
June 1, 1992

Chapter 1

The Light Was Born

I

Once upon a time, about 2,600 years ago, there lived a teacher whose name was unknown. Because people recognized him as having lived for many generations and knew that the wisdom of his teaching surpassed time and age, they believed he was ageless and called him Ageless Teacher. That name was appropriate. The ageless truth of millions of years of human experience had been passed down to him by immortals. He was a popular teacher; many people went to him looking for answers to their personal questions. Many students wished to learn the ageless truth from him and find out the secret of how to achieve a long and happy life. Some came to him for the purpose of exploring the possibility of immortality.

As he was a developed and experienced person in many ways, he was able to understand patterns of the rise and fall of society. When competition for central leadership grew stronger, he knew that the disturbance and turmoil of war would soon follow the decline of central government and the decrease in the health of society. The wise one saw that violence would soon begin, so before the trouble started he fulfilled his duty by teaching cooperation, which would bring benefit to people instead of sacrifice brought about by competing for power and self-aggrandizement. What people did was left to their own choice. He decided to move to a rural place where peace still prevailed, and thus he traveled on his buffalo to the vast western region of the continent where there were fewer people and the over-established culture had not touched them.

Thus, long before trouble began, he was already leisurely on his way, leaving behind the turbulence where the flames of human desire were burning strongly. He went to the scarcely populated, rural West, traveling through areas where there were only occasional villages in the forest, centered around some spots of fertile land. The villages were small, usually consisting of only a few huts, and people there spoke a different language, had different customs and lived simple lives.

His intuition led him to the high land of Kun Lun, a place where there were only a few small communities scattered across the highlands. He stayed there for a long time and was respected by people for the service that he gave and for his teaching, which began to influence people. Because he followed what he taught, and from doing special practices (the Way of Organic Life), he became physically like a young boy, with a clear, pink complexion, full of vigor and energy, healthy and alert. His special practice (the Way of Unspoiled Natural Life), which came from ancient, ageless wisdom, also made him become physically very light. He could even visit high mountain peaks to meet other equally achieved beings. He and his direct students, several dozen people who stayed with him and helped him, were respected by local villagers, because they disturbed nothing but cured people of their diseases and helped them with the problems of their lives.

The Ageless Master periodically went to the mountains to visit his friends. One day he made preparations for a longer trip from which he would not return. Before leaving his students, he said to them, "After five hundred years have passed, a wise young person will come to this place searching for the teachings of the Way. The important teachings should be passed to that person, especially because he will have come from a faraway land that nobody knows much about. This is my bidding for all of you to remember." Then he departed.

The elders and the younger students stayed in the rural place for generations and continued to practice the ageless truth, which their teacher had taught them. The ageless truth is sometimes also called the Way, or the Subtle Law of the universe. It is called subtle because it is unformalized and unwritten, yet, if you call it "the Subtle Law" you are calling it "law." The Subtle Law is not enforceable by men. It can only be learned by people according to their own spiritual development. This is also why the Subtle Law is known as the Way.

A person who lives with the Subtle Law is supported by it. Living according to the Subtle Law is also called "following the Way." Thus, the Way is the Subtle Law, and the Subtle Law is the Way. The Way of Universal Nature, or the Subtle Law, is continually in expanse. Its own law is like the action of stretching a bow: the high part comes down and the low part moves up. This decreases what is too much and increases what is not enough. Thus it could be said that self-balancing is the way of universal nature. The ancient developed ones subtly recognized it. They automatically followed the Subtle

Law, because they felt that the only law in the universe is to support life. An individual whose life is devoted to spiritual awakening must see that the Subtle Law of the universe is installed in their life and be respectfully compliant with it. There is a limited range to the exercise of free will and personal inclination or interest. One must learn and develop one's free will, however one always needs to correct oneself to meet the Subtle Law. Because of the corruption of their original nature, people tend to do things differently from the Way; in their lives, they increase what is already too much and decrease what is not enough, thus they come to extremes and end up in trouble much of the time.

The Way was discovered by the ancients. They knew that the universe endures because it is in concordance with the Way. Therefore, when a person follows the Way and obeys and lives with the Subtle Way, he or she lives with universal vitality. When a person disobeys the Subtle Law and lives differently from the Way, going against the flow of universal vitality, then destruction and death approach.

In the surroundings of the highland, in all the small villages and communities everywhere, people naturally followed the Way because their lives were simple and they loved peace. Because they lived in obedience to the Subtle Law, they enjoyed peaceful, happy and long lives.

II

The Ageless Master himself had gone to stay in the higher places where no unachieved person could stand the cold and the drastically different living conditions. By the time 500 years had passed after his departure, several generations of teachers had already come and gone. At this significant time, the new generation of elder teachers gathered together to discuss the Ageless Master's bidding to pass the highest instruction to the stranger who would come from the foreign land. Because the elders had their own spiritual achievements and thus had the powers of preknowledge and premonition, they decided that it was necessary to directly contact the young person who would later come to them to learn the great Way. They used the *I Ching*, and their decision was confirmed.

Three of the elders were selected to go on a trip to look for the young sage. Although the three were old, they were light of foot. They gathered some items and started their trip west across the desert wilderness. To find him, they followed their inspiration and their own achievement and development. It was a long trip of many days duration.

They traveled at night and during the cool hours of the day, and rested during the hottest part of the day. They used the sun to guide them in the early morning and evening, and used the stars to guide their path at night, as they were accomplished in the practical knowledge of astronomy and astrology. Several nights after they began their journey, they noticed an unusual event in the heavens. Three stars were moving in the sky in such a way that their paths would meet in one spot.[1] This celestial event was obviously related to the purpose of their journey. Without discussion, the three sages traveled in the direction of the point of congruence of the three stars.

After several months of travel, the wise ones were stopped by the messengers of the local ruler, who had heard of the arrival of the sages in the land and of their search for the special child. "Our ruler wishes also to know his whereabouts," the messengers said. "After you find him, send word directly to the palace." The wise ones said, "If the stars are willing that we find him," and continued on their way, aware of the danger.

About seven days later, one of them said, "I feel that the special child must be somewhere near here, in these surroundings, but where exactly shall we search?" Another sage replied, "Last night I had a dream, a vision that showed me a small building. I would recognize it if I saw it again." The third said, "Let us rest here for several hours. I will meditate to enhance my sensitivity. It has become somewhat dull because of so much physical activity." When he came out of his meditation, he saw and felt a strong aura surrounding a modest location. They went over to it, and the sage recognized the shelter from the vision he had seen. They addressed the child's parents, bowing silently to indicate their respect and wished the family blessings. They did not need to tell the father and mother that the child would be of great influence and importance, but they instructed the parents that at age 14, the boy needed to go east

---

[1]Some say that they are planets, probably Saturn and Jupiter conjuncting Venus or a bright star.

to find his teacher. The elders bestowed their gifts of frankincense, myrrh and gold, all highly prized items with spiritual significance.[2] Then they bid farewell and left.

The boy's youth was typical of that of a carpenter's son. The parents were not wealthy, but they were respected for their integrity and hard work. The boy looked like a typical child in his village, but a few people noticed that he had great sincerity and natural spiritual piety. According to local religious custom, he visited the temples and observed the spiritual rituals. He listened to scholars and teachers discuss all types of spiritual subjects. He asked many questions, which surprised the teachers, but he did not comment upon what he heard. At age 13, he visited the main temple where the ancestors of his people were inspired by God.

At age 14, the father and mother approved that the boy make a trip to the East with a slightly older boy, his cousin. They traveled with a merchant caravan for safety. They voyaged through the southern lands on main roads, and absorbed much from seeing new territories and from the activity of people they saw on the roadside. They particularly paid attention to spiritual and religious matters of those new people. They conversed with priests, magicians and healers. They had been on the road already for several years when the cousin decided to stay and learn from spiritual teachers in the South. The young boy continued to travel north with a different group of travelers to search for the villages where the wise ones said his teacher would be found. This took him another several years. When he finally reached the village that he had been told to visit, he was met by a student of the teacher, a man who looked around 30 to 40 years old. He wore ordinary clothing and did not look particularly distinguished. After he introduced himself with a hand posture, he said, "We will find a place for you to stay." The communication was also done in a similar way. With his travelling experience, he seemed to understand him with no great difficulty. The boy thanked him and then bid his traveling companions farewell. He knew that he would be there for some time.

---

[2]Frankincense and myrrh are still used in natural medicine and present the fragrance of life. Gold represents the goal of Internal Alchemy, the attainment of the undecaying spiritual immortality.

Chapter 2

Informal Teaching
Is of Greater Service Than Formal

The young one settled down to live in the small village. He was given a small, independent hut in which to live where he was able to feel free and comfortable. The host was a family which had observed the Way for generations. A boy close to his own age, the youngest grandson, lived next door. The family provided food and other necessities for the newcomer, and they also helped him learn the language.

The villagers were genuine and natural, yet respectful, with no trace of having been schooled. Having adopted no special customs, they were simple and easy to get along with. He was impressed by how different the people of the village were than those of his homeland and where he had traveled. There were no crowded market places or temples. He also observed that they did not seem to have stonings or similar activities as public punishment. There were no government officials or soldiers around, only an informal automatic government. The whole region was safe for all people.

After resting a few days and orienting himself in his new environment, the boy had thousands of questions which he thought anxiously needed to be answered by the highest teacher. During the first several months, he worked diligently with expectation in overcoming his language problem. With the help of the host family, his progress was amazing. Months later, he was greeted by the student who had first met him and he requested: "I need to see the teacher. I have thousands of questions to ask him."

The student replied, "The teacher does not teach any more. Right now, he lives among people as an ordinary person. That is what we call achievement. To live the ordinary way is what we call achievement. He can hardly be traced. The highly achieved one keeps moving. He does not enjoy exhibiting his wisdom as high attainment. He often wanders to the deep forests and high mountains. I am now at the stage to be recognized as a teacher, and I am specifically authorized to be your mentor and teach you what I have learned."

Then the young one asked, "I would like to begin right away."

His mentor answered, "Your learning will proceed by living quietly and in a relaxed way. You can walk around the neighborhood. Nature itself is a great teacher to all of us. I will explain to you what nature has taught us and what inspired the ancient achieved ones.

"It is a training that while you walk, sit, lie and move, pay attention to your self and to your mind. From there you will dissolve the self and the mind by slowing down your thoughts and eliminating all unnecessary mental activity. Then you will be able to see yourself and the world. Pay attention to what you are feeling within yourself. Self-discovery is the first step in learning the Way."

The boy said, "I trust in God. I do not need to discover myself; I do not have a self. It is God who has the power to help people, not myself."

His mentor smiled and answered, "All that is at the nameable level are creations. Only what is at the unnameable level is the creator. Is God a creation or the creator? What is created really has no self. The beingness of everything created is an expression of the self-nature of the creator. Do you know how to know God? If God is known by a self or if God is known by no self, God and self join together as Oneness right away.

"To an individual being, no self is God, because he or she has taken God as Self, so God is selflessness. Only after becoming spiritually selfless can a person become responsive to God and all, and have the ability to respond to real problems and the real needs of people. Only a selfless mind can have true love for all others. Most people are busy-minded because they have a strong sense of themselves. They separate themselves from God either by their sense of self or their sense of God. Because they have not consciously resolved the question of what is their self, they cannot join God.

"Once self is established, God becomes only one object on the other side of the world. It is to say that when the deep self and God are established at the same time, then they can never be one. When concepts of the deep self and God are dissolved, the oneness of deep self, or the spiritual self, and God can be reached. To set God apart from people's spiritual nature is the indirect teaching of religions. To unite God and the spiritual nature of all people is the teaching of the Integral Way.

"Where there is too much external establishment, a person remains blocked from seeing and being the truth. After learning the established teaching, one is blocked even more from seeing the truth that brings peace and the reward of life."

This conversation took place mostly on the spiritual plane with the help of some language. Almost all of their other meetings were conducted in the same way. This reduced the over-eagerness of the young one, and he was encouraged not to rely too much upon language.

Weeks passed, and one day the young one returned to his mentor.

The boy said, "When I am selfless and see that God is not outside of my own spiritual nature, I am God."

The mentor said, "Yes, you are God." He then asked the boy, "You have been in the temples of your own country and those of the South. What have you learned from the teachers you have contacted?"

"Teachers in the temples in my own country follow a written book, which is the ancient tradition of my people," replied the boy. "It is mostly a code of behavior. People follow it strictly, but it seems to bring no real benefit to them. It only seems to cause inconvenience by creating a stiff life. People who follow it become more rigid than they were to begin with. This is why I am looking for a deeper truth. I have talked with the teachers in the temple, and I do not think many of them know about the truth of self or about God. God has long become only like the bit in the mouth of the horse.

"When we were in the South, we learned to pray through a special language. It took a while to learn to speak it, because it was so different. We must say all these prayers in that way. They said that it was a holy language."

The mentor said, "Please give me an example."

"What impressed me the most was a mantra that goes something like this:

"Aditya Heidyam Punyam.
Sarv Shatru Bena Shanam."

The mentor asked, "What does that mean?"

"It means, no evil will come to him who keeps the sun in his heart."

Smiling, the mentor said, "All language is holy when properly applied, not just one special language. It is all right to say mantras, but can you tell me, what is the sun?"

The boy said, "The sun is light."

The mentor said, "Right. Here, we do a different practice than just saying it; we directly cherish the light within. The light is Life. The light is God. Keeping light within will produce a power so strong that no evil will come to the person who practices it."

Then the boy said, "Can thinking produce light?"

The mentor replied, "When you think about light, there is light. Whatever you think, you are."

The boy said firmly, "Then, I am light."

The mentor said, "You are light."

Another pause, and then, the inquisitive mind of the boy asked the mentor, "But I still feel that there is something important that I would like to learn. What is the Way? The reason that I have traveled thousands of miles to come here was to search for the Way."

The mentor smiled, "The Way is the power of life."

The boy said, "What is the power of life?

The mentor said, "The power of life means that you do not need to become rich or noble in order to live a fully developed life. It also means you do not need to rob, cheat or harm others in order to have a good life. You only need to live a plain and honest life. Uprightness is the power of life."

The boy said, "It is hard for all people to remain plain and honest, but how do they attain the power of life?"

The mentor said, "The power of life is to become one with God without separating the self and other people."

The boy asked, "How do people nurture this power?"

The mentor said, "By living a simple life with independence; expecting no one to help you, but giving help to the needy. Independence and kindness are qualities to be nurtured at all times."

The boy said, "Is not the purpose of life to serve God?"

The mentor said, "The purpose of life is to be God, not in the sense of a ruler, but as a helpful and productive power of life."

The boy asked, "I have an independent, helpful spirit as the power of my life, so I am God."

The mentor said, "You are God." Then after a pause, he asked, "By the way, were you lost on the way when you traveled here?"

"No, we were not, although we had experienced some difficulty."

"Did you reach the destination by your determination and right choices?"

The boy said, "Yes, we did."

The mentor confirmed the boy again, "So you are the Way."

Yet the boy requested, "I need to learn something more distinct which can be applied to everything."

The mentor said, "You can apply this new learning to everything. The Way is known by its opposite. When a mistake occurs, the generally unnoticeable Way is recognized, because the Way can only be known by what is against the Way, just as light is known by darkness. Healthy people do not notice their well-being unless they become sick.

"The Way is known when you attract a problem to yourself. Because the Way is everywhere and always in a state of constant harmony, only when something is not right or is not suitable can lack of the Way be known. In other words, the Way is constant normalcy. When something is not normal, then the corrected normalcy is can be perceived or known. Thus, a person can know the Way from something that is not the Way."

The boy said innocently, "Then, I am on the Way."

The mentor said, "You are on the Way. The Way is nothing other than the truthful self-nature of a thing itself. It is the Way for a fish to live in water. It is to say that wrong projection enables you to see the right behavior, but that does not mean that you must do a wrong thing in order to reach the right. It means to learn the Way is to avoid mistakes in the first place."

That was the first teaching from the mentor to the boy. It was given in an informal style, because the most meaningful and useful teaching between a teacher and student is done in a direct and informal, not a stiff way.

Chapter 3

Through Spiritual Learning
One Becomes Less, Not More

The young one was wise, and when he was alone he kept thinking about what his teacher had given to him. He worked with it again and again to make sure that he had received it and learned correctly.

After he started to become more familiar with the new environment, he discovered by himself that the people in the village were not materially rich, but there was a quiet enjoyment in their lives. They were simple, quiet and attentive. They did not engage in restless activity but mostly went about their own business. The people did not communicate much verbally, but all of them seemed to have great understanding. They were not much on social manners, but they were sincere. It seemed that they were all illiterate, but they seemed wise. Although there was no ruling system in the village, everybody fulfilled their duty.

To his surprise, the boy saw people walking along the edge of a high cliff with as much confidence as if they were walking on flat land; they had no fear. Because the village was in a rural place, a fierce animal occasionally wandered in, but he observed that the people, although cautious, were not disturbed by it. That roused his curiosity, so he requested an explanation of his mentor, because the mentor was responsible for providing any answers he needed, if he knew.

He presented himself to his mentor and said, "I have continued to ponder self and God, light and power, the Way and how people go astray. I have been working on trying to simplify and unify my mind as you have instructed me. I have been working on trying to eliminate concern and lower emotion for myself. I think this is why people here live so peacefully and spontaneously. What I do not understand is why the people are not afraid on the high cliff or when the tiger comes near the village."

The mentor smiled and answered, "Fear comes from the sense of self. If in your mind you diminish the size of your life to a single being like yourself, anything that confronts you in your life will cause worry, fear or anger, and you will try to destroy anything in your way. Worry, fear and anger are products of the mind. Memory and built-up imagination come from projecting the past into the future, especially self-harming anger. This type of mental activity will weaken your natural spiritual power.

"To eliminate mental worry, emotional fear and anger, one must stay in safety and take proper care of one's self. I am saying that oneness of spiritual being can increase one's inner light and power.

"However, a student of the Way needs to learn and practice being with nature. 'Being with nature' has several meanings. The first is to enlarge and develop one's sense of being to include the vast universe and all lives so that one sees all people and all other types of life as expressions of the big natural life. You are a part of natural life. Which part of life can you call yourself? All of your life is nature. Your heart beats, your digestion, your breath, etc., all function naturally and are not under the command of the mind. Can you truly say that the entire being of your own self is not part of nature?

"Most of the time, people do the reverse of enlarging their sense of being. They mentally limit themselves and thus make their range of beingness smaller and smaller. By so doing, they push themselves into a corner where they do not enjoy the world any more, because their sense of self binds them so strongly. Once a person can dissolve or relax the sense of self and change it from being only the body, then the scope of beingness can begin to include the whole universe. The Ageless Master called this 'living beyond the bodily life.'

"The practical instruction you have to remember is that the sense of self is caused by worry and fear. If you hold yourself too tight, you will lose the healthy condition of life or not develop well. The secret of life is not to hold your life too tight by spending time worrying that the entire world will hurt you at any moment. Such a person is too sensitive and becomes weakened by the mind's activity. Set the mind aside and allow no oversensitive reaction, but release the natural spiritual power that nature endowed you with. Then there is no fear.

"People who come here to learn from us do not learn much from the verbal teachings. What they learn is the practice of fearlessness. When a person does not have fear, worry or anger, their spiritual nature is not damaged, and the entire world appears to consist of different powers and strengths. The source of true strength is the spiritual nature of the universe: God, the Light, the Way. Each of us is born with the ability to do this. However, cultural development and certain activities overemphasize tension and concern for the self. When people focus on nervousness of the mind, this mental nervousness replaces the light within. Learning to calm the mind to eliminate worry and fear, straightforwardly facing reality, and acting correctly are the best things that can be done to decrease concern for self. Doing what is right for others, when it is also right for yourself, increases your power. It is not actually that you are increasing your power, but that you are on the Way. The Way is selfless, worryless, fearless and without anger."

The boy responded, "I wish to learn the power above nature, then I can help my people who are in trouble. How can I attain my power? Then I will be different and can truly help people."

The mentor smiled and said, "You are wise in wishing to use power to help other people rather than to benefit yourself. You shall come to understand that power does not depend upon prayer or upon any performance. It depends upon your pure spirit which is fearless. As your spirit becomes stronger and your fear decreases, you will become more like the local people who have the ability to walk over fire, live next to dangerous animals and walk on the cliff. Natural spiritual power and the fearlessness that comes with it can overcome any possible problem.

"However, again I repeat, fearlessness does not mean that a person becomes violent, radical or daredevil. Fearlessness means to maintain a state of inner calm and balance, and grow the all-knowing light within. As the light grows, no matter what happens, you will not have fear.

"For example, people become afraid at night because they cannot see. There is always more fear in the darkness. On a bright day, you can see and distinguish things, and you know the right approach to take. The light makes your vision steady and clear. Thus, fearlessness comes with having light. You could say that it is similar to having courage, but there is a difference.

"If you live a life of few cares, then you will live better. Learn to be above all useless concern, but handle useful concerns by learning and practicing the Way. The Way is prudence, fearlessness, righteousness and suitability. The Way can help you accomplish your life perfectly and excellently, or at least harmlessly and with different levels of success. This is also to answer the question about your search for power. Power is not external; power is within. Power comes from the spiritual nature within. Power is not produced by any special ritual performance. There are many different symbolic postures and ceremonies that are designed to create a spiritual affect, but symbols are superficial. They are not the essence itself.

"A wise student learns 'the Way is that God, light and power are one.' Once you attain the Way within yourself, you are the Way; you are the Way of truth, the Way of power, the Way of life. The Way is power. The Way is light. The Way is truth. The Way is one with light. The Way is everything in its right order and right function. You do not need to learn God, then the light, then the truth, and then the Way. One is all. All is one, spiritually, but the one is the achievement. It is not God, the light, the truth or the Way. The one is power."

The boy received the instruction from the mentor. He knew in his sensitive young heart, which possessed a high level of great understanding, that it was not hard to understand the mentor's words, but it was hard to practice such a simple thing as fearlessness and oneness in all moments of everyday life. Yet as he lived among the simple people, he quietly and subtly learned their strength and selflessness. The new environment and culture helped him progress on his Way to practice higher instructions. It can sometimes take a long, long time to attain such power as worrylessness, fearlessness, selflessness and no anger through oneness with the high nature.

Chapter 4

Truth is for the Developed Ones

A mentor is still a student, no matter how old. While a mentor uses his or her own experience to help another spiritual student, he or she is still in the process of growth. He or she is aware that giving help to a student is just like a hen hatching her chicks; both require patience and constancy. The temperature, enthusiasm, and amount of attention provided cannot suddenly be hot and then cold. Too much heat will damage a growing life; too much cold, and the new life will not develop at all. Because he knew this, most of the time the mentor allowed the boy the freedom to do whatever he felt was right for himself. At the same time, the mentor watched his student and made himself available when needed.

On one occasion, the boy told the mentor, "I know that spiritual truth is not hard to understand, but it is hard to do. Spiritual truth can be understood in only a few days, but it takes a lifetime to be or to do the truth."

His mentor smiled. "You are right," he said. "Spiritual learning is contrary to the world's learning. In worldly learning, it is hard to understand what you are doing, but it is much easier to just do it. In other words, it takes a long process to understand a thing of the world, although it can be easy to do. On the contrary, spiritual learning is easy to know and hard to do."

"Why is that so?" asked the boy.

The mentor replied, "Spiritual learning is easy to know because the spiritual truth is already contained in our natural beingness. This is why when we meet with inspiration, the sleepy mind is easily lighted up, and the truth naturally runs through the locked shield of the mind and is easily understood. But spiritual learning is hard to achieve because it requires changing the internal flow of energy. Typically a person is accustomed to repeating certain patterns of thought and behavior which might also be called habits. The habitual internal energy flow needs to be rechanneled, but not just once. It requires willingness or desire to change and then constancy in thinking new thought patterns and performing new behavior. It is also related to being open to new positive energies and adapting to and raising one's vibrational frequency. For many people, this takes a long time, but the reward is improvement in one's personality and increased spiritual flexibility.

"On the other hand, worldly learning competes with what is natural. Sometimes worldly learning looks natural but is not; sometimes it seems necessary, but is not. Worldly learning can bring small success, but at other times, it brings big failure. Even so, we do not say that all worldly learning should stop, yet we do not encourage the development of competition with nature, which not only damages nature but also damages what we are.

"Humans can apply their creative energy according to the natural truth of the Subtle Law. If they do so, what they create will be serviceable and beneficial. The human mind is certainly capable of achieving something unnatural that competes with or defeats nature, but this is not necessarily beneficial."

The boy said, "This seems to be true, because as you said, truth comes from oneself. But in that case, then I am the truth. I do not doubt it. Do you think that people will accept me as the truth?"

The mentor said, "There are two levels of truth. There is absolute truth and relative truth. You might ask me, 'Is truth one?' Yes, truth is one, but when it comes to the relative sphere, the truth must be described in relative terms and relative expressions, just as a coin always has two sides. Non-verbal truth is absolute truth. It is the light within the human mind of wise people."

"How do I handle both spheres of the truth?" asked the boy.

The mentor smiled and said, "We always need to pay attention to follow the absolute truth, not the relative truth. If we do not follow the absolute truth well, we go against our own spiritual nature and become untruthful to the universal nature, which is the same as our own self-nature. However, once truth is verbalized, conflict arises because of the ways in which the verbal expression is perceived. Words always have two sides. This is why we must apply gentleness, softness and weakness in argument; this allows us to remain flexible for when we better perceive the truth during the unfolding knot of a conflict in the process of discussion. This is why we must be flexible enough to allow for adjustment when we face a relative situation.

"Fundamentally, do not consider the truth of the relative sphere as absolute. That truth is on a level of being that can be expressed in different ways.

"Ordinary people consider verbal truth to be absolute, and this causes them to be unyielding. When it comes to the understandings of the mind, they should seriously drop mentalization and practice following the subtle truth.

"It need not be recognized as a problem that people have different understandings or different views of the same thing. Such is the nature of the mind. It takes patience to accept and be open to different expressions or outlines of the truth rather than always going down the same blind alley, insisting that one's belief is superior to another's. Different expressions of the same truth can easily bring a different understanding; this is why people should avoid insisting upon any one terminology or system of thought. People also become confused because different understandings of the truth lead to different expressions. It is not the same final truth which is different, especially spiritually. People compromise or even sacrifice themselves for a relative truth or for different expressions of that truth. In depth, the absolute truth cannot be sacrificed. Somebody's supposed "absolute truth" is only a personal concept or thought that is not even connected with the absolute truth. It is merely a betrayal of the mind.

"People even become warlike when an important point is connected with their personal interest and considered as the absolute truth. They are unable to see the balanced co-existence where all points join together to express one truth. To compromise is to join together with people in a positive way; it is not a betrayal or sacrifice of the high, absolute truth. The absolute truth of beingness is inherent in healthy conditions of harmony. Compromise only sacrifices the relative truth which separates people. The absolute truth always remains neutral. Thus, in an argument or conflict, people can compromise.

"This is to say, when an important point connected with people's personal interest and considered by themselves to be absolute truth is questioned, they usually will not compromise but will defend themselves or attack one another. This is a betrayal of oneself and others, and it seriously obstructs the potential to change from personal perception to objective truth.

Truth, at a certain stage, is balanced co-existence in which all points and people are joined together harmoniously.

"When it comes to the relative sphere of the truth, people forget how to practice flexibility, how to compromise and how to exercise their understanding. This comes with lack of spiritual depth.

"A spiritual person always remembers that individual attainment is much higher than any truth that can be put into words and communicated in different ways to different people. People all have different standpoints because of their level of attainment, thus they can be allowed to have different understandings of any verbal truth you might express. It is impossible for all people to attain the same growth at the same time. Understanding different levels of growth is often the key point of an argument.

"Teaching or writing can help to lay the foundation for greater understanding in ordinary circumstances. It is much harder to reach agreement when one or both sides still need a lot of education, particularly self-education and discipline. Therefore, it is always right to keep your own perception, but at the same time allow the further correction to be made to your previous perception. That attitude is a correct mental attainment. It is right to keep your own conception of the truth, your own way of stating your principles, your own understanding and attainment. However, the best way to bring your opponent to see what you see is to give the person enough time to understand you. You need to be clear about your own thoughts, and not intend to express your superiority. Be quiet and not argumentative. Be flexible, soft, gentle and constructive about the problem of truth in the relative sphere."

Then the boy said, "I greatly appreciate your instruction. It seems to me that I need power more than anything else, even more than the truth which I can teach to help my people."

The mentor smiled and answered, "The Way is power. It is the power to live honestly and unadorned. The Way is the power to be upright. It is power to take less and help more. It is power to face pressure and misunderstanding. The Way is the power to yield in conflicts, and the power to tolerate insults. The Way is the power to accept disfavor and to withdraw from a fight. The Way is the power to provide a normal life.

"The power you admire in your mind must be spiritual. Power is natural. You do not need to do anything to attain power.

"Ordinary people understand 'power' differently; they mistake fear for 'power.' For example, he fears somebody, then he creates the power of the other person. All those fearful powers in society or the mind are created by darkness. Darkness can create fear of others. People misunderstand their fear as power. They think that fear is natural power. This is an unhealthy way of thinking. The healthy mind understands that the power which comes from nature does not use fear to create or recognize power. Any power which is created by fear, or recognized by the subjective side which has fear, is untruthful power.

"Now, I would like to know what kind of power you are interested in."

The boy answered unhesitatingly, "Surely I am not looking for any power created by fear that others might have of me. I also reject the fear of darkness created by leaders of society or the culture. I also will hold fearlessness toward other people's darkness or any power which society will try to impose on me. I am looking for natural power."

The mentor said, "Can you be more specific? Are you talking about magic power?"

The boy nodded his head, "Yes, I admire magic power. I need that type of power to help my people, to deliver my people from the bitterness of their suffering and from their darkness."

The mentor smiled and said, "People of ordinary society think we are a type of magician that deserves respect. We do not refuse what people think of us, but we also do not accept it. We only know one truth; there are two types of magic: small magic and big magic."

The boy asked, "Please, I would like to know what is small magic and what is big magic."

"Small magic," replied his mentor, "is doing something that makes people astonished at your capability, such as sowing some seeds in a pot, covering the pot with a cloth, and in a few minutes to have the flowers blossom.

"Big magic is related to life and death. Life itself is magic. After death, you rise again. After death, you do not become smoke, but you can shape yourself with your power, and walk again among people.

"Learning small magic, which can startle people momentarily, stirs them up and makes them interested in seeing you. We do not appreciate that level very much.

"For generations our teachers have studied, practiced and devoted themselves to the main subject of the magic of life and death. What we are interested in is the immortality of life. What kind of magic are you interested in?"

The boy pondered a while, because although he had always been impressed by small magic, he never had any chance to learn big magic. Soon he answered, "I would like to learn both. Something that can make people interested and marvel, and something that can truthfully help me if I meet danger."

The mentor said, "I cannot teach you any small magic, but I can refer you to someone who can. If you are interested in big magic, you need to wait until the right time. We shall go to see our highly achieved teacher for that, or our teacher will instruct me, the humble beginner, to teach you such truth."

This meeting brought joy and happiness to the boy, because although he was wise, he was still a boy.

Chapter 5

The Highest Magic is Being Spiritually Self-Centered

The young one was happy about receiving the promise to fulfill his personal wish to learn magic. At that time, in that part of the world, everyone admired and respected magic, except the militant rascals who relied on the position of rulership. People had developed different kinds of magic to meet different needs and anxieties. Some magic could make a person suddenly become rich and powerful and greatly respected. Even the nobles were in awe of a person who could perform magic, yet this type of motivation was not in the boy at all. He only thought of his people who were in trouble. Because his people were lost, he wished to learn something that would help deliver them from the misery of being a conquered race. He was excited by the opportunity to learn unusual capabilities, and he was prepared to spend a long time learning them. No matter how long it would take or how much trouble it would be, he looked forward to the opportunity and the achievement of these special capabilities.

At their next meeting, the mentor asked, "I now know your interest in learning magic. Popular magic is the smallest of small magic. It is not difficult to learn. I have told you that there are two types of magic: big magic and small magic. Today I would like to tell you something about them. Big magic is the transformation of life and death. To us, there is no death. Death is just a superficial transformation of reality from one stage of life to another. A person who knows big magic is ready for a new life after physical death. In three to seven days, someone who is highly achieved can get rid of the body in the snap of a finger and become a totally spiritualized new life being. That is what we call big magic.

"Small magic is an everyday matter. Waking up each day from sleep is magic. Each morning, after we get up, everything that happens to us is magic, then we go to sleep again in the evening. Are your expectations of big magic and small magic what I have described or are they the common magic which you can find in the street? Whatever the case, I promise that your wish to learn magic will be fulfilled since you are our honored guest."

The boy said, "No, I am a student. I have come here to learn. To me, magic is the performance of wonders, of miracles that untrained people cannot do."

The mentor smiled and said, "That is all right, but can you be more specific about what you wish to learn? There are thousands of kinds of that type of magic."

The boy thought it over but could not answer. His mentor continued, "Do not worry. Around 200 to 300 miles from here is a town much larger than this village. Each month on the fifteenth day, during the full moon, they have a market, and magicians and merchants come to gather there. They have it on that day because some people need to travel day and night to get there, so they make use of the moonlight. That market has been going on for many generations. I think you might be interested in going to the next one[1] to see how the magicians there inspire you. See if there is something you really desire to learn from them.

"This coming market will be on the Autumn Moon, so it will be the biggest gathering of magicians and merchants from far away, even from other provinces. You shall have a great opportunity to see wonders. The only thing is that you must go there with the villagers. They have things to sell such as deer horns, herbs and furs. I myself have not gone to the market for over thirty years. That is no longer a great enjoyment to me, but I promise you, it will be great enjoyment for you and others. I will entrust the elders with your care and safety. Do not worry, they are all good, trustworthy people. But when you come back, try to let me know your real interest."

After some time, preparations began for the journey to the big festival. People were excited about going to the market for trading, and some younger people wanted to go just for fun. Quite a number of people, old and young, many men and a few women, prepared to go with their donkeys and mules loaded with different goods. The day was long, with lots of bright light from the sun and nights were well lit by the moon. The journey was happy and light.

---

[1] The ancient type of market was held in the open air in a location near main travel routes.

When they approached the market, it was amazing to see people wearing different clothing and speaking different languages. Many types of food and other things were displayed on the ground and arranged in different rows. With each step there was another novelty. The young boys and girls were delighted with all the different things they saw. The village elders were busy with the trading, but the boys had time to watch all kind of shows.

One special street had many tents with signs on them. Magicians, witch doctors and medicinal people were healing in the tents, flocked by people with different needs. Some traded herbs, others were taking care of the belongings and so forth.

In another place a circle of people was packed so tightly around something that he could not see through them, which piqued the boy's curiosity. Just like all the other people, pushing and crawling, he managed to penetrate the human wall. In the center of the circle was a magician. A huge pot was supported by some stones which was above a big fire. The pot was full of oil so hot that it was smoking. The magician threw a small green branch from a tree into the oil; you could only hear a hissing sound as the object was rapidly fried in the oil.

The magician rolled up his sleeves and walked around the circle, showing everybody his bare hands. No one breathed. Although there were many people, silence descended on the crowd as the magician walked toward the pot and plunged both his hands into the boiling hot oil. The crowd gasped. He kept his hands there in the hot oil for a long time, then took them out, and walked around the circle to show everybody that his hands were perfectly safe. He wiped away some remaining oil, smiled, and nodded to the crowd. This was an amazing sight to the boy. How could he do that? After a short while, the magician repeated his performance. Some people threw some money into a hat he had placed on the ground to reward him for the show. Other people did not, but the magician simply continued performing.

The human wall was alive with people coming and going, and the boy followed some of the people to a new circle to see a new show. Inside the new circle was an old man who held two long bamboo chopsticks in his hands, two feet long. Nobody knew what he would do, but everybody stood there, watching quietly. In front of all the people, the old man took the two chopsticks and gently inserted them into his two nostrils. Everybody in the crowd was nervous about that, because they did not know what he would do. Then the old man then began to push the chopsticks in; he put them quite far in, many inches. It seemed like it was one third or one fourth of the length of the chopsticks. The old man walked around to let people examine this. He let people take one out and then he put it back safely inside. The boy felt nervous about this. It created no respect in him, but he was amazed. He walked away.

Now he approached an open tent with a big group of people standing in front of it. A cow had been taken into the big circle, placed on a big piece of wood, killed and cut into eight pieces. Its head was off and you could see blood and all the internal organs were out. The magician, a small skinny person, walked into the center and bowed and addressed the audience. He pointed to the cow and had somebody from the audience come to examine the pieces. Then he put a big sheet over the pile and said an incantation. After a long moment he lifted the sheet, and the cow jumped up whole. The magician put a rope around the cow's neck and walked it around the circle in front of all the people. The boy wondered, how the man could do that, but it also created no great respect in him.

He continued on and on, looking at all the different circles of people. In one circle there was a man who showed the audience a long nail around 12" long. It was very sharp. He put the tip of the nail up to his chest and used a hammer to drive the nail into his heart. After it had gone in about four inches, he asked people in the audience to take the hammer and drive the nail in further, but nobody would do it, so he himself hit the nail until it was almost totally driven into his chest. He did not fall down and there was no bleeding. He walked around and let people examine it. He turned around so that people could see that the nail went all the way through to his back. Then he used his right hand and pulled it out. He walked around some more to let people examine him again; they could see that there was no hole and no scar. The boy marveled at this but this too failed to create any special respect or interest.

There was another circle of people standing around a magician who was in front of a young woman lying on a large blanket. The blanket was in front of a sword which had been embedded in the sand. After he said a few words, the woman suddenly began to float straight up in the air. The boy was amazed, because he had never seen anyone levitate before. She rose up several feet and then over to balance on top of the sword. Then the magician used another sharp sword to cut her into pieces which still floated in the air. Then he put the pieces in mixed up order with the hands, trunk, limbs and internal organs in a different order. The magician held the end of the blanket and, at the moment when the blanket was almost fully spread over her, shouted, "Rise!" The blanket opened up to show the beautiful young woman, who jumped up in front of the audience with a complete, attractive body and a big smile on her sweet face. The audience did not breathe freely until this moment of relief, then great excitement came with loud and long applause.

Now that he had seen all of this, and several other magic performances, the boy became less and less interested, so he went back to the street with all the tents, some with walls and others more like a canopy which was open to all four directions. Behind the tents were tethered the animals used to carry them. Some tents had horses, some had camels and others had mules or donkeys. This street was special; it was the location of all kinds of doctors. The boy was particularly interested in seeing how people could cure the sick. Some doctors did acupuncture. Others did magic healing. He stopped in front of a tent where there was a human figure cut out of several layers of linen cloth. It was flat, front and back; two dimensional. The figure itself was rather uninteresting, but what was interesting to see was that it was standing straight in the air just like a person. Both of its hands were up in the air, and it was carrying a real stone of 200 or 300 pounds. It did not have any special support; it was just standing there. This was marvelous. He went inside the stick-marked gates. There he saw a doctor and his patient, a man who had some kind of tumor on his back that had grown into a big lump about the size of a small melon. Even the healing was done somewhat like a show with several people standing around watching. The patient was on one side of the tent, sitting on a chair and facing the wall. An attendant was standing next to the patient. The doctor stood on the other side of the tent with a dry branch in one hand. On the ground, he simply drew a human figure with a lump on its back. He stopped and asked his attendants to get ready for the blood and pus which would drain from the tumor of the real person. Then, from across the room, the doctor used a small bamboo knife to draw a line that looked like an incision on the lump in the picture. On the other side of the room, the tumor opened, and blood and pus began to come out. The people all saw it, and the attendant went to help clean the wound. They cleaned it and then put some incense powder on it, and the patient thanked the doctor and happily left. The boy wondered, how could that happen? The doctor did not directly cut the patient or touch the body, because he was several yards away on the other side of the tent. He marveled at that. Then the next patient sat on the chair, this time facing the doctor. It was a person who limped because of a leg problem. This time the doctor used yellow clay which he picked up from the earth, and added to it some water from a jar. With his hands, the doctor made a small clay person by his fingers just like the lame man. Then he pulled the mis-shapen leg of the doll, and everyone in the audience could see that the lame man's leg started to shake. The doctor did it again, and the man's leg shook again. After a while, the doctor said, "We are finished now." He put the doll away, and he said to the man, "Stand up and try your leg." The man got up and walked around without showing any limp.

He then went to another tent where the doctor was a woman. People came around, and the woman drew small pictures or written words that nobody could recognize upon small pieces of cloth. It was a different kind of writing. A crowd of people came up to ask her for help. She said, "Write down your misdoings, then throw your misdoings into the stream. Let the stream carry the confession away[2] or just burn it in the air. Then, take this talisman that I have drawn for you, burn it and put the ashes in a cup of water. Then drink the water, and you will become well." This woman had gone to the market for decades and she had earned people's

---

[2] There was a stream running through the other side of the market.

trust, so she had more patients than the other doctors. Her treatment was much simpler, too.

Now, the boy went to a tent where acupuncture was practiced. Nine types of needles of different shapes and sizes were displayed on a plate. Sharp edged stones were also often used to cut certain spots of the patient's skin to take blood to cure the congestion of internal and external problems. It was done by making two shallow incisions like a cross; thus, a slightly bleeding red cross was seen on the patient. This healing technique was simple and effective.

On another street, a large number of women and a few men were crowded around the sides of the tent of a medium who channeled the spirits of people's ancestors or relatives in the shadow world. There were other people on the same street doing practices such as oracle explanation, fortune telling, etc. Among them was a medium surrounded by a group of clients. She responded to their questions and carried the communication to the entire crowd. It seemed that a group of spirits was using her body, because she spoke in different tones, voices and emotion with each person. Each of the clients seemed to catch the message clearly and threw money into the plate before walking away.

The boy watched everything. However, he did not understand the language well. He was interested in learning how to heal like the people of power, but not exactly as the woman doctor did. However, he could not directly communicate with any of the doctors because of language, so in the evening, he went to his elders and begged them to help. "I would like to contact one of the magic doctors to understand how their healing skill can be learned." There was no need to make an appointment, so they just went over and talked to her.

With the help of the elders, the magic doctor told him, "My trade was passed to us by the ancients. We have to take a serious vow. A student needs to be tested a long time, maybe several years, until the teacher says that proficiency has been achieved to accomplish the work. When you accept, you need to make a vow. Not only that, you need to declare your way of life. You need to choose poverty, or celibacy, or maim yourself in some way. Only when you have accepted one of those conditions will the teacher teach you. We learn a power that can affect people greatly. Because you have power over people, you might take money or women, so the discipline is strong. To us it is a tradition, and because we have been here for years, we are used to it. To you, a handsome boy from abroad, I am not so sure that you would like to live our type of life. We live only to serve people with a few skills and earn only enough money for our survival. We cannot earn too much or become rich. We have to follow and obey a teacher for our whole lifetime. No student can surpass the teacher; this is the tradition. This is the rule for all magic students in general. Think it over carefully." The boy said, "Some things I can do, some things I cannot do, but I really believe that this is what I want to learn. I will think it over carefully."

By the end of the market, the boy did not follow the medicinal people or the magicians, but followed the elders and went back to the village.

Chapter 6

The Power that Comes from Patience is Greater than the Power that Comes from Magic - the Sudden Gathered Faith

The young one returned to the village with mixed emotions. He did not want to see his mentor until he could decide what he wanted to learn, yet he needed assistance in clearly understanding all that he had seen. After a number of days, the boy still could not see clearly enough by himself to make a decision. He was interested in knowing how all those exceptional things were done by those special people, but at the same time, he felt certain that this was not his direction.

He was close friends with the boy from the host family, who was also a student and attendant of the mentor, although the mentor was independent and usually did not need anyone to attend to him. After having been quiet about his exciting experience at the market, he finally asked his friend, "Are those magic performances all true?"

His friend answered, "With my knowledge and small attainment, I could say that some of them have more truth than others, but all of them, whether true or untrue, are attainable only after long training in one type of knowledge and skill. Even the true ones are still on a level which controls people's senses. They make you see what they would like you to see. The way they affect you is through your eyes, ears, nostrils, taste, feeling, etc., for a certain period of time. When the performance is over, there is no more effect.

"I have been to the market many times. Once I understood this, I cultivated or trained my senses not to be controlled by anyone else. I do not think it is fun to exchange the healthy condition of my senses for the momentary control of entertainment. But you may ask your question of my father. He is the one who may be able to provide you with some advice. People in this region consider him as the most authoritative master of nature, because he requested rain from the sky during a drought and has done other similar types of service."

So the young one talked about this to the elder. The father said, "I know only a little bit of magic. If it is your interest, I will tell you what I know."

The young one said, 'Please tell me about it."

"The first magic I learned," said the father, "was to protect our dwellings. By putting a few stones in different spots of the land inside the yard and outside of the house, any intruder who comes will be confused and will not be able to achieve his purpose. I make no use of this practice here, but on one occasion when I visited a friend and was going to stay overnight, my intuition gave me a strange feeling. I told my host, 'Tonight, you may have a surprise intruder who is interested in your fortune. Please follow my advice and arrange the bench and footstools, etc. on the ground according to my instruction, and tomorrow you shall see who is there.' During the night, the intruder entered the house, but once inside, all he could feel in any direction were walls and obstacles. He kept struggling to be on his way, but he could not get back out. All night long, the thief groped in the darkness, trying unsuccessfully to find a way out, until he became exhausted and collapsed on the ground. The next morning, it was easy for the owner to catch him and turn him in to the local authority.

"The second type of magic that I know is when you are in a critical situation, such as when someone wishes to capture and harm you, it is simple to take a branch from a tree or a use rope or your own belt. Lay it out on the road and cast an incantation on it. Then, the enemy cannot go over the line, and you can walk away safely. I heard of an example of this practice. Once a magician was being chased by a group of soldiers because he had made a disrespectful statement about the ruler and was ordered to be arrested. He escaped by untying his belt and putting an incantation on it, and then put it across the road before the soldiers arrived. When the soldiers came to that point, they all saw a big river which stopped them from going any further, so they returned to the citadel and the magician escaped. The magician probably walked home holding his pants up because he had no belt!

"The first type of magic power comes from training the subtle sphere of mind. The second type of magic power comes from the subtle mind as faith responding to an emergency."

The young one requested, "May I know what was the incantation to stop the bad people?"

The elder smiled and answered, "The incantation is simple; it is just one word: 'Stop.' Incantations are different from the short effective prayers which gather energy. Incantations cast the faith of the mind. Actually, both effects are created by faith. Intuitive foreknowledge is the product of a quiet mind. Both faith and a quiet mind must work together with a disciplined life and doing the practice regularly. If one element is missing, the spiritual function is not complete.

"It is clear to me that power comes from the faith of your mind. If you have no faith, then magic does not work. I tried using the second practice to stop a nasty dog. The effect was not clear, because when I went to the tree to take a branch, the dog ran away. I cannot prove whether it was my power or whether the dog just lost interest in chasing me around.

"When I was young, I liked magic so I spent my time learning about it. In my experience, if I am qualified to say so, the supportive magic in our daily life is the faith of the mind itself. Magic is not hard to know and learn. To make magic work requires training the mind. That takes time.

"In his early years, my father was around to help me. He told me about his father's experience. I would like to tell you about their experiences. He lived in the middle land before he moved over here.

"First my grandpa studied magic, but later, he became a student of the Way. He told my father, 'The highest magic is the magic of accomplishing any meaningful thing, and life itself is magic. These are the most valuable types of magic.

"When he was a young boy, his family life was supported by farming the land and harvesting the crops. My elders were students of different types of magic, but their power was concentrated in living a pleasant life. My elders always said, 'The magic of life is the faith of mind. If you have faith, a big thing can be done as easily as cutting a small branch from a tall tree. If you do not have faith in your life and in your mind, then moving a small pile of dirt away from the road would be as difficult as moving a mountain. You could never accomplish the smallest thing; you would see it as a difficult task beyond your own strength. Casting the faith of mind is the secret of the magic of life.'

"One day my great grandfather pointed to a piece of land and put it under my young grandpa's charge. It was raw land with lots of thorns and weeds which first needed to be cleared. On some mornings, he took his hoe and went to the land, and divided it into small sections and worked on tilling one or two. He cast his faith by saying, 'This is nothing; it can be done easily.' His faith was reasonable and the work was accomplished pleasantly.

"On other mornings, he went out to look at the land and saw many thistles, weeds and bushes everywhere. Then he said to himself, how can I, without the help of other hands, ever possibly accomplish the cleaning of the land? The weeds could be burned away, but it is not the right approach there, so I will have to use the hoe to clean them. On those days, when he thought the job was too big for him, he could only work for a few minutes, before he became tired and returned home.

"My grandpa said, 'I totally understand from my own training of working on the land with my hoe, how to cast the faith of mind. That is the secret of magic.'

"When I was older, my elders also taught me the teaching of the Ageless Master. I believe they only gave me a few lines to use as maxims in my life:

"'A tree so huge you cannot even measure it by your two arms started from a tiny seed.

'A thousand mile trip starts with the step right under your foot.'

"All big things are accomplished by small beginnings. All difficult things are accomplished by attacking the easy part. When you accomplish only the small, in the long run you suddenly notice and are pleasantly surprised to see that you have accomplished a big thing. Therefore, sages do not try to do anything big. Unbridled ambition only creates frustration and the feeling of failure in life. Sages like to do small things and allow the accumulation of small things to become a big thing. That is what happens when you set the right direction for your work. This is the magic of accomplishment.

"My elders also said that life is not easy. Sometimes there are natural disasters, like a flood or a long drought. Whatever kind of work you do in life always creates difficulty for you. Not only that, you also have internal pressure or problems in your relationships. These all become challenges in your life. Too many people are killed by the feeling of their life experience. They are killed by their fear of life. They lack faith in their life. My elders said that type of life lacks spiritual essence. Spiritual essence, spiritual power, is the faith in life.

"A swallow is born from a mother swallow. It comes into the world, but its parents never built a fortune for it. How does a swallow live? It was taught to catch worms in the field and small fish in the lake. The simple reality is that the life force is built into all lives. Once you express this life force from the inside out, then the life can be a simple accomplishment. No need to worry or brew bitterness. In the process of life, you only need to straightly express the life force you are born with.

"People consider tigers and lions the strongest, fiercest animals of all. If a tiger or lion is overprotected and overfed with good meat, if they do not need to take a single step because everything just comes to their mouths, they lose their life nature or life force after a time. Then they are not a tiger or lion anymore, and so it is with humans. All life is born with its own life strength. Therefore, a good life is not how much fortune your parents build to protect you. It is the life force you nurture inside that is fulfilled outside. This life force should not be damaged by being overly ambitious. This life force needs to be used to maintain your life correctly.

"Therefore, I understand faith in life. Faith in life is produced by a powerful mind. If a mind lacks faith in life, the mind becomes powerless. The magic of life is much bigger than the magic of amusement which entertains others for small change.

"Big magic is the Heavenly Way. It resides in an earnest life and in the nature of each moment. People do have magic power, but it is best used only for emergencies, otherwise it will cause your character to become low. It is more important to be aware of the spiritual power which responds to an emergency. This power can be evenly distributed every day to the earnest life. It is the source of an earnest life.

"Life can be helped by two things: good faith in yourself and finding the right way or tools to do the right thing. These two things help bring about the realization of an earnest life of the highest magic."

The young one reassured his host of his correct under-standing by saying, "I have noticed that one needs to be selective in learning magic. Some types of magic are insignificant, like the magic done for entertainment. I feel that the nature of that kind of practice would affect my spiritual quality if I were to take it up. It is of no benefit for true spiritual fulfillment or spiritual cultivation. It is just a superficial feat. I also feel that the magic that is most appropriate to learn is the spiritual power that should be exercised with faith in an earnest life, such as healing power which can cure people's disease."

The elder said, "Healing power can come from the natural environment, from natural herbs, from nutritious food and from a healthy way of life. Especially, healing power can come from the individual's own body, mind and spirit. All in all, healing power comes from the cooperation of faith and being methodical. The healing power in oneself is respected by the student of the Way. External medicine just assists one's own self-healing power. Magic can summon energy that is already there. Magic cannot summon the energy if there is none. We use the same power to treat ourselves and to help others. All healers must achieve knowledge of the internal truth of life, otherwise their service is partial and segmented. This is how the immortal tradition earned its reputation from being integral. Magic also makes hungry people not feel hungry any more; although that is useful, it still not substantial.

"Besides that, learning how to use spiritual power can help one know what will happen and know how a specific individual can develop. It takes spiritual self-development to know these things.

"So the fulfillment of a healthy life comes from the realization of the proper knowledge of life. This serves as a supplement to the outward vision, the desire to conquer one's difficulties, and the desire to establish a system of knowledge to make the world manageable by the mind. Why are those services good? Because they come from two conditions: a healthy condition of life, and a healthy condition of spiritual knowledge which includes the knowledge of possible negative side effects.

"Each person has healing power. Healing power needs to be applied properly on the right occasion, otherwise it will not bring positive result, and will cause a student to become frustrated or to lack courage or the right faith in oneself. All people have to learn that the good performance of life is the practice of tolerance; a spiritual person has to be a student of life and have the virtue of being patient and yielding emotionally. All possible accomplishment comes from the practice of being patient; and yielding to eliminate the negative conflict. That is the highest power of mind. Spirits have no need of patience, because they are able to directly know things, but they cannot give explanations. The human mind can explain things, but the virtue of patience and yielding are still the power of accomplishment."

The boy could not express agreement or disagreement. He just kept quiet and continued to wonder and think over all of his experiences. He saved all his questions, maybe to be answered and confirmed later by the mentor.

Chapter 7

Option and Choice offer Humans The Freedom to be Unchained from their Animal Nature

The boy did not see the mentor for several weeks. Sometimes he stayed in the hut, sometimes he walked in the forest, in the mountains and by the creek. Sometimes he helped the neighbor boy clean the surroundings, plant flowers, mend stone walls, and do all types of useful help. When the local boy did stretching and breathing, a type of gentle physical movement, he was always interested in doing it with him. Finally, he asked his neighbor where the mentor was. The neighbor was a cheerful person who had similar qualities as the boy, so they got along well. He replied, "I have been instructed to take you to him whenever you were ready to see him." The neighbor had no hesitation in taking him to see his mentor. They went on a path which lead to the mountains. After climbing over a pass and through a valley to the base of another mountain range, they came to a wide river with a fast current. His friend said, "We need to cross here."

The boy started looking around and said, "There is probably a bridge here somewhere."

Then his friend asked, "How do you know?"

"Because each time our mentor came to see us, there was no indication that his clothes had been wet."

His friend smiled and said, "That's because he walks over the water without touching it. He lives on the other side of the river so that the village people do not bother him; no one else can cross it because there is no bridge. No other person lives there, either. Many years ago, although he lived over there, he used to come back and forth each day to help the villagers.

"Sometimes if someone stands here and prays, he knows about it and comes over. Because he was my great grandfather's friend, I am especially favored, so I can occasionally go to see him. Sometimes he also teaches me."

The boy said, "How can he be the friend of your great grandfather? He is young. He looks like he is only 30 or 40 years at most."

The neighbor smiled. "Teachers cannot be judged by age or by appearance. My father and my grandfather told me that when my great grandfather saw him, our mentor was the same age as he is now. Occasionally he looks old. He can also look like somebody else if he wants to. How he looks depends upon how he wishes to show himself."

The boy thought about these words. He remembered that the mentor had told him he had not gone to the market for over thirty years. Because the mentor looked like he was around 40 years old, he had wondered how a nine or ten year old had gone to the market because the trip was too long and rigorous for such a child, but now he understood that the mentor was much older than he looked.

The young one asked his friend, "How shall I formally address our teacher?"

"We are in the west high section of the big land," replied the boy. "There is a small population here. In this culture, teachers are always called 'Tzu.'"

"What does Tzu mean?"

"Tzu means the 'son of man,'" replied the local boy.

"Why would a teacher be called that?" asked the curious young one.

His friend replied, "This is a title given to teachers and all learned men and women. It distinguishes a person from the 'son of beasts.' I was told that human people developed from and lived with animals. Thus, they also contain part of the nature of an animal. However, when human people attain spiritual development, they feel ashamed to be considered the same as a beast. Thus, 'son of man' represents the spiritual awakening of human life. If any human culture strays from this center or direction too far, either too high or too low, either too spiritual or too material, it establishes an unhealthy or negative element of human society. It is the same principal in each individual. All social rules and cultural establishment should follow the core. A 'son of man' is a person who does not shame their parents by the life they live. Anyway, as I know him, our teacher watches the heart. Titles are not a big deal to him. Just feel relaxed when you are around him."

The young one asked, "Why is our teacher always smiling?"

His friends replied, "I think it is because smiling makes people young and it presents the well-being of one's personal internal situation."

Now the boy tried to hurry his friend, saying, "Let's cross over there where the water is not as deep," but the water was not shallow enough or calm enough for crossing.

His friend told him, "This time I will carry you on my back."

"No," the boy said, "I would like to try to cross by myself," but each time he put his foot in the water, the current was too strong. There was not even any way to stand in the water, not to mention crossing. The boy had mixed emotions; on the one hand, he misjudged the current, but on the other, he had a strong desire to see the mentor to help resolve something his own mind could not decide. Thus, he climbed on his neighbor's back, held tightly to his neck and shoulder, and they started across the river. The local boy held him well, despite the fact that they were both about the same size, and walked across the water about six inches under the water's surface. Half way across, the local friend said, "Look over to the left. Still farther up the river is a big waterfall. About five miles above that waterfall is really good water for drinking; it's the best! Next time, if you serve our teacher, go over to that spot to bring water for him."

This was all a new experience for the boy. Although the water's current was so strong, his neighbor just carried him as if he were walking on flat land. He did not know how his friend managed it, but they made it safely to the other side. After crossing, they straightened up their clothing, and the boy looked around. It was a beautiful land. Flowers were everywhere. Birds were singing and animals were walking gently. Everything was so green and beautiful, he was almost enchanted by its loveliness. They walked down a path and finally reached the hut where the mentor lived. He came out as they approached.

The mentor smiled. "Did you have a good time at the market?" The boy nodded his head.

"Did you make your decision?"

The boy shook his head. It was difficult to find words to describe his feelings. At the beginning he had felt so high and confident; it seemed that he could see things much easier before than now. He even thought, "How long will it take me to learn, as my friend who carried me on his back without even deeply entering the water?"

The local boy picked up a big water pot and went to fill it, so the boy was alone with the mentor. The mentor tried to console him. Finally the boy said, "I saw many things in the market, things that were amazing. You asked me to find out what I would like to learn, but it seems that it is not my life goal to learn all of those things."

Then the mentor said, "You do not need them; you only need to say what is your interest."

"I would like to treat ill people, to make people well," said the boy without hesitation. "I would also like to have the power to do as I wish."

The mentor smiled, "Well, that is a direction. You can say it. I am going to help you because you do not know how the people in the market did their small magic that so amazed you. Before you can learn any kind of magic, though, first you need to know what human people are made of."

"That I know," the boy said. "People are made of muscles, bones, hair, teeth and internal organs."

It was the mentor's turn to shake his head. "No, no. Those physical parts of a person are the foundation, but muscle, teeth, hair and bones alone do not comprise a human being. There is something else which cannot be seen. A person cannot exist unless there is that something inside the form made by the bones, muscles, internals, hair and teeth. These are what everybody has that is the same, with no doubt, but above these is the human soul and spirit. I would like you to confirm this for yourself.

"Have you ever witnessed a human death or an animal death?"

The boy replied, "Yes."

"After something dies," asked the mentor, "do you still see the body or corpse of the animal or person?"

"Yes. "

"What you cannot see is the life. What you still see is the shape of life."

The boy said, "I believe in God. God is in Heaven, and God decides everything for us."

The mentor smiled. "You can think that way. If God is an individual who lives high above with lots of helpers to carry his work, who are the helpers?"

The boy said, "The angels."

"What are angels?"

The boy said, "I don't know, but everything is made by God."

"Can I provide you with a different fact? God is one being, but he has split himself to be all lives. He split to become angels, human spirits and everything else. In totality, or considered as a group, spirits are God; when they are split up as individual entities, we call them spirits.

"Each spirit is the same as God, because it is split from God. God is a common name for all spirits in totality. Spirits carry the function of God. Please remember the principle 'One is all, and all is one.' When you contact any spirit, you contact God himself."

The boy said, "I never heard such a thing, but I have always intuitively felt its truth in me, so I do not doubt it. But how is this connected with magic performance and healing power?"

The mentor patiently explained to him, "Each person is made up of a number of spirits. The entire universe is made up of countless spirits. When a trained person's spirit becomes powerful enough, he can command spirits of a similar or lower vibration. Now may I ask you again, what is human life made of?"

The boy said, "The physical body and spirits."

The mentor said, "Plus your conscious mind, because you have a brain. The physical brain is the tool or the vehicle of the main soul or spirit. The body itself is made of numerous spirits.

"Now I can help you know the three levels of spirit. The physical spirits are called chi spirits; they come from what your body and the universe are made of. In human life, above the chi spirits is the mind. The body cannot understand that when there is a thought in the mind, the spirits of the organs and of all parts of the body know the thoughts. There is immediate communication between the mind and body. Yet, these spirits are not part of the nervous system. Because they are developed throughout the body, they know the mental projection which is about to happen in the brain. Once the conscious mind issues a thought, it is a projection and, right or wrong, it receives agreement or disagreement from some or all of one's spirits. When the mind remains still and does not shape itself, it is pure spiritual substance or mental essence. It is to say, when the spirits of the mind stay in the mind and do not formed themselves into thoughts, they are simply pure spiritual substance or the essence of mind.

"People have three levels of spirit. The bodily chi spirits, the spirits of the mind and the spirits of the spiritual level of the life being. The spiritual level consists of spirits which sometimes function as conscience, inspiration, enlightenment, insight, deep reflection and rational strength, which is higher than the mind.

"When a person dies, the part of his being that was unseeable leaves the part that is seeable. The unseeable part is called spirits or the soul. It is to say, when the unseeable spirits or soul leave the body of a person, the so-called "person" appears dead. The trained achieved person can command the soul to return to the body of the dying person, if he sees that such action is feasible and proper.

"You have seen that there are many levels of magic. The level that you have seen affects only your senses; what your eyes can see, your ears can hear, your nostrils can smell, your tongue can taste, your hands can touch, and your body can feel. The level of magic that can be seen, heard, smelled, tasted and touched, even the higher level magic performances that can change one material substance into another or someone walking on air, is still limited. It depends upon something else to create an effect. As for the magic show, which is still much lower, that is a further limited power, which can only have a temporary effect. People believe what they see, what they hear, what they smell, taste, feel, etc., but in reality, they are temporarily controlled, because they are too unachieved to resist the illusion created by someone who has been trained to temporarily alter your spiritual and mental perception. It means that all the people in the audience agree that they have heard it, seen it, smelled, tasted or felt it, but the reality is that they have been temporarily controlled by something outside themselves and they still trust their unachieved level of perception. This type of magic power has a temporary effect;

what you see is unreal, although it is still a good show. When people watch it and are thus controlled by it, it is like being hypnotized under another person's power.

"An achieved person is not interested in this level of magic, because to him, there is no magic. The clarity that he has achieved makes everything in front of him very bright, and what others call magic is an ordinary skill to him. An achieved person does not participate in such performances, because there is no need to do anything for show. He just accepts that all things in daily life, right in front of him, are true magic.

"At a deeper level, it is the same for what is considered 'reliable knowledge' which is related to the general level of untrained and unachieved eyes, ears, nostrils, tongue and pores of the palms and the body. That is the physical level which ordinary people perceive as being solid. However, the physical level is not as solid as it looks. The belief in the solidity of the physical world is a misunderstanding. The strength of people's habitual way of thinking that the world is solid makes it appear to be so to them.

"The reality of the physical world, that which is seeable, audible, touchable and so forth, is limited. The physical world is the surface; it is only a small portion of the unseeable vastness of the potence of nature. If you understand this, really understand it, then for you all things are possible.

"The possibility of having spiritual power of unlimited potential is recognized through denial of the mind's concept of solidity. As the Ageless Master said, 'The power comes as nothingness, but it is able to penetrate what is called solidity.' If you accept the concept of solidity, you become limited to what your eye can see, what your ear can hear, and what your hand can touch.

"Magic exists only for ordinary people. Learned, achieved people have no magic, because everything 'magic' that happens is natural. You are a special person. You already have developed spirits, so you will probably not take too long to deeply understand that truth."

At this point, the boy asked an interesting question. He asked, "All the magic and all the healing power I saw happened by incantation. It seems to me that incantation is the most powerful and most important thing I need to learn. If I learn the most powerful incantations, then I will be able to do everything."

The mentor calmly and encouragingly told him, "Yes, you are right, but you need to go one step further, because you have been to the South. Did the southern people do magic?"

"Yes," replied the boy, "There is lots of magic there. One man threw a long rope straight up into the sky and climbed up it. He climbed so high that you could not see him any more; he took off his outer garments and one by one, threw them down on the ground. He was so high that the people on the ground could not longer see him, but we could hear his laughter. It was a marvelous thing to see. I have also seen people hang themselves on a high, tall pole as worship. They had sharp knives inserted in through one side of the chin and out the other, and they were hung from hooks through their palms, suspended from the top of pole. I saw them hang there in front of a temple for days; they did not die or even show any pain. And I have seen many other things, such as snake dancing, etc."

Then the teacher said, "Did those people say incantations?"

"Yes, they said incantations all the time. "

"Were those incantations the same incantations that you heard in the market?"

The boy thought a minute and replied, "No, all the incantations were different. They were all in different languages. Even the ones that were in the same language were different. Some were written and others were spoken."

"If all incantations are different, then how can they all get a similar type of unusual power?" asked the mentor.

The boy pondered a while and then said, "I wonder if it was the different languages or if language itself has power."

"It is not the incantation which is powerful," the mentor said, "it is the intention behind the mind which has power. It is the deep intention of the person that makes him able to project his mind and make something 'miraculous' happen.

"The highest training or cultivation is not to learn incantations one by one, it is to first purify and strengthen your intention, and then direct your mind. The mind can create whatever it intends to. This is how several months ago, you learned to be worryless and fearless. Your decrease in fear happened through cultivating the power of mind, which contains the spirit energy. This is where you start."

The boy said, "I see. I need to learn how to cultivate the power of the mind, which can then nurture my spiritual power. I would like to learn how to attain a powerful mind."

The mentor said, "Each person was endowed with spiritual power, but it becomes scattered, or people are confused by it and thus make themselves powerless. There are two ways that the power of the mind can be nurtured. One way is through incantations and invocations; their function is mostly to help remind your mind or thoughts to come back to their own spiritual center. The second way is to use it to affect people or the environment in a good way, such as healing, etc.

"Once you learn to control your mind, you can be above all untrained and unachieved minds. By being virtuous and righteous, the mind is powerful. If someone's mind is quick and sharp, but he does not have a good heart and a virtuous being, he can sometimes make people do his bidding, but in the long run, it will only lead to self-destruction."

At this point the local boy came over with some wild fruit. "This fruit was over by the waterfall," he said. "It's really ripe now."

It was a good time for them to take a short break. The mentor always instructed the boy in an amount that the boy could digest and absorb. The two boys ate well, but the mentor just took a small one and smelled it as his way of participating in the meal.

Then the mentor continued, "Spiritual learning is different from intellectual learning. In intellectual learning, one must avoid subjective involvement. When you study a tree, you do not have subjective involvement because you are not a tree, although life itself is somewhat like a tree. When you study grapes, you are not a grape vine. You are more than the grape vine or tree. You may wonder that if everything is God, (one is all, all is one), then how can you ever be more than anything? The answer is that you know nothing and nothing needs to be known, either.

"In spiritual learning, when you learn about God, you cannot regard God as somebody who is rich or authoritative or even wise. This would be to miss the mark, and, the learning would not benefit you at all. In spiritual learning, each individual's own good energy joins God; thus, you are God.

"You have to have faith in your own spiritual energy in order to accomplish your spiritual task or ordinary life. An external search for God leads to failure. If you do not change your own internal energy to participate in the positive universal spiritual flow, you will not reward yourself for your learning or pursuit.

"When you do something which is either beneficial for yourself or for another person, it was first issued or projected from your mind. Therefore, you have to have faith in your mind. A good mental being is expressed, through your behavior. After some time of constancy of good mental being, the mind is part of God itself. Because the mind has multiple functions, it takes God as its source to project in different areas and bring different positive results.

No positive result can be brought about by a mind which lacks faith in itself. To have insufficient faith in the mind is to doubt. It leads to unfulfillment. It is self-intimidation. Losing direct faith in the mind could turn a person to the negative sphere because that person will project his life in a different direction. It is the same as lacking faith in life. Such a person will become irresponsible, dependent or have a low moral character. That is all the result of lack of faith in one's own mind.

"The mind is the eye of the life; if you do not have faith or trust in your mind, what more trustworthy thing do you have? Have faith in the substance of the mind as you trust your eyes. Then the positive quality of the mind leads you upward and forward to a better place or condition of life all the time. One who does not have faith in the mind or in one's own spiritual energy remains at the level of a beginner in spiritual practice because truthfully, the performance of spiritual power is the performance of one's own personal faith in life, in the mind and in spirit itself. It is one's own doubt and lack of faith in the mind and lack of faith in a decent life which holds one in the tar pit and keeps one from lifting oneself up to any better self-condition.

"God, truth, the Way and the light are nothing different from the mind which is healthy enough to contain all of them. Sometimes the external pursuit of God, truth, light and the

Way misses the entire point of seeing the mind. Once the mind or the spirit of the mind functions positively in real life, God, the truth, the light and the Way become its description.

"The pure energy substance of the mind, spirit or physical being, before being projected in any direction, cannot be judged good or bad, or defined by any relative description. Because this 'nothing' cannot be described, the ancient sages called it the pre-Heaven stage. I utilize the word 'nothingness' to describe it; this term has been passed down from the teaching of the Ageless Master. However, once you project your mind, spirit or physical energy as positive or negative or in between, then it can be judged or decided.

"A spiritually achieved one's spirit lives in the stage of pre-Heaven. Living in this way can be considered spiritual training or discipline for all hopeful spiritual students. Once a person forms an idea or a motivation, then he must immediately be aware of whether it comes from the godly source or the physical source. It also could be from the mind itself because of its random habit. Yet, in general, because the mind is in the middle, it can go either way.

"If a person discovers that his motivation is wrong, he can stop without actually engaging in the real behavior or he can stop in the middle of the behavior. This is because human life has already evolved much higher than animals. For example, if a group of wolves attack someone, there will often be some wolves who did not involve themselves in the attack. You cannot say that the wolves who did not join in the attack are good-hearted wolves, and it is not necessary to guard oneself against those particular wolves. The fundamental truth is that wolf nature attacks all the flesh life which it can handle or manage.

"Human nature is more highly evolved and human nature is different from animal nature. Although human life possesses an animal foundation, it has other options. Because some humans have grown to attain a divine nature, this creates the possibility to join with God, to be the Truth, to give the Light and to live on the Way. Option and choice give human nature its freedom.

Chapter 8

It is not a Matter of Giving Life to Truth But Embracing the Truth of Eternal Life

The young one felt that it was difficult to train the mind, even though he had a strong ambition to do so. Because the mind is not visible, it is not easy to manage; this was true not only for him, but for anyone. The best practice is one which stabilizes the mind and strengthens the spirit. This type of practice is typically called "non-doing." It is achieved by reducing all thought and other types of mental activity. This allows the healthy spiritual function to be implemented directly without using the mind as interpreter, which would distort the spiritual purity. It is the mind which holds a position or sense of individuality, self and personal interest. Desire either comes from the mind, the body, or habitual patterns.

The boy also knew that the practice of peaceful mind is not to be used to rigidify the mind, but to develop it, so he requested that the teacher instruct him in the practice. His mentor responded, "You already know that there are thousands of techniques for visualization, finger postures and incantations. Not only that, but there are also thousands of rituals that go with the incantations. All these have been created since the time when people started to do spiritual practices, and new teachers continually create new techniques for their students. Confusion about which ones to use occur when there are too many indirect systems of practice. Each student wishes to learn the most powerful incantation, and each teacher says, 'My incantation, my method and my medicine is the most powerful.' Is that type of statement trustworthy?"

The boy said, "I don't know, but I suppose there must be some powerful ones."

The mentor continued, "Now, think. Does the power you seek come from the incantation, ritual, invocation, finger posture or visualization or ritual itself, or does it come from the mind? Yet even behind the mind is something more subtle, something which does not live totally in the body or the brain. It is energy, and it can be summoned, gathered or assembled to accomplish anything."

The boy said, "I still request to know how I can start to achieve it."

The mentor responded patiently and instinctively, "I have already pointed out that the most powerful element is what you put into the form, ritual or voiced vibration. However, all spiritual practices still have different levels. Some people enjoy higher things than others, depending upon who they are and their own level of spiritual quality and intelligence, etc. In art, for example, the quality of some works is higher than others. The same truth applies in selecting a spiritual practice. Yet, choosing a spiritual practice is not a matter of taste, it is a matter of how useful it is as a learning tool and in application. Some things are truthfully more useful and others are more ornamental.

"In answer to your request, I recommend the most ancient spiritual practice which inspired the development of the *I Ching* system, which is recognized as an effective system to train a useful mind, although, some people use this system of divination excessively and thus weaken their minds. Since you do not have time to learn the *I Ching* itself, I will teach you the spiritual practice which is considered the mother of the *I Ching*.

"It is not that the *I Ching* developed first and then people had a spiritual practice, it was the other way around. Spiritual practices helped people develop themselves as sages, and the sages helped the development of the *I Ching*, which is sometimes also called the *Book of Changes*. That occurred a long time ago when there was no other system of knowledge. The first systems of knowledge were developed from spiritual practices. Some early spiritual attainments become worldly life knowledge, some developed into religion, and some remained as the plain truth, the Way, because they expressed universal nature so directly.

"To do this practice, you need to clearly understand where the power comes from. It is channelled by the strength of the mind, but the mind itself is not the source of the power. Perhaps we could say that the mind is the source of personal power but not of universal power itself. Do you know the source of spiritual potency in the universe?

"In the teachings of the Ageless Master, spiritual potency is called the Mystical Mother or the Mother of All Differences, or Tao. Mystical means something that is invisible, inaudible and untouchable. Mother means something giving form to life. The two types of energy, the mystical energy and the motherly energy, always need to come together. If the mystical energy is separated from the motherly energy, then nothing can be expressed, experienced or applied.

"The Ageless Master taught that the Way has two spheres. It is through the exploration of these two spheres that the Way is reached. One sphere is describable and the other is inde-scribable. Only through the describable sphere can the indescribable sphere be expressed.

"It was also taught that there was a subtle level which exists above the level of form. When both levels come together, wonders, miracles, great performances and great achievement happens. Great things cannot occur without both elements: the mystical part, which is called spirit, and the forming part, which is called material. When both parts are married, befriend each other or come together, things appear. Each of the two parts are needed to accomplish the other. Each attracts the other, each needs the other.

"In spiritual teaching, people tend to exalt the mystical and put down the level of form. That is not the teaching of the Ageless Master. To find the Way, one must look for coopera-tion, harmony, balance, equilibrium and symmetry between the two great energies."

The young one asked, "If the universal source is the Mystical Mother, what is the position of God?"

The mentor smiled and answered, "How does God express itself?"

"Through creation," answered the boy.

"Right." The mentor continued, "Creation is the impetus of nature having expressed itself. The impetus of nature is the source of all changes, variety and differences. However, if you view the impetus of the creation of universal nature as God, then you leave out divine law; that is not complete. Also, if you only view divine law as God, you leave out the impetus of creation; that is also incomplete. God is both divine law and the impetus of creation.

"Universal divinity does not express itself only through the impetus of nature. The impetus of the universe and of univer-sal nature exhibits the subtle law, orderliness, harmony, unity, balance, symmetry and equilibrium within each creation and within the totality of creation. This Subtle Law is the Godly law in everything in the world. The Subtle Way is the way of universal nature and is what the Ageless Master teaches.

"It is partial to recognize God as either the creator or as the supreme ruler. All creations are not finished at once; the creation is continued. The late comer, humankind, thinks that creation was complete before they entered the stage. However, it was not; creation is always ongoing. The creation of the universe is not done all at once, nor was it done in a short period of time. Most people are unable to see that creation is a long, unceasing process. It is also impossible to conclude the creation that is done.

"Yet all creations, no matter what stage they are at, express a common source and the subtle law which exists among all creations. This subtle source can also be called the creator or production which only can be manifested through the interplay of two main forces. Thus, the subtle is exhibited by the interplay of these two main forces to accomplish, assist and supplement each other. The two forces are yang and yin. When one is shown, the other must be brought into existence too. Thus, the human mind also expresses the same nature as universal creation and its law. It is to say, the Subtle Law expresses the same nature as the human mind. The human mind is also an extension of the universal nature; it creates, and is therefore subject to the same principle of continual creation of one subtle source. There is no wisdom of forming the world from a pre-designed plan before the formed reality of the world, and there will be no wisdom left after the formed reality is fulfilled. The formation, the transformation, and the reformation of the world comes from nature. Nature itself contains all wisdom, or the Law. Simply, the wisdom or the law is just the universal nature. The Subtle Law is contained within the continually forming reality of the universe at all levels. It can also be viewed as the universe continually forming itself in accordance with the Subtle Law at different levels. Surely, there is the unformed before something is formed. When a thing is unformed, it is substance; when it becomes formed, it expresses the substance.

"The Universal Mother, which is the mother of all creation and differences, is the nature of God. God is the name for the powerful sphere of being which always keeps forming, reforming, coming to life, dying and renewing."

Then the boy[1] asked, "People of most places believe God is like the supreme emperor. Is God really like a king who can watch over people, punish them for their mistakes and decide their lives and deaths? Even though God is called different names in different places, the basic belief in God is the same in all parts of the world."

The mentor responded, "Each life receives the same spiritual seeds. Those spiritual seeds are not different from God. God is not a watchman; God is nature itself. God has four virtues: originalness, proceeding, benefitting and persistence. God is persistent in being original, persistent in being proceeding and persistent in being beneficial. If you consider God as a being, then aside from him, there is still non-being. In that type of thought, God is still beneath what is non-being. That is not the truth, because God is both being and non-being."

The mentor patiently waited for clear understanding in the boy. He continued, "The entire universe is one being. After the stage of pre-Heaven, all lives and beings are individualized, so we call the common source of all lives God. At the same time, the universe is one being and is also a combination of all individual lives and beings, but each individual life such as human life contains the potential of God.

"In general, after the human mind is individualized, we conceive of God as a separate being. If you consider God only as the creative energy of universal impetus, then you leave out the integration and unity of all creations. God is not a separate being.

"On the other hand, some people treat God as a ruler and the dispenser of divine law among all of creation. This too conceives of God as separate from all creation and the expanse of universal impetus.

"Both of these partial visions are incomplete. If God is not just a ruler or the Subtle Law in all creation, what then is the correct way to think about God? The correct way is with integral vision and the Integral Way.

---

[1]According to local custom, before marriage and fatherhood, all males were considered boys.

"The perception of some sages is that when human beings are born into the world, creation is accomplished, but in reality no single creation is ever accomplished. In its entirety, creation never stops, it only begins. For example, when a father and mother give birth to a child, a human being has been born, but its life has not even begun; its creation actually never stops. A person's life takes many years and many stages of development, each of which is a creation of the self-nature of life. It can never be said that God's work is accomplished. This is why good teachers', sages', leaders' and inventors' lives further creation. If you understand this, then you know this is why you can have a role in an unaccomplished, Godly task, and you can understand the valuable teaching, vision and direction of the *Book of Changes*. The *Book of Changes* states that what is accomplished dies and what is unaccomplished lives."

Then the boy asked why people become bad. The mentor answered, "That is a question of deviation from one's original nature or God. It often happens when people live within a small environment in which they find a means of survival. From this they develop a secondary nature which is concerned only with individual physical survival. This nature is different from their original Godly nature, but they become lost in the secondary nature. Therefore, spiritual teaching has value as an educational instrument to guide people to tame their unhealthy secondary nature and help them unite themselves with their original Godly nature. This is the teaching of the Way.

"To respond to your request, I must show you the correct spiritual practice. Since the Ageless Master gave his teaching in writing five hundred years ago, three types of spiritual teaching have developed. It may also be true that these three ways of spiritual teaching already existed prior to the time of the Ageless Master's writing. The three ways are:

1) In one's spiritual cultivation and meditation, depend on nothing but sitting quietly, almost like a statue, but still breathing. Stillness is required in bodily posture, mind and spiritual activity. The principle of the practice is to do nothing, search for nothing and achieve nothing, just allow whatever

spiritual phenomena occur to pass through. This became the one school of the practice of holding oneness.[2]

2) The next kind of cultivation is overly methodic. It is the opposite of holding only the indescribable simple essence. There are thousands of theories, ideologies and small techniques to follow. As the proverb says, 'By too many bypaths, one loses one's sheep. Almost every teacher has his own theory and own small technique for how to cultivate in this way. Thus, no student knows which techniques can help him the most, and no student can ever achieve himself beyond the state of confusion.[3]

3) The Integral Way knows the shortcoming of both. The rigid practice of non-dualistic mentality causes stiffness; too many small practices cause confusion. Ideologies, theologies and exaltation of individual small techniques as secret or esoteric teachings exert control over students, and never allow them to achieve higher than the teacher.

The Integral Way was not created in response to the disadvantages of the above two ways. It offers an effective and simple way which depends upon nothing. Without the Integral Way, it takes too long to prove the stiffness of the first way and the scatteredness of the second. All spiritual powers come from spiritual energy itself and are produced by following good and simple methods of spiritual practice. Correct spiritual practices do not damage one's original spirit, but correctly display it.

"This is the Integral Way I teach. It is simple, useful and truthful. It contains no religious exaggerations of spiritual power or the power of God. It clearly recognizes that spiritual power and the power of God are more subtle than physical force. It requires gentleness and delicacy to connect to the subtle reality of personal life and of nature. No lofty and unrealistic ideologies, no untruthful theologies, and no misleading or exaggerated small techniques are necessary. There is also no need to control anyone. Yet, the teaching of the Integral Way needs to find the right student to whom to pass this spiritual attainment. When a student learns the plain and

---

[2]Note from Master Ni: This later led to the development of the practice of the Zhan (Zen) school.

[3]Note from Master Ni: This lead to the development of folk Taoism.

unadorned truth, the proper methodic approach can be applied to guide his achievement. This is the fundamental principle of the teaching of the Integral Way. I will surely give the necessary practices for you to achieve yourself.

"I know you urgently need some useful practices that will enable you to voyage far in the spiritual world. The most powerful and essential practice is a set of simple but effective practices to unite your mind with your spiritual energy. Among them, the shortest prayer or incantation is 'Wu.' The image of Wu is 无 or 無 . Wu is the sound that represents the subtle source of all power. The ageless one said, 'All beings and things come from Wu - nothingness or non-beingness. From nothingness comes a great many beingnesses.' He also said, 'The power of nothingness can enter the density of beingness.' In meditation, the sound 'Wu' does not need to be voiced; it can be done by thought only. On other occasions, you can voice it. When you do, the vibration originates from the three cavities of the body, which are also called the 'tan tien.' Those three cavities are the head, the chest or thoracic cavity and the abdomino-pelvic cavity. Practicing making the sound Wu brings the power of great peace. Even God needs to yield authority to it.

"Wu is a way to start one's spiritual practice. Wu is also the destination of high spiritual practices. The correct mouth shape to use when practicing the sound is to smile.

"The purpose of spiritual cultivation is to make things unseen or unnoticed because everything is in a state of normalcy. Typically, people practice spiritual cultivation by exalting some particular spirits to command a specific spiritual function or power. However, doing so arouses the spirits to compete with each other internally and externally. It is not helpful to do some kind of spiritual cultivation that increases conflict.

"An equally powerful and short incantation is 'Mu.' The image of Mu is 母 , and it means the Mother of All. Mu represents or symbolizes the power to increase personal confidence and chase away evil spirits or demons. The sound Mu also does not need to be voiced in your meditation. However, if you do voice the sound, the vibration must originate from the brain. The correct mouth shape to use in voicing the sound Mu is to have a stern look on one's face. Mu establishes internal control to influence the external spiritual environment.

"The most commonly used incantation for self-cultivation is 'My heart emits the auspicious light.' If you prefer to use the one syllable words, they are "Su Shing, Da Fan Hsiang Kung." Gently, silently recite those words, or produce the non-verbal image by the mind in meditation; stop when the mind and the entire bodily energy become one. Then you shall see your own light. Consistent practice helps attain the light body.

"If you wish to align your energy vertically from the top of the head (the yang meeting point) to the perineum (the yin meeting point), you can focus your energy by thinking of the following order: the ring of the crown, the ring of throat, the ring of spiritual heart (the center of the chest), the ring of navel, and the ring of perineum. Each ring has a specific associated color that follows the same order: purple, lavender, blue, green, yellow, orange and red, respectively. This will help you attain the correspondence of the bodily subtle energy. The rings are energy rings formed by your mind. In other words, they are your own internal projection. One ring can be developed into three rings with the smallest in the center, and two bigger ones outside. The six rings are to be arranged vertically in the center of the head and the body. The size of the ring can be as big as the index finger and the thumb coiled together, or as small as the thickness of a chopstick to store in the spine. This greatly helps your spiritual health and strength. This will further develop the ability to see the straight yellow light penetrating the center of all the rings. Then, your mental energy will be powerful enough to know many things which you have never learned.

"The above achievement is safe and helpful in your spiritual development. There is also a practice that involves the power to govern internal as well as external spirits. It was the knowledge of the ancient achieved ones that the spirits above the Great Dipper are Heavenly spirits. They do not need to be governed. However, the spirits beneath the seven stars of the Great Dipper are spirits of the earth, and they need to be governed.

"The next practice which I am about to teach you is related to the spiritual power of the seven stars. Practically speaking, the seven stars are just a spiritual symbol for this practice.

Walking in the pattern of the seven stars and reciting each of the star's vibration produces powers. This practice is not suitable for people with too heavy worldly ambition or sexual interest, because a further imbalance will be created by increasing the earthly tendency. Yet some people need to do it for professional purposes such as exercise instructors or some spiritual magicians. If you control yourself well, it helps bring longevity.

"Choose a clean spot which is safe from disturbances. Mentally image the Great Dipper on the ground. Then, walk on it as follows:

★

                                                      1 ★

           6 ★

               5 ★   4 ★

7 ★

                                      2 ★

                    3 ★

"As you do so, recite the seven word incantation Tou 剋 , Shao 尠 , Chuan 尵 , Heng 尶 , Pi 尷 , Fu 尹 , Piao 尰 . These are just vibrations of the subtle energy of the seven stars. The English meaning is like the leading powers of natural balancing. If you wish, you can render service to heal people, especially those with spiritual disorders, but not mental ones. In order to do this, you need to do the practice and attain its authority. Remember one thing: if you do this practice, you need to eat some meat and have some sexual activity for harmony, because it is the level of spiritual reality which is close to human life. Surely, those spirits can be developed to be united with high heavenly spirits.

"A short, useful incantation for circumstances of needing protection is to silently recite with the mind, 'My chi protects me.' In one syllable words, this incantation is 'Wu chi pao wu sen.' 'Wu' in this instance means 'I' or 'my.'

"To go deeper, I already mentioned the source of spiritual practice to you. We call the universe 'the Mystical Mother' because 'mystical' means something that you cannot totally understand. It cannot be determined whether something has been accomplished or not. 'Mother' means that which produces lives or gives life. This means that no one can ever fully understand how life is produced. Yet, the universe is developed under the same law as the life of human individuals.

"Thus, there are two key points to recognize. One, in the universe there is the mystical power or subtle power. That mystical power is the universe itself, it is great nature, and we take provision and support from it. Two, God or Heaven has four virtues, as I described before. God is the creation and at the same time God is the orderliness of the creation.

"To remind yourself of your Godly nature, you can do this practice, which is the practice of the universal mystical source.

"Hold your thumb in the four fingers of your right hand. This is called a baby fist. Then touch the throat with the outside knuckle of the second finger and say 'Chyan.' Then move the hand in the same position to the left shoulder, say 'Yuan.' Then move the hand to the forehead and say: 'Heng.' Then move the hand to the right shoulder and say, 'Li.' At last, move the hand to the center of the chest and say 'Chen.' Then, put the left palm over the right baby fist and say, "Ta Dao Fung Quang Ming." This means, 'God of four virtues produces all virtues and gives its light to all lives.'[4]

"These words also represent the spiritual level of the five elements. There are always five types of spiritual energy which interplay in personal life or in the big universe: vitality, prosperity, astringency, hidden (sinking) and the equilibrium among them which keeps any force from becoming extreme. Yi, Shi and Vi also represent the spiritual levels of the three tan tien just like the three divisions of the universe: spiritual sphere, material sphere and the intermediate life sphere which is the midpoint that can go either way."

The mentor continued, "In the world, things can be expressed in three levels; what you see, hear and touch. The level behind these things is what you cannot see, what you cannot hear and what you cannot touch. That which cannot be seen, heard or touched is the source of what you see, hear and touch. The source of everything you see is called Shi. The

---

[4]More explanation on this system is also given in the book *Mysticism: Empowering the Spirit Within.*

source of everything you hear is called Yi. The source of everything solid that you can touch is called Vi. When this understanding is applied to the body, three divisions can be made: spirituality, mentality and physics. Put in three levels, they are how Yi, Shi and Vi.

"When you practice this with the baby fist, the four fingers of your right hand touch the forehead and you say, "Yi." Then, move to touch the human heart, the center of the chest and say, "Shi." Then move the fist to touch the center of the lower abdomen and say, "Vi." This is the foundation, then you nurture your special wish or special desire. It must be upright, righteous, straight and direct in order to be powerful. This will guide you to the next step, which is the most direct way.

"These two practices are to start to reach the internal and external energy flow of nature. There are thousands of practices and small techniques, but it is not necessarily true that each of them can lead you to the place you would like to be. You have shown me that you are looking for the Great Way and are not confused by the small techniques or the small path of confused worldly spiritual culture. This is why I have taught you the practices essential for your direct achievement. After your achievement, you can go to learn magic or remain with the pure spiritual practice."

The boy carefully repeated what was to be done, pronounced the vibrations and remembered the instructions as the foundation for his great development.

The mentor continued, "The basic nature of most incantations is to ask for something or give a command. If your spiritual practice only extends to the side of controlling or suggesting to your mind, and if it is not associated with the spirits of your entire being, then the spiritual practice is limited to the mind. If your spiritual energy does not go together with your mental or verbal practice, it will not work, and will thus be on the same level as religious practice.

"Spiritual self-cultivation needs to cause the response of all the spirits of the entire being. The highest level of practice is to put all reachable and responsive healthy spiritual energy inside and outside of the body together as one. This is what you have been taught. How diligently you do the practice and how great an achievement you attain depends upon you now. When you eliminate the extra, unnecessary activities in your life, and you do the practice, you will become stronger. Eating correctly and doing normal things also attracts no harm.

"The main thing that prevents spiritual achievement is that the mind is too active. This is the same for all people. People create excitement in their lives, then they have to experience frustration. The mind builds a pattern by doing this over and over, and continually struggles between frustration and excitement. However, if they do not establish frustration, then they do not need excitement and vice versa. Therefore, discipline of mind is important. There are so many mental creations in the world which the wise ones developed to try to help people stay calm-minded, but correct practices do not use strange language to cheat your mind. It is to say that the wise ones created mantras - useless worded prayers in all types of strange language - to occupy the mind. However, the best practice is not to use the mind to do and to repeat something that robs you of your energy all the time. A true practice puts your mind together with your spiritual and physical being and at least reaches well-being on all levels.

"The best practice is to concentrate or focus on uniting the three partners of the spirit being, mental being and physical being harmoniously and cooperatively. This is the only valuable direction of spiritual practice. Otherwise, spiritual practices tend to guide more energy on one side than another. This only causes faster divorce, dissembly or separation of the trio of body, mind and spirit. If you know this point, you shall enjoy the benefit of the practice you received. It is called 'The Spiritual Practice of the Son (or Daughter) of God.'"

The boy said, "I still have one question."

His teacher said, "You may ask."

"Is religion good or bad?" wondered the boy.

"Be a teacher to respond to the spiritual problem of the time," replied the mentor. "Do not be a person who creates problems for the future. What you face is the spiritually deadlocked condition of a society. Once your message is given, you can leave. The ancient wise one said, 'Give your life to the truth, but do not sacrifice truth for your life.' You might be resented for awakening those who prefer to stay asleep."

Chapter 9

The Most Worthwhile Learning
Is How to Cross the Torrent of Life

After receiving the instruction, the young one seriously worked on his mind. After a long while, he developed special mental capacities. Now he could understand things that were previously vague. He saw that the benefit of such a practice is not directly knowing and learning it, nor even being able to practice it skillfully. Its true value is the blossoming or opening of the heart, mind and spiritual reality. This practice almost opened him up completely to all the universal spiritual subtlety.

When he thought that it was a suitable time to return to his teacher, he went to the stream, however his mind told him the same thing that it told him before: if he entered, the torrent would carry him away. He had learned to be spiritually fearless but he still hesitated to cross that stream. He thought about it: "Should I go into the stream and try to cross? No, it is not right." He still thought that the current of the stream was too strong and would carry him away if he tried to cross, so he went back to the village and asked his friend to take him across. The local boy did not hesitate and immediately went with him.

The boy mentioned his progress to his mentor, who seemed happy with what he said. The boy then mentioned his hesitation about trying to cross the stream. His mentor also accepted that and did not scold him for being cautious. Still his fear made the boy tense; maybe he felt ashamed of holding onto fear in the face of the raging torrent. However, his mentor said, "You do not need to be ashamed. It is irrational to do something that is beyond one's capacity or experience. Actually, you have exercised good judgement not to try something that you are not ready to do. You have not yet developed your full capability. I am glad to hear that you are doing the practices I gave you. Walking over water is not an important one."

Then the boy said, "How can I freely come to see you? I would like to request the practice that will enable me to cross the water. It is not a matter of being fearful, it is a matter of real danger that my mind can see. Now, my mind can only see the real danger of the torrent. In other words, I do not want to learn how to swim across the water or to have a long rope tied to my waist and attached to a big tree, I want to learn how to walk over it."

The mentor said, "If you see water as water, and if you see fire as fire, then because you take the position of physics, it will take a long time to promote yourself from the physical level to the spiritual level. It is only when you are on the spiritual level that no harm can come to you. Come along, I will show you."

The mentor took the boy outside in the sunshine. "Look!" he said. "Does my physical being create a shadow?"

The boy looked and discovered that truly his mentor had no shadow, but he himself had a big shadow which looked like a large duplicate of himself on the ground. The mentor said, "Now do you know? When you are a physical being, you only fit physical law. You can not deny it. One day, however, when everything in your life is exactly the same, you will stand in the sun or in any bright light and you will not have a shadow. Then you are spiritualized, and you can walk into fire, go through walls, walk on water, etc. You can do that because at that level, there is no water. Water and fire belong to the earthly level of the five elements. Human bodies are made from five elements - the essences of metal, vegetation, water, fire and earth - and that is why people are controlled by and stay at that level. Not until you achieve yourself above the five elements can the five elements cease to harm you. When that happens, no knife can harm you, no wooden or earthen wall or stone can stop you; you can go right through them, or them through you."

The mentor usually taught the boy in a big log shack at the side of the hut. The shack and hut were on the side of a meadow, next to some beautiful trees. Far away was the stream with the strong waterfall, but the noise of the water did not affect the hut. On the other side of the house were some hilly places and a big rock. The mentor asked the boy, "Can you feel how hard the rock is? The senses are deceptive. My room is not in this hut; my room is in the rock. I need to go into my room now to bring some material to share with you. Wait here and watch."

The mentor went over to the rock, faced it and then suddenly disappeared. The young boy went over to the rock, and although he felt everywhere, he did not find any hole that the mentor could possibly enter. After a few moments, the mentor came back out of the rock carrying a bunch of bamboo pieces with written characters. He told the boy that the bamboo book had two parts. He said, "We will discuss one part today. You are not yet ready to receive the other part.

"Today, I am going to teach you a breathing technique that will to reduce the physical control over your spirit. If you only develop the mind without learning the breathing, then the level of physics is too strong and wonders and other things stay in the realm of the impossible.

"Fearlessness is not something that can only be commanded by the mind. When your mind has fear, it has fear. When your mind has joy, it has joy. Ordinary people try to hard to command their minds, but their minds are unable to reach or do those things. Do not make the same mistake and have the same problem as ordinary people. When people do not know something, they make up a story about it to try to explain it. Their minds become wrongly active. They create whole knowledge systems this way; at most, it is the blind teaching the blind. By doing so, they never reach the final truth."

The young boy thought to himself, This is what I want, to learn the practice so that I can be powerful and be able to come here, just like my friend who carried me over.

The mentor looked startled and shook his head, "No," he said, "Everybody's spiritual mission is different, and everybody's spiritual potential is different. Do you know what? In ancient times, some sages were born, not through intercourse between their mother and father. The mothers were women who lived a single life and had an unusual experience, such as one who had a star falling into her bosom or one who walked over a giant footstep. Suddenly, the women felt a little tipsy or had a kind of sexy feeling, then soon discovered the pregnancy. They later gave birth to a person destined to be a social leader or sage. On other occasions, a dragon would fall down from the sky alongside an unmarried woman, and she would give birth to a special person. This was the experience of generations of people in ancient times. How can people not understand that life can be brought about by energy intercourse? People insist that only physical intercourse between man and woman can bring a child. It is only one way. It was not that way when the first human was brought into the world."

After hearing that, the boy's face was aglow and he said, "I have long wondered and been frustrated and dismayed by the similar question. After listening to you, I feel I am assured of my own birth."

The mentor smiled and said, "In each stage of life, we open up to new realities and new things that we have not known previously. Some things are worth knowing and other things are not.

"Sometime around 2,200 years ago or earlier, a big deluge happened on the land. A hero called the Great Yu lead people to conduct the flood waters to the ocean by developing small channels to become bigger and deeper, and linking together those water channels to pour their water into the Yellow River and other rivers. At that time he had an assistant named 'I.' Everywhere they went, 'I' wrote down all the unusual things, people and creatures that they met or saw and made his writings into a book called *The Book of Mountains and Seas.* In his record, he described some people whose shape is hard to imagine. Their strange and unusual shapes were the result of mixed-up sex. A human having sex with different animals or other strange creatures produced such strange species. Bestiality was considered the greatest sin of human people; that is what caused the rage of the Heavenly God. The ancients believed this was why the big water was sent, to wash away those ugly creatures that were born from human mixed sex and punish the human people. However, those creatures no longer exist. They were naturally extinguished as quickly as they came to earth. This is why we say that Heavenly Law or natural law is installed within human life. Mixed or confused sex produces no positive results.

"Prime minister 'I' who accompanied the Great Yu wrote his records over 2,000 years ago (the deluge happened around 2307 B.C. and the success of the great Yu happened around 2205 B.C.).[5]

---

[5]Niao (reign 2357-2258 B.C.) assigned Yu's father to fight the large amount of stagnant water over the land. Shun (reign 2257-2208 B.C.) assigned Yu to fight the flood. After Yu's success in 2205, he also accepted the throne and reigned from 2205-2197 B.C.

"A life is formed by different types of energy; a good life is brought about by the intercourse of two healthy positive energies. By understanding this fact, we know that all good people, good leaders and sages who provided long generations of virtuous influence were good energy born on earth.

"According to legend, the Ageless Master was born under a plum tree, thus his mother adopted the word 'Li' which means plum as the last name for her child. This is one account of a divine birth from energies which came from Heaven. The mother of the Ageless Master was a spiritual woman, thus her pure energy attracted pure energy. Likewise, mixed energy will attract mixed energy. Spiritual cultivation and discipline can help purify a person's life energy.

"Everybody needs to know that the simple fact of choosing a partner influences their lives and that it also causes an adverse effect to have intercourse with the wrong kind of partner. Even if a well-matched pair does not know the right time or is not in an environment with the right energy, the result can bring trouble to the person or society or generation. Irresponsible behavior bears bitter fruit. You will have the mission of warning people now for generations to come.

"Today, in this meeting, you will learn breathing practice. It is one method, but it is not the way I achieved myself. My capability came by following the Way. Thus, I do not even know how I achieved myself. There are many different breathing systems, thus there are many ways that can help you come to see me.

"When you do this practice, stay in a quiet, safe room with the door closed. Remember that all spiritual practices need to be done alone, away from friends or family. After completing your practice, then you can go back to join them again. It is not necessary for you to stay in seclusion all the time.

"Lie down comfortably on your bed, on your back, using a pillow that is only about the height of a finger. Maintain your body almost level. Close your eyes and then begin to pay attention to and control your breathing. Put a feather under your nostril. When you breathe, the feather is not allowed to be disturbed. An inhale and an exhale is called one breath. Do three hundred breaths; make your ear not hear anything, your eye not see anything, and your mind not think anything. This cannot be accomplished at the beginning; it takes some time, even years, to achieve. If you eat cold or spicy food, or things like fish and meat, or are emotional, either happy, angry, worried or resentful, and you do this practice at the same time, then it is unbeneficial or harmful. Not only that, it will increase your emotional problem.

"In doing your practice, remember this principle: just breathe delicately as many times as feels natural, then remove the feather and go back to breathing normally. It may only be for three, five or seven breaths at first. Then put the feather on your nostril again and repeat the process. When you can do 12 breaths without needing to breathe differently, it means you have made a small achievement. When you can do 120 breaths, you have a medium achievement.

"The time you do this practice must be after midnight and before noon of the next day. Because earthly life follows the solar cycle, we consider the hours from midnight to noon as life-giving energy. The time from noon to midnight is death energy and are not suitable for this practice. Neither is it suitable to practice it in the afternoon; yet, during the hour of Yu, which is from five to seven in the evening, you can do this practice. Use the four energy hours to do the practice. The right hours are Tzu (midnight), Wu (noon), Mao (5:00 to 7:00 in the morning) and Yu (5:00 to 7:00 in the afternoon).

"In winter time, do not do the practice during the hours at midnight, because it is too cold. During the three months of summertime, do not do it at noon, because it is too hot.

"You need to adjust the timing of this practice yourself; if you feel too cold in your stomach, do the practice closer to the hours of stronger sunlight. If you feel too hot, use the hours just after midnight. If the winter weather is too cold where you live, you can make a fire in the fireplace.

"When you practice this, your whole body must be comfortable. Usually you are lying on your back. Always remember to do it gently; do not hurry or push, that only slows down the progress and causes problems.

"When you slowly guide the energy into your body, you feel full. Then use an energy conducting exercise to move the energy throughout the whole body. If you do this practice, you will have no sickness during your lifetime.

"Once you are achieved, if you blow out the energy from your mouth with a 'poofing' sound toward water, the water flowing downstream will turn back upstream. When you 'poof' a fire, it will go out, even if it is a big fire. If you 'poof' a fierce animal like a tiger or panther, it will be tame and obey you. If people are bleeding from injury or bleeding from a lump, then you can stop the bleeding by your 'poof.'

"This practice can also teach you levitation. If you are fully achieved from doing this practice, you can levitate as high as you wish. Do not do anything, just command the mind to tell the bodily energy to float up. Then walking over water is a simple thing. Remember, it is not the breathing but the practice of uniting the mind and the body. When there is no more separation, then true power is produced."

The young boy was happy to receive this practice. "I do not know how to describe it," he said, "but I know that this is what I have been searching for. This practice does not need a talisman, charm, costume or ritual. I do not need to sit in a high chair and look very stern to summon the spirits from East, West, North or South, or ask God to come to help me. It is done just by breathing. I promise you that I will learn it faithfully, no matter how long it takes. The next time I come to see you, I hope I will not need any help. That will be my pride."

The mentor smiled with encouragement.

Chapter 10

Spiritual Achievement Overcomes
The Power of Yin and Yang

I

Soon the boy was no longer a young boy, but a young gentleman although according to local custom, he was still called a boy. He diligently nurtured his energy, daily practicing according to the instruction of his mentor. Because he had spent several years doing this concentrated cultivation, he had achieved himself on several levels. He could foresee the problems of the villagers and also cure their illnesses. He knew the importance of the Way, the law, and the chi or power. Thus, he knew about things that had been hidden or that had not yet happened, and could see the near and the far. His power of understanding had been greatly improved by his learning. However, he knew his position as student. He became more independent from his teacher and friend. He did well with his emotions and in the psychological sphere of worldly necessities as a stranger in the place. The cultivation and practices that the teacher gave him were to strengthen him in all levels so that he could cope with all the travail of life by himself. On the one hand, he did not like to bother his teacher or his friend, yet on the other, it was his growth to have remained quiet for several years and simply do his practice.

By living with a family who observed the Way and by being in an environment containing all types of magic and semi-spiritual and semi-magic practices, the boy came to know that there were 36 big kinds of magic and 72 small kinds of magic, none of which were serious spiritual practices. Even so, his young heart was sometimes curious about them. Yet, among all kinds of magic, the Way is the most truthful and useful; it is just hard to take it in and absorb it into one's life being. However, the young one had clearly learned that an earnest life is the root of all wonders.

During this time, he came into contact with some people who could make themselves invisible. He also met some people with the knowledge of five methods of escape from danger or death. This practice employed the elements in the five element system. He came to know how to appear at the same time with hundreds or thousands of similar semi-bodily figures which could confuse a hostile energy. He saw that people could part the water in a lake or river on both sides of a person standing there. He witnessed people fishing in a bucket and catching the same fish as in a river thousands of miles away. He saw people spill beans on the roadside and make a whole army appear to act as guards. He also learned that there were many other practices. The host family had volumes of books related to these and other types of magic, yet no one in the family paid much attention to those things. It seemed to the boy the power of no curiosity and the power of earnest living had a higher value. Even so, his hosts explained a number of magic practices to him, which he could try for fun.

Because he practiced the breathing so diligently, he had no doubt that one day he could walk over the water without getting wet or being swept away. He wanted to test himself so he decided to go over the water by himself, but he was summoned by the teacher before having achieved it. His neighbor came over one day and said, "Come, let us go to see the teacher."

The young one replied, "I wonder if this is the right time for me to see our teacher. I might still need to ride on your back."

His friend smiled. "I will let you ride on my back. Some day, maybe thousands of people will need to ride on your back to cross the torrent of life."

The young one was calm now. He was ready and willing to see the teacher, no matter what his level of achievement. He was happy to go with the support of his friend, the neighbor boy, and he crossed the water with the help of the neighbor to see the teacher. The mentor greeted him affectionately. "This time, it is I who wish to see you and see how you are doing."

The young man said, "I hope that I am humble enough to present myself to you. I wish that I myself could walk over the water to see you, yet after several years, I am still unable to do it."

The mentor smiled and said, "There is no hurry. In spiritual learning, impatience only creates stronger obstacles. Just relax and allow things to happen naturally. Nothing can be accomplished by an urgent, hasty mind."

Then the young gentleman said, "Thank you for your kindness to allow me, a slow student, to present myself to you without shame, although I am still unachieved. I am especially grateful that you told me my understanding would come by itself. Now I understand people better, and I can also practice some healing and am doing some prophecy.

"Several years ago, when I went to the market, I saw performers, magicians and witch doctors. They told me that anyone who chose to learn from them would be required to make a heavy vow, to be tested and to offer a lifetime of obedience. However, you have never tested me or asked me to live in poverty, be lonely or become disabled, but you taught me many great things. You helped me change from ordinary to start to enter the gate of the Way.

"I know have a long way to go, but I always cherish this sweet gratitude in my heart. It is hard to tell you, but this is truly what I feel."

The mentor smiled and said, "I do not need you to take a heavy vow or promise that you will observe a lot of unreasonable ascetic practices. I do not need you to recognize me or have me as your life-long teacher. However, I would like you to remember one thing.

"When all spiritual people are moving toward coming back inside of themselves, there is no difference between God and the devil. When they outwardly issue their mind in using their hands or their power, there is a great difference between God and devil. In the outer approach, it is clear who and what is God and who and what is the devil. Still, the distance between God and devil is as thin as a thread. Only the truly achieved ones see that fragile boundary.

"One day, when you are achieved, you can do or command whatever you wish. What you do depends upon your own choice. If an achieved person is still intimidated by disbenefit, disfavor or disadvantage, or something that is not in his interest and refuses the moral consideration for the benefit of others, then his achievement cannot be considered complete. In other words, if personal consideration is still higher than moral consideration, it will make a person a moral coward. The moment of choosing between personal interest or moral behavior is when a person is known to be God or devil. Particularly when one suffers from another person's mischief, can he be strong enough to avoid revenge?

"The Ageless Master did not teach commandments, but some of his special words that were handed down through generations were, 'Repay evil with good-heartedness.'

The young man said, "I do not understand the importance of this teaching. My life experience has mostly been enveloped by my family and the several years that I have stayed here being helped by you. Some day, when I am in a situation where I have all the power to do what I wish, I will come to understand this."

"Oh!" the mentor said. "This is not the purpose of my asking you to come see me today. I have seen you make amazing progress. Today I am going to continue to prepare your mind for higher learning."

II

The young gentleman said, "I have received the practice of how to develop my mind," he said. "It seems to me that using a certain system like a mental drill to develop or distract the mind is easier to maintain a calm mind than practicing plain peace of mind. Therefore, I request to see some particular model which could give me an example, or serve as a model, to set my mind right. Then I will not have any doubts."

The mentor answered, "This is a good question. In spiritual cultivation, age does not matter. A person's mental health is easily neglected. The reason for this is that the mind is not like the body. With the body, if you watch your diet, follow a good regimen - which means right time to rise, right time to go to sleep and right amount of work, etc., plus you do some suitable exercise - then there are no more physical problems as a human being.

"Most people do not notice that they have a spiritual being; they only notice that sometimes their mind is troubled. They do not notice that the mind can shape the spirit. Although the spirit is invisible, it stays inside the body. During the period of time when you are a human being or when you live in the world, every day you constantly issue different thoughts and emotions. Maybe the outer world does not notice, but if you are bothered or disturbed, you keep shaping, diminishing or twisting your spiritual being. Your mind not only affects your spiritual being, but it also affects your physical being too.

"Faith is what you project. The power of faith is how you project. The health of faith is the direction of your projection. The faith you project is your exact spiritual being. Therefore, faith in the high God is your own projection of your own strong image which forms and shapes your spirits. Thus, it is important to set your Godly image right. Your God must be kind, loving and gentle. He must be caring, righteous and reasonable. He must be all able, and must be the everlasting life. He must not be brutal. One must not lose faith in God, because that is what you are going to be.

"Therefore, all people need to pay attention to the health of their mental being. It is essential for your own spiritual self-image. The Ageless Master always said, we can take a child as the model of a healthy mental being. A child is full of potential, full of organic health, full of the life force."

The young gentleman asked, "How we could take a child as an example? Self-achievement takes so long, and is so difficult. A child does nothing."

The mentor smiled. "A childlike mind is the goal of a spiritual student. A child recovers quickly from any trouble," he said. "Sometimes a child is unhappy. Sometimes he dislikes something, but he does not stay unhappy all the time; it is only a momentary reaction. When he dislikes someone, he will not brood over destroying the other person. If he feels mistreated by his friend, mother, brother or sister, or has some other type of trouble, he easily forgets all about it. He keeps nothing in his mind.

"Look at adults. They take a small thing that bothers them, and wait for an opportunity for revenge. Revenge is another thing altogether, but the mere fact of keeping such a memory or emotion in the deep mind is harmful to a person's mental health. Adults nurture hatred, jealousy or prejudice as part of their mental being from all kinds of life conditions. These thoughts and emotions are unconsciously stored and subtly planted in the invisible mind like a seed that will become future trouble.

"A baby or child does not do that. If you trust that there is paradise somewhere, you can trust that an innocent child carries paradise with him. Adults are people who have lost their paradise. They can no longer enjoy their attainments as much as when they were in their childhood paradise. They have no more pure enjoyment because they have lost the paradise of their innocent childhood. The wise one takes simplicity as high wisdom. The unwise one takes simplicity as foolishness.

"When people grow older, the mind is worn out from being too nervous and from contamination by different unhealthy emotions which brings them close to death. Mental rejuvenation is the key to physical and spiritual rejuvenation. When a person decides to be reborn again spiritually and mentally, and take the image of a child into his heart, he hopes to restore paradise in his life.

"Cultivating oneself to achieve proficiency in small magic is not difficult. Cultivating oneself to achieve immortality is also not difficult. The difficulty lies in watching your mind and keeping it from stealing the fruit of your natural being. Left to its own devices, the mind can make your natural being turn out to be sour and of no value. It can corrupt or decay the fruit of your pure, untouched spiritual being. It is important for spiritual students to know that.

"Thus, in each moment, a childlike mind receives new life. It is reborn. To rebirth yourself anew in each moment is the fundamental practice of everlasting life."

The young man quietly and carefully took each word into his mind. He knew that such things are important. Without discipline of mind, without nurturing the mind, immortality will be devalued. He remained quietly sitting on the side, waiting for his mentor to speak again.

At this moment, the mentor said, "No individual person can stop self-regenerating and refreshing. In other words, each individual needs to refresh oneself all the time. Similarly, if a society or nation does not refresh itself, if it cannot accept new things or new light, it will become worn out and lack flexibility. If it still exists, its left-over shell may still keep the society together, but its vitality has been badly damaged. Therefore, it is the responsibility of sages and leaders of society to keep their own minds attuned. To receive the rebirth of life by attuning the mind is like a musical instrument that is recently tuned; it gives the best music. In tuning a fiddle, if you pull the string too tight or loosen it too much, the instrument will not produce a harmonious melody.

"Spiritual cultivation is internal work. We always need to attune ourselves to be not too hyper and also not to be too low key. It takes persistence to keep our mind light and cheerful but not excited, calm but not stagnant. This is important for one who pursues immortal life or even someone who lives a general mortal life. Mortal life is no different from immortal life; mortal life is the foundation of the immortal. Supernature comes from nature.

"If you understand what I have been telling you about controlling the mind and can do it, you have almost achieved yourself. Never feel tired or bored with your life; never feel bored with the living opportunity. This is how to conduct yourself toward the sunshine and the light side of life.

"The Ageless Master spoke about yin and yang. Yang is light, yin is dark. Yang is positive, yin is negative. What you move toward is how you determine what you are going to be. Yet, there is yang in the yin, there is yin in the yang; there is positive in negative, there is negative in positive. Learning life is the effort of purifying a situation."

Chapter 11

A Successful Future Lies in Preparation

The young one offered to do whatever chores his host family had for him to do, but his host introduced him to the villagers who needed help. Each day, the young one brought a lunch that was prepared by his host and went on his way to give help to others, but not for payment. During these last few days, he helped an old widow and her children. It was a long summer day. Then he went to see his teacher and asked, "Today, I would like to know what the Ageless One said about God. It is important to me."

The mentor smiled and answered, "The Ageless One did not present God as an individual, the Ageless One presented God as a Way."

The young one asked, "May I know what is the difference between presenting God as an individual and presenting God by his way?"

The mentor answered, "To present God as an individual being would limit God to the experiences of some human ancestors, only to become a partial expression. Presenting God as a Way must come from the universal experience and inspiration of prophets of all places and all generations. The Way helps people recognize the choice of the Godly Way as the direction to conduct a good life."

The young one asked, "May I know now what the Ageless One has said?"

The mentor considered. His language was simple and direct. "I can tell you everything written by the Ageless One, line by line, in his words. There are only eleven places in his writing which mentioned the Way of Heaven. It can be called the Spiritual Way or the Godly Way. The Ageless Master only mentioned God once. He said, 'The Way comes before God.' What he mentioned was the Heavenly Way. Another name for God is Heaven.

"The Ageless One mentioned the following:

1. It is the Godly Way to retreat after a contribution is made to people. Do not become attached to the name and credit for what you have accomplished for others.

2. The Godly Way puts an end to all struggle through being non-competitive.

3. The Godly Way is responsive; it does not proclaim.

4. The Godly Way comes to people by itself, not by anyone's invitation.

6. The Godly Way is not meticulously designed, yet it is the complete plan of all lives.

7. The Godly Way is like a mesh net; nothing and no one can escape its justice.

8. The Godly Way is like pulling a bow; the high part is made lower and the low is raised higher; what is excessive is taken, what is insufficient is given more.

9. The Godly Way leaves what is excessive to support the insufficient. (Here, the Ageless Master repeated the advice for self-balancing.)

10. The Godly Way is to benefit, not to harm.

11. The Godly Way is not partial to anyone or anything, yet it is as always at the side of the one of righteousness and virtue."

The young one asked, "Can God be an individual?"

The mentor answered, "Yes, God can be individualized as a single being. When an individual lives up to the Godly Way, he or she is a holy individual; if a spirit lives up to the Godly Way, it is a holy spirit. On a shallower level, when humans perceive the spiritual world, they cannot distinguish between the spirits. To the human being, any individualized spirit which is holy is God. It is also good to know that in the spiritual realm, one is all and all is one. All holy spirits are God, yet each individual is God also."

The young one asked, "I have already known that it is important to live up to the Godly Way, but I just did not do enough. Is there anything else that I need to know from the teaching of the Ageless One?"

The mentor smiled and answered, "Yes, he said that the Godly Way is to not respond with violence or revenge for the wrongdoing of others."

The young one said, "Then, is there any punishment for doing wrong and evil? And is there any reward for doing right and good?"

"The reward is everlasting life," replied his teacher. "Improper behavior has its own punishment installed within it, just as the Ageless One described: 'Any action that is over-stretched or over-expanded is against the Way and will soon end one's life.'"

Then the young one asked, "How does an individual person realize God?"

The mentor replied, "By forgiving. The power of forgiveness is the power of God, but if you forgive somebody, do not proclaim that you are God. Otherwise, satan's test must be met, because the forgiveness was given out of pride. Forgiving must come from the kind nature of the Godly individual. Forgiving must naturally flow out from one's nature to meet the circumstance. May the godly nature be recognized by people of high spiritual nature."

There were so many questions in the mind of the young one. After he was able to communicate well in the new language, he liked to solve all the riddles in his mind. He would ask about things that were far from his own life to things that were near to his life.

He asked, "We know that God created the world and humankind and animals, but how did God himself come forth?"

The mentor smiled again and said, "It is beyond the experience of all humankind. We have not lived long enough to witness how the world began. However, the source of spiritual knowledge is the immortal spirits. Their experience is that all beings come from non-being. Non-being is the source of all."

The young one asked, "What is the source of non-being?"

The mentor answered, "It is the Way. According to the Way, beingness and non-beingness give birth to each other. It is similar to the question, 'Which came first, the chicken or the egg?' The Way expresses the interdependence of form and the subtle essence."

The young one asked, "What existed before the chicken and the egg?"

The mentor smiled and answered, "There was nothing that could be distinguished. It was not totally nothing. It was the subtle energy before it became apparent and formed. The immortal spirits with their growing spiritual function, discerned that the world developed from the prime energy. This prime energy has two phases: light and heavy. The light energy is spirit, and the heavy is form. It takes a long time for the light and the heavy to meet each other and produce the form of life.

"Life also went through a long process of development to attain the growth of the mind in the form of humankind. Upon reaching the full growth of mind, the spirit of humankind recognized its own source as God.

"At that stage, God was the self-recognition of the human spirit. They established the three divisions of nature as Heaven or the spiritual sphere, Earth or the material sphere, and Life or the human sphere. Humankind was the new integration of spiritual energy and material energy. This was discovered through the development of spiritual discernment in our human ancestors.

"They saw that nature comes from one - the prime energy. One was divided into two: light yang energy and heavy yin energy. Then came the third, which is the integration of yang and yin. Beyond this third level there are numerous things. All of nature was roughly classified into these three divisions."

The young one said, "Who are the immortal spirits?"

The mentor answered, "The light energy or spirits do not die. Their form of life, as a new integration, is subject to transformation; they cannot stay the same all the time. Not only are lives transformed, but so are the stars in the sky. Even the earth itself does not stay in the same location all the time but makes a whirlpool movement and experiences all types of things.

"The learning of the Way comes from the spiritual growth of our human ancestors. They knew all the forms of movements and transformation in nature. There is no other ruler than self-law or the Word. The learning of the Way is the study of self-law or the Word. God is the universal self-law, the Word. As the self-law or the Word, God is not only the lord of creation, God is also the lord of movement and transformation."

The young one asked, "You have mentioned that God is the self-recognition of the spirit of human ancestors. Why is the world full of darkness?"

The mentor answered, "Spiritual growth is not the same among all people. It is a precious attainment to distinguish oneself from one's animal nature. The effort was made by a few sages, and it attracted the spiritual resonance of other people because all human life contains spiritual energy. The spiritual development of humankind came about through the struggle between people's spiritual nature and their animal nature. It happens differently in each individual. Some people are more successful at it than others.

"The basic direction of human life is toward spiritual development. Surely, there are failures in the forward and upward movement of a newly integrated human nature, but the effort continues until it successfully reaches liberation from the animal basis of life. Few people overlook their animal instinct. Most people overlook their spiritual nature. In other words, fewer people can live with God; it is easier for them to live with their animal selves. Thus, the dark force is in expansion, and the light force is yielding.

"The *I Ching* describes a negative phase when yin energy grows and yang decreases. When inferior-spirited people take the lead, virtuous-spirited people are suppressed. This is what you have seen in your own homeland and other places."

The young one asked, "What is God's function in an individual person?"

The mentor answered, "God lives in the individual to as one's complete spiritual faculties. This could be called the Angel of Conscience when it gives a person moral power, the Angel of Inspiration when it gives advice in times of difficulty, the Angel of Enlightenment when it brings light to one's search in the darkness, the Angel of Intuition when it bestows knowledge without any learning or experience, such as the knowledge of God, the knowledge of ethics and the knowledge of invention in breaking through where there is no precedence or examples, etc. Other faculties might be called the Angel of Rationality when balance is established or restored, and the Archangel of Power when accomplishment in all good directions is achieved.

"Putting all these spiritual faculties together is the wisdom of God as well as the God of wisdom. God is the heart of the Infinite Mother. Everyone should obey and offer their highest."

The young one asked, "Why doesn't God punish evil people immediately and directly?"

The mentor answered, "God punishes all types of evil, yet God's punishment is not always immediately apparent, because God is both internal and external. Punishment works on the inside of life. All angels and spiritual faculties leave an evil person in gradual steps and then his tree of life is slowly toppled or sudden death is received. People of God watch even their smallest mistakes and do not allow them to develop into lifetaking problems."

The young one said, "Who are the immortal spirits?"

The mentor answered, "Immortal spirits are natural spirits who took human form and then left their forms after attaining higher spiritual evolution in worldly life experience. Their spiritual attainment was fulfilled by constantly giving spiritual help to people. They are the Gods of people on Earth.

"The attainment of Godhood comes about through self-recognition and self-realization. The attainment of the God-head is inside-out, not outside-in as it was in earlier human spiritual development when there were no examples.

"To follow the Way means to have one's attainment come from inside out. Attainment means to achieve the balance of the interplay of natural yin and yang forces. In other words, when learning the Way, it is helpful to allow the inside-out and the outside-in meet each other. This does not mean that one does not have any personal experiences of enlightenment."

The young one asked, "Isn't self-recognition easy for everyone?"

The mentor smiled and answered, "It is easy for some people who identify with self-responsibility or self-duty of life and who extend the love of life to all beings. It is not easy for those who identify with self-aggrandizement and jealousy and who extend darkness to all. People must first develop spiritual awareness to improve their spiritual self-recognition. Only then can they hope to attain Godhood."

The Young one said, "I still am not totally clear about this."

The mentor patiently answered, "All right, I will discuss it further. Self-recognition is the projection of a thought.

Thought comes from the mind. One first needs to recognize the power of mind in one's life. Whatever you think is what you become spiritually.

"I would like to give you a worldly example. A neighbor boy stole your sheep and you suspected or truly knew him to be the thief. When you accused him face-to-face of having stolen the sheep, he denied it with a flushed face. Because his stealing was associated with his mind, but not with his life spirit, he does not recognize himself as a thief. Thus, there is still hope that the boy will correct his behavior. If he had recognized himself as a thief, it would have been a hard situation for him.

"A person's occasional mistakes are a similar situation. For example, a man or a woman sometimes makes mistakes in sexual matters or in making a commitment to someone. Spiritually supporting the behavior may not be so serious, but that behavior could bring more trouble. The direction in which you set your mind and will is an important matter; it determines in what direction you will move forward."

"Self-recognition as God comes as the good fruit of the hard work of enlightenment. It is different from the general level of mind."

The young one asked, "Who were the three sages who came to my birth and gave me gifts and blessings?"

The mentor smiled and said, "They were three achieved ones: the Messenger of Unsurpassable Virtue, the Messenger of Everlasting Life and the Messenger of Heavenly Triumph."

The young one asked, "Where are they now?"

The mentor answered, "They have lived among people in order to fulfil their mission and they are all in different places now giving help to people."

The young one asked, "Who was the Ageless Master?"

The mentor answered, "The Ageless One is an immortal spirit. He has been born into the world at different times, in different places and among different people to help them through selfless service."

Then, the young one asked, "Why was I chosen to study the Way?"

"It has become a traditional rule for the teacher to find the student for worldly service," replied his teacher. "In this important matter, it is not the student who finds us, it is we who look for the student in whom Heavenly virtue can be realized and a teacher be built for helping people. We also choose someone to whom we can pass down important spiritual secrets. Because you will be the one to go to the masses to do the teaching, I am in the position to provide spiritual knowledge for your general service and the secrets of the spiritual world which are just for you.

"Why do we go out in the world to look for students? There are few people who posses the willingness to serve the world and, at the same time, have no personal ambition to become a ruler. We need to search long for such a one. The typical general student does not need to search for an achieved teacher, although there is certainly the same difficulty in finding a truly achieved teacher.

"Yet, among ordinary spiritual students, who would not like to become invisible or become a flying, wingless angel to meet friends they enjoy? Who would not like to find the way to refine the bulky life of the body to be a tiny flying shien, a high and complete spiritual being with all the achievements of profundity to converse with you so that you can receive all knowledge? Everlasting life relies on nothing.

"Only the student of selfless piety is allowed to know the secret of God's Kingdom. Who else should be given this privilege? By what spiritual merit can an ordinary person invite the attention of Heaven?"

The young one bowed and withdrew himself with tremendous joy. He knew that his learning had not yet reached its depth and that his teacher was only preparing him to be a teacher.

Chapter 12

Love of People

This time the young one came to the teacher. The teacher asked to see his palms. Both palms were callused from hard work and showed that his kind heart was stronger than his palms. The mentor smiled and asked him to soak his hands in newly drawn water from the deep well and carefully wash them. The young one obeyed and did so. With joy, he returned to the teacher and said, "My hands are clean and all the callouses are gone." The mentor was pleased.

The young one asked, "I would like to know more about the teaching of the Ageless One. What is everlasting life?"

The mentor answered, "The Way is the way of everlasting life. This is the essence of the Ageless One's teaching. I will recite his own words for you, slowly to help you catch them carefully. I will do it in no particular order. I will just tell you whatever comes into my mind first."

The young one said, "All right."

The mentor paused briefly as he did when he used to recite this as part of his own practice. He began, "The Ageless One said,

'The spirit of the universe has no death.
It is the hidden reproductive power of nature,
    and is the subtle origin of all.
Thus, it is the root of the universe.'"

The young one asked, "How does it live?"
The mentor answered, "The Ageless One said,

'The universal source is everlasting.
It is subtle and gentle
    and exists beyond the knowledge of senses.
By being subtle and gentle in using itself
It never exhausts itself."

The young one asked, "Is the spirit of the universe an individual or is it a thing?"

The mentor smiled and answered, "It is not an individual. It is the foundation of all individual beings and things. It is the subtle level of universal existence.

"As the Ageless One said,

'The spirit of the universe is long-living.
Why can the spirit of the universe live long?
Because it does not live for itself.
Thus, it lives an everlasting life.'"

The young one asked: "What can people learn from the spirit of the universe?"

The mentor answered, "The Ageless One said,

'The wise one puts his own life concerns
*   after all other people's lives.*
Thus, he is found to be the foremost.
Because his spirit lives beyond his physical life,
*   he finds his everlasting being everywhere.*
Not because one does not take care of oneself
*   but because one loves the lives of all people.*
*   he accomplishes his life in peace.'"*

The young one asked again, "I would like to know more about how people should treat other people."

The mentor answered, "As the Ageless One said:

'To know everlasting life is to become receptive.
By becoming receptive, one becomes selfless.
By becoming selfless, one extends one's life to all lives.
By loving all lives, one becomes God.
To be God is to be one with the Way.
The Way is everlasting.
Then one's life is with the Way and never ends.'"

The young one asked, "I know now that the wise one serves God through serving all people, and the foolish one makes people serve his ego and therefore abandons God. Yet, I would like to know what is the right way to achieve this."

The mentor answered, "As the Ageless One said,

'To help others live an orderly life and to serve God
    there is nothing better than
    a self-disciplined, balanced life.
By practicing a self-disciplined, balanced life,
    one reaches the way of everlasting life.
By living a self-disciplined, balanced life,
There is no obstacle that cannot be overcome in one's life.
Thus, one moves toward the infinite.
Practically, one enlarges one's spiritual territory
    to enjoy endless development.
This is to deeply root one's life
    in the everlasting life of universal potency."

The young one asked again, "What is worth doing other than things related to physical life?"

The mentor answered, "As the Ageless One said,

'What is strongly built,
    is found in ruins someday.
Yet the upright character of a person
    cannot be removed.
What is tenaciously adhered to,
    is sometimes seen falling apart.
Yet, the loving nature of an individual toward all lives
    cannot be destroyed.'"

The young one asked again, "What is the general practice for obtaining everlasting life?"

The mentor answered, "As the Ageless One said,

'The universe has its beginning.
The beginning is the mother of all.
From knowing the mother - the spirit of the universe
    one knows the offspring, all the beings and things
    of the manifest world.
We are among the offspring of the subtle origin.
Knowing oneself to be one of the offspring,
    but staying united
    with the inexhaustible subtle source,
    is how to attain everlasting life.

Keep away from the distraction of the sensory surface.
Stay with the deep subtle origin
  which is beyond all differences and conflict,
  then you will find the deep truth of eternal life.
One who runs after the superficial differences
  of the offspring
  loses the connection
  with the subtle source of oneness
  and is found to be helpless in the end.'"

The young one asked again, "How does one use the mind in order to achieve spiritually?"

The mentor answered, "As the Ageless Master said,

'To know what is too subtle or too small to be observed
  is to become bright minded all the time.
To keep to the gentle and soft
  is to become stronger every day.
Use the light of your own spiritual energy
  in all life activity.
Remain with the subtle source of all,
  and you shall have no trouble in your life.
This is learning the Way of Everlasting Life.'"

The young one asked again, "I have received the most invaluable guidance for spiritual practice, yet I would like to know more about how to practice it in general worldly life."

The mentor answered, "As the Ageless One said,

'It is intelligent to know others.
Yet, it is truly wise to know oneself.
It is tough to conquer others.
Yet, it is truly strong to conquer oneself.
It is rich to own a lot of things.
Yet, it is truly rich to be self-contented.
It is willful to impose one's ideas on others.
Yet, it is truly unshakable to move straightly
  toward an unselfish goal.
One is long standing to hold onto one's position.
Yet truly lasting means not to die by continuing
  to give good service to all lives.'"

The young one asked, "Is there any warning about learning everlasting life?"

The mentor answered, "As the Ageless One said,

'If you are too fond of something,
  it becomes too costly.
If you have too many things,
  you will have a great loss.
Humiliation is the end to the one
  who does not know how much is enough.
The durable life force is attained
  by knowing when and where to stop.'"

The young one asked, "What is good and healthy for all people?"

The mentor smiled and said, "It is your divine nature to always remember to benefit all other people. Now listen to what the Ageless One said:

'Blessings reside in being humble.
Straight is seen from the wrongdoing of others.
Benefit is received by being insufficient.
Renewal happens to what is worn out.
Gain more by taking less.
Waste comes from having too much."

The young one happily concluded the meeting by saying, "Today I received enough for my entire lifetime."

The mentor smiled and said, "Concerning immortality, it is almost ready in you. Your life mission is to teach people the truth that there is everlasting life."

The young one said firmly, "I will teach the faith of everlasting life to my people. They are in trouble; they need help."

The mentor said, "Sometimes one finds that a piece of old wood is harder to carve. Their stiff minds have lost flexibility. You may find a new place with different people which is more fertile ground for this new seed."

The young one answered, "But I love my people."

The meeting stopped here.

Chapter 13

Spiritual Teaching is Undoing the Student

The young one remembered very well what the teacher told him: it is harder to be a teacher than it is to become immortal. For his service, he had to be well-versed with all the important points at the level of mind, so he patiently followed and learned to prepare himself to be a good teacher.

The young one requested, "What did the Ageless Master say about worldly power?"

"The Ageless Master spoke about worldly rulership from two different points of view," replied his mentor. "When he spoke to those whose ambition was to conquer the world, he said,

'One takes the world by having no trouble.
If you have a lot of trouble,
Then the world is not worthy for you,
*   and you are not worthy for the world, either.'*

"When the Master spoke to those of moral motivation who wished to help the world, he said,

'The one who considers the world
*   as if it were his own life*
*   should be assigned to take care of the world.*
The one who serves the world with his life
*   can be entrusted with the world.'*

"In my own words,

The one who values the world as equal
*   to the value of his own life,*
*   can be assigned the duties of the world.*
The one who loves the world as much
*   as he loves his own body,*
*   can be entrusted with the safety of the world."*

"Did the Ageless Master say anything about how to value one's own life and love one's own body?" queried the young one.

The mentor answered, "Certainly. He gave valuable guidance. The Ageless Master used the metaphor of governing a kingdom when talking about governing the life of one's own body. He said,

'Can one love the people
*   and govern the kingdom*
*   without applying intelligence?*

"This means, can you love all the parts of your body, even the ones that cause you problems or are unattractive, and take care of yourself using your natural instinct and intuition rather than your intellectual capability? The Ageless Master also said,

'When the government is incapable,
*   the people will be capable.*
When the government asserts control,
*   the people become poor.*
When the government is clever,
*   the people become useless dependents.*
When the government plays dumb,
*   the people come to help.*

"This means, govern your bodily kingdom according to the Heavenly Way. Allow the people of the kingdom, which are all the parts of the bodily kingdom, to enjoy their own organic, healthy nature. Do not do anything that would damage your kingdom's well being or naturalness.

"In the physical sphere of life, each individual life is a kingdom. Many people can accept this truth because they know that a life is composed of different parts, such as different organs and systems, etc. At least, people know that in their lives, there are two partners: the body and the mind.

"In the deep spiritual sphere, each individual life is also a kingdom. There are different spiritual agents which carry different spiritual functions. If one agent of the life is lost, then the spiritual function of the corresponding physical organs or system is dissolved. If one or more agents which are related to the mind are lost, the function of the mind also appears incomplete.

"Fully knowing this deep reality of life requires spiritual learning and cultivation which will bring about self-discovery of the internal truth of life.

"In the system of spiritual knowledge, the word 'kingdom' describes all general, individual life. 'Heavenly Kingdom' or 'Kingdom of God' describes an individual life which has developed its own spiritual sphere. The spiritual faculties and spiritual friends are known and can communicate to the mind of the individual by different subtle signals. Inside the individual different internal agents or spirits exist and function in the bodily life. Outside the individual are spiritual friends who come to visit. Spiritual friends sometimes communicate when one is in a meditative state of mind. In general, the communication is simple. It can be done in any way. The individual only needs to keep his own mind quiet.

"Self-discovery of the internal spiritual system can be achieved in two ways. One way is natural. Older people with correct spiritual cultivation know the hidden truth through dreams and different critical life experiences and learning.

"Another way is to bring out all spiritual agents and entities during an intense 49-day spiritual cultivation. This can be a great challenge to an individual who is used to thinking he is a single spirit alone, or merely a conscious mind in a physical being without knowing that an individual is the convergence of numerous spiritual and semi-physical entitles. Now suddenly, he faces the multiple differences of activities within. He experiences feelings of panic and perplexity, the feeling of no peace and the feeling of being unsafe. He experiences these things, because when the energy vibration of your physical and mental bodies change, a person is like a teenager who suddenly receives the throne of a big kingdom and does not know what to do with it, internally or externally."

The young one asked, "Should I learn this art?"

The mentor responded, "It seems you have no other choice than to quickly bring about all necessary knowledge to your pre-decided life destiny. This specific practice will be taught to you separately from these study meetings. Now we will only discuss the general practice that will satisfy the inquisitiveness of your healthy, young mind and help you understand the direction of your practice.

"Since I have already given you the important definitions of the Kingdom, I will share more of the Ageless Master's teaching with you.

'In the Kingdom of God,
the pursuit of improper wisdom comes to an end.
The use of intelligence is abandoned.
By doing so, the people[1] are benefitted a hundred times.

In the Kingdom of God,
the preaching of love is quieted;
the argument of righteousness is forgotten.
People return to genuine love and honesty.

When the play of smartness ceases,
the pursuit of profit is given up.
Robbery or theft no longer occur.'

"These three verses convey the principle that people should not work on the cosmetic or superficial part of life any longer but remain with their deep nature.

'Thus, one sees the simple essence of life.
One needs to embrace the simple essence.
One does not extend oneself to become too selfish.
One rarefies all types of desire.
One is not pushed into external learning and has no worry,
but appreciates the pure joy of life."

"The Kingdom of God is given to those who have developed themselves to reach such sweet immortal fruit.
"Now, I would like to tell you what the Ageless Master said about the Godly government of the bodily and mental life.

'This spiritual ruler of life, the main developed spirit,
has no personal opinions or ideas.
He reacts to the needs of the people.[2]

---

[1]"People" means all parts of the body or life being of an individual.

[2]All parts of natural life.

He extends his good will to the good.
He also extends his good will to the bad
because he is the being of good will.

He extends his faith to the faithful.
He also extends his faith to the unfaithful
because he is the being of faith.

As the dutiful ruler,
he is cautious.
He blends the conflict of different interest of all people
and allows people
to have different interests.
He helps each spirit on the physical and mental level
to attain growth.
He helps them all without discrimination."

In this meeting, the young one said, "Each time you teach me, I feel I have to give up what I thought I had before. You teach me more, yet I become less occupied. I have almost reached a state of nothingness. I feel clean and clear. It is this way each time after I listen to you; the weight of the world is lifted from me. I feel emptied. I feel like I have received a new life, not a fleshly one but a spiritual life."

Chapter 14

Do you Have a Godly Government Within Yourself?

Through the practice which the mentor taught him, the young one came to the stage where he proved that spirits are internal and external, yet he needed to confirm his attainment. Thus, he said, "On the conceptual level, I am not yet totally used to the truth that God is internal and at the same time external. In general, a kingdom is a society. Are you telling me that the bodily form of individual life and the developed spiritual realm of the spiritual achieved ones should be also like a kingdom? To understand this, I need more help."

The mentor responded, "In all individual lives, there are three souls. The conscious mind, with its own spirit, is the middle soul. Above the mind is the upper divine soul, the God in a person. Beneath the mind is the lower physical soul.

"The divine soul is the spiritual king in a person; the conscious mind is the prime minister of one's life; and the physical soul is the population of the kingdom. The divine soul is highest and the physical soul is the foundation.

"In undeveloped people (I am talking about human people here, not the physical soul), the conscious mind is the ruler. Yet, in developed people, the ones who live in the Kingdom of God, the divine soul is the 'unruling ruler' who does nothing to interfere with the people. 'People' here means all less powerful spiritual entities and the physical and mental partners.

"Yet, even in developed people, the conscious mind depends on its own development in order to attain high spiritual attainment. If it is not developed, it inclines to meddle in anything that happens internally and externally, but that does not mean it brings the best things to the kingdom of the individual life. It tends to dominate with its intent to like or dislike things. It takes advantage of its important position, but it does poorly. The mind is like a devious and tyrannical ruler which demands the people to hail it as King but it eventually brings all departments of life to the trenches and dunghills.

"The purpose of spiritual learning is to attain spiritual achievement. From this, there is a process of transferring internal leadership of one's life being from the mind, which consists of worldly experiences, nervous pressure and education, to God, which is the spiritual being within. The Godly part of each person is like magnetism to the needle of a compass. The needle or the mind must connect with the magnetic field.

"It is to say, the relationship between the mind and spirit in life is like the magnetic pole of a compass point. One does not know the correct direction unless the cardinal points of the compass' surface are lined up correctly with the needle. In the human being, the magnetic field is universal life, the magnetic pole is the spiritual being of oneself, and the flat surface of the compass is the mind.

"You see, because the life of a human individual is a small universe, it has its own magnetic field. Spiritual cultivation changes and improves the personal magnetic field of an individual. The ancient sages recognized the importance of spiritual cultivation even before the invention of the compass.

"Now, I will continue the important message of the Ageless Master:

'To the people of the Heavenly kingdom:

To have complete spiritual power
is like the full life energy of the red baby.
Poisonous insects do not bite it.
Fierce animals do not attack it.
Birds of prey do not grasp it.
Its bone is soft and its muscles tender,
yet its grip is firm.
Its sexual organ stirs to express the health of life,
yet it knows nothing of the intercourse of yin and yang.
Because of its great harmony inside,
it is not hoarse after crying the whole day long.'"

The young one asked, "What is the red baby?"

"A red baby," replied his teacher, "was also a spiritual experience of the ancient spiritually achieved ones. It is deeply related to each individual's own spiritual development. It is a truthful spiritual attainment that is used as a metaphor of how to nurture one's spirit within and form the supreme vitality to be like a baby. In this metaphoric guidance, the image of the red baby was a spiritual reality when the first sky energy and earth energy integrated to become the first human ancestor as an unclothed child. Pink or red refers to the skin color of a newborn.

"When formed with the two types of energy, the spirit can already speak, walk and run around. All creatures on earth respect, love and protect it. It enjoys tremendous freedom and happiness. The birth of a red baby is an auspicious event. The sky shines with all the colors and there is joy and peace on the earth. The spirits in Heaven quietly await the formation of the red child. At the moment when the unclothed red child radiating a fiery aura appeared on earth, it was the only true God formed into human shape. It walked seven steps forward, a finger of one hand pointing to the sky and a finger of the other hand pointing to the earth to express 'Up to Heaven, down to Earth. I am the one, unique, most respectful being.' However, some achieved ones made this as a declaration of independence to rank humankind as equal to the other two partners. The position of humankind in the universe was established and expressed the gallantry of the new species.

"The pink baby, which is also called the red baby, was the unclothed, childlike first being who radiated a red aura. It was the earliest spiritual form of God, as well as the earliest stage of the spiritual human form. This stage of evolution occurred when the human shape of life was greatly formed with two types of energy: earthly physical energy and heavenly spiritual energy or the subtle rays of the sky. There was a period of time when 'red babies' lived happily among giant animals, birds, snakes and insects. They were not human adults.

"The first human form was the best developed of all forms of life on earth. It was the greatest integration of universal spiritual energy and the highest form of physical energy."

The young one broke in by saying, "Pardon me, but I was told that all lives are the creation of God. Is that correct?"

The mentor smiled and responded to him by saying, "That is a metaphoric way of describing it. In the beginning, God had no form at all. God - or the red baby or the universal spirit - formed itself many times with various shapes and forms and left many kinds of descendants on earth at the very beginning during a trial stage. At last, it formed itself with the human form. This new form expressed the progress of integration of physics and spirit. In other words, the best form was produced through the integration of spiritual and earthly energy in the human form. Then the mind was added later. Thus, the new human form is the perfect integration of three types of energies, Godly energy, physical energy and mental energy. From that time on, there existed three lords in a human life. The upper one is the spiritual, the middle one is the mental, and the lower one is the physical.

"At the time of the red baby, the baby itself was just a well converged energy form. It directly absorbed the natural energy surrounding it and matured. Then later, the new partner, the rapidly growing mind became associated with the lord of the lower physical region and squeezed the upper natural lordship of the spirit, causing it to give up its leadership to the new, mixed leadership of good and bad, the mind.

"That is to say that eventually, the development of the mind became dominant to collaborate with the 'lord' of the physical body. This partnership suppressed the spiritual part. Then, the quality of life plummeted rapidly."

The young one excused himself for interrupting, but he felt he had understood something important, so he said, "I see the importance of teaching the Kingdom of God in order to restore the joy of pure life. Yet, can we go back to living like a red baby again?"

The mentor smiled and answered, "Your intuition is strong. You have sensed the importance of the red baby. Here is the secret of everlasting life. The integration of different energies produces human life, and human life is a small model of nature. Through spiritual cultivation, the two types of energy within an individual human life can give birth to a new, more highly evolved being: a pure, subtle red baby that is not physical but spiritual. We will discuss more about this later. The practice for how to produce one will be given to you separately.

"Now we have come to the point: can people go back to the early stage of living in a natural paradise? No, they cannot, nor do they need to. A good answer to this is found in the *I Ching:* straighten the order of the three natural spheres in order to balance your life. This is the advanced guidance produced by the ancient developed ones after having done a great amount of spiritual cultivation. We know that we cannot go back anymore to the early stage of innocent life. No one can stop the downfall of modern culture or become anti-cultural in order to return to nature. When any aspect of human development lacks spiritual leadership, people shall eat the fruit they have sown. Therefore, spiritual development, balanced leadership and a healthy culture are needed. Knowing this need, no spiritually developed people should abandon the world to its own ruin. We can only focus upon the way of balance, which is the way of everlasting life of God. This means not to move too much in any one direction. This is the guidance of the Ageless Truth, which is contained in the teaching of the Ageless Master.

"In the later stage of cultural development that we are now in, the middle sphere of mind is continuously expanding, yet the real position of the mind should be that of prime minister of the three spheres of life. Its correct function is to serve the subtle sphere and the well-being of one's life. A healthy government has a healthy constitution, and its prime minister should fulfill its duty only according to the constitution. In the Kingdom of God, the 'constitution' is the Way.

"As the Ageless Master said,

'When the government is simple,
 the people enjoy happiness.
When the government enforces meticulous control
 the people suffer from the difficulty."

and

'When smart ideas and approaches are applied
 in governing a kingdom,
 the people are robbed.
When no smart ideas and clever approaches
 are applied to govern a kingdom,
 the people are blessed.'

"Smart idea means the partial interest of single mental intent, which usually lacks an integral vision of life. For broader wisdom, it must be applied in association with spiritual energy.

"It is true that benefit can be brought about from smart ideas and clever approaches. Yet, trouble is produced from benefit and so, even smarter ideas and more clever approaches are then needed to handle the new problem. This type of vicious cycle continues to grow with no real benefit to anyone.

"Spiritual leadership of the individual self and of society, as taught by the *Tao Teh Ching,* the Ageless Teaching, would allow natural development to all, the individual and society. All wasteful struggle could be avoided.

"The entire book of the Ageless Master can be considered as the teaching of the Godly government of each individual self. However, the teaching is so condensed that it also contains all other important spiritual treasures."

Chapter 15

The Opportunity for Survival
Is Found from Death

The young boy had grown a great deal since his last meeting with the mentor. Now he understood many things he did not understand before, because the new knowledge came through personal proof from the special practices he had received. One by one, each thing the mentor told him was proven through his practice and the wish to do something for the world became ever strong within him. Clearly, this was the purpose of his learning. Thus, in the next meeting, the young one asked his teacher, "The world has become bad. What salvation does God have for people?"

The mentor replied, "If God is accepted as the faith to fight evil, people of moral courage are respectable. Their fighting serves people directly, yet their offering is only a temporary solution. The greatest contribution to the world is spiritual teaching and making a real example of Godly love. It is your divine nature that never forgets the suffering of the world. I think you are asking me if the Ageless Master said anything about it. He said,

"The one good at conduct leaves no trace
because he follows the Way.
The one good at speaking makes no flaw
because he speaks coherently with the Way.

The one good at calculation needs no calculation
because he lives beyond the calculating mind.
The one good at shutting out all divergence needs no doors
because his true being embraces all.

The one good at tying knots with no rope
can still untie one
because he ties nothing down to himself.

Therefore, the sage is always good at saving people.
He does not give up on anyone.
He is always good at making the right use of things.

He does not abandon anything
because he continues the light in the dark.
This is why he is good at saving others.
Good people are teachers of people who are no good.
People of no good are the "working objects" of good people.
The student who does not value the teacher,
and the teacher who does not accept those
on whom he needs to work,
may be smart and clever
but they miss the deep natural law
of interdependency.'

"The Ageless Master said,

'There are three precious things that I treasure.
The first is love.
The second is simple living.
The third is moderation.

With love, one can be brave.
With simple living, one can offer help to others.
With moderation, one can accomplish others.

The one who is brave but has no love,
stretches himself broadly among people,
but does not simplify his own life.
The one who expresses self-importance but
has no moderation,
follows the way to death.

With love, one can win in war,
one can fortify the defense.
God helps the one who helps others with love.'"

The young one asked, "Did the Ageless Master say anything about sin?"

The mentor smiled and answered, "Two times. He said, *'The greatest sin is to extend oneself to what is desired,'* and

'Since ancient times, the Way has been respected.
Why?

The Way is greatly valued in the world
*   as the Way to learn to avoid all sins.*
The one who looks for the Way can find it."'

    The young one asked again, "What about punishment?"
    The mentor smiled and answered, "The Ageless Master said,

'When people are not afraid of death,
*   it is of no use to kill them*
*   in order to stop them from killing each other.*
The positive approach is to teach people to love life.
This is the way to reduce killing.

People who kill and like to brandish
*   the heavy ax of the great master in forest*
*   can hardly avoid hurting themselves.*
They do not see that only God has the authority
*   to take away life from someone."'*

    The young one said, "What I have learned is of great importance, but the question now is how to make use of this great teaching."
    The mentor smiled and said,

"My teaching is easy to know and easy to do.
Yet people under Heaven cannot know its benefit
*   and do not follow it.*
My teaching has the purpose of loving people.
My master's love is unselfish heavenly love.

Because of ignorance,
*   people do not know me.*
I am known to few.
Those who follow me are valuable.
Therefore, the sage holds treasures within
*   but appears garbed in common cloth."*

    The young one asked, "It is sad if all sages must remain hidden. Did the Ageless Master mention how to realize the Way in our lives?"

The mentor smiled and answered, "The Ageless Master was not interested in running a kingdom. He did hope the Way would be accepted by the people of the world. He knew a great cooperative universal society of spiritual development could not be realized by a few people, or in a single day, but only by all people over a long period of time. Thus, he left us his writing and expected that the sages of the future would come to realize the Way in the world.

"It has now been five hundred years since he retired to the subtle realm. His prophecy has been partially fulfilled that a young sage would come from the West to search for his Way. It seems that it will take an even longer time for the Kingdom of Heaven to be realized among all people. He gave some guidance about how to teach the Way to the people of the world. He said,

'Realize the Heavenly Kingdom within the individual self
  and the spiritual gain will be truthful.
Realize the Heavenly Kingdom within the family,
  and the spiritual gain will be rich.
Realize the Heavenly Kingdom within the community
  and the spiritual gain will be growing.
Realize the Heavenly Kingdom within the nation,
  and the spiritual gain will be prosperous.
Realize the Heavenly Kingdom with all people under heaven,
  and the spiritual gain will benefit people universally.

An individual should observe another individual
  in order to have what meets the Way
  and to remove what does not meet the Way.
A family does the same; by observing another family,
  it learns what meets the Way
  and removes what does not meet the Way.
A community does the same; by observing and learning
  from another community, it can meet the Way.
A nation does the same; by observing and learning
  from another nation, it can meet the Way.

People of the world also observe and learn
  from people of other places.

We know the world and offer our help
   by learning what is right and getting rid of the trouble
of our own making.'

The young one requested, "Through my contact with the people of neighboring villages for many years, I have observed that people differ from one another in how they do spiritual practice, but all of them are unified in the way they trust their calendar to tell them what is suitable to do on different days.

"I asked the head of my host family, who often gives such service to people, and he explained that the Yellow Calendar is a combination of many cycles.

"The date is numbered by the lunar cycle. Each day in a month corresponds to one of the 28 constellations, because the moon stays overnight in one of the 28 lodges. For correspondence with the solar cycle, each month has 29 or 30 days.

"There are also 24 climatic periods during the year which express the differences in the solar cycle.

"Each day's energy in the five elementary system is given by the system of 60 heavenly stems and earthly branches.

"There are seven-day cycles in the solar system.

"Then there are 12-day cycles of heavenly energy proceeding in the order as the day of construction, the day of removal, the day of fully storing, the day of evenly distributing, the day of decision making, the day of action, the day of decision related to all things and the day of breaking, which is the day when energy opposes the handle of Big Dipper. It is not a good day to start constructive purposed activity, but the day of damage suits activities whose purpose is destructive. The day of reception, the day of initiating and the day of shutting off is not suitable for adventure.

"I would like to know more about the seven-day cycle, because my people also observe this cycle."

The mentor smiled and said, "The day of the sun is not used for official activity in order to avoid competing with the sun which symbolizes dictatorship. Yet, it is a day for animal husbandry, taking trips, seeing doctors, curing disease, writing prescriptions, entering school, etc.

"The day of the moon is a good day for friendly gatherings and merry making, furniture making, setting office, digging trenches, doing work connected with kitchens and wells, trading, trying on new clothes.   Monday is a good day for meditation and spiritual practice.

"The day of Mars is a day of verdicts and sentencing criminals, hunting and arresting thieves or robbers, cattle trading, military action and weapon making.   It is also a good day for drilling troops.   It is a triumphant day to attack outlaws.   It is also a day for initiating litigation for justice.

"The day of Mercury is suitable for initiating learning and attending to elders and teachers to absorb their experience and wisdom.   It is good for learning all skills and crafts.   It is also good for handling money, but not for starting to build a house for oneself.

"The day of Jupiter is good for making friends, trying on new clothes, planting, taming horses, receiving helpers, marriage, etc.

"The day of Venus is good for visiting high ranking authorities, washing hair and body, dressing up formally, social activities, making friends, purchasing plates and silverware, moving into a new house, etc.

"This is not fixed or rigid knowledge about each day, because the day's energy is still affected by the relationship of the 28 constellations.

"The ancient spiritually developed ones observed that because we live in nature, the near-by sun, moon and first five planets affect people's behavior.

"Each season has its own strong energy corresponding to the direction according to the solar cycle: East in spring, South in summer, West in autumn, and North in winter.   The strong energy of the seasons needs to be taken into consideration. One must avoid conflict with the strong energy.   Thus, do not plan to make a northward trip in winter, build a house facing north without protection, or make a southward trip in summer, etc.   Seasonal changes can turn a favorable direction into a disfavorable one.

"Colors can be used to stabilize and harmonize people's emotion and benefit the nervous system.   In cold climates, especially in winter, red and yellow should be used.   In hot regions or hot seasons, greens, blues and light greens and light blues will help.   This is for your own reference.

"The most useful type of knowledge for almost all people is the daily cycle according to solar energy:

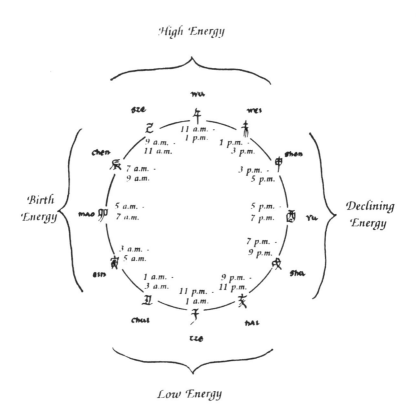

"Whatever a person does in general life activity, it is good to use the energy cycle of birth and high energy, but not declining energy times."

The young one asked, "Why do we choose the death section for doing our cultivation?"

The mentor smiled and said, "This is called 'finding the opportunity for survival in death.'"

Chapter 16

Spiritual Essence Needs to Live with Form

The young one was instructed to see the teacher in the mornings for the yang energy of the day's cycle, and on the days of the first quarter of the waxing moon. He would rest for a day before seeing the teacher in order to prepare himself spiritually, and then rest for three to five days to digest what he had learned from the teacher. The teacher thought he was bright, but the learning had to be rooted in his being after first being memorized and absorbed by his mind. The meeting between the teacher and the student usually took place irregularly according to the situation of the instructor. There were practices to do and some achievement for the boy to attain.

"You need to learn the art of immortality so that you will become deathless," the mentor said to him. "Otherwise, you will not be ready to live in the world. After you learn it, there will be no one who can damage your great soul.

"The great soul born in the world uses its worldly life and teaching to show the way of eternal life. The reward is not here or in the world, thus there is no value in establishing a kingdom for oneself. Instead, each one needs to fulfill a clean, positive life. In addition, if one can give pure spiritual help to the world without any intention to separate people by establishing personal influence, the true God has descended from to the world to elevate all people's spiritual quality. Keep this in mind, and your immortality can be achieved naturally. All people can achieve the same if they all learn unselfish broad spiritual self-upliftment.

"There is no need for you to worry about fulfilling your great spiritual mission. Your physical body will be taken and your soul will ascend to accomplish your achievement. Are you interested in that?" The mentor waited for his reply.

The young one quickly answered, "Surely, I will devotedly learn and practice whatever you teach me, but so far, I still have not achieved the last practice you taught to me."

The mentor smiled. "You do not need to achieve the ability to walk over water before you learn immortality. That is not a priority or a necessity. Anyone can learn immortality, at least anybody with the potential to be a god. However, be careful: that godly potence is the same potential that people call the devil. Yet in your case I firmly trust that you are God. A devil is an unachieved god or a god who has failed. Only God can teach a god; God would not be interested in teaching a devil.

"Immortality has special importance in your life, so you must begin to learn right away. You do not need to wait for the day you can walk over the water with dry shoes. Now let us start."

The young man said, "I am grateful that you have sufficient belief in me and think I am worthy to learn to conquer death. Thank you. I am willing to learn what you teach me."

The young man began to kneel before the teacher, but the teacher would not let him. "I do not need rituals," said the mentor, "I need the real heart. That is something that you already have. Every word and deed that a spiritual person says and does is part of his spiritual being in the spiritual world, because it is how spiritual reality unfolds. Today, I am teaching you the basic understanding, then later I will give you the practice."

The young gentleman said, "Thank you. I am ready."

The teacher said, "A number of years ago, we discussed what life consists of. Now do you know what life is?"

"Yes," responded the young man. "We have a physical body which externally consists of skin, flesh, bones, organs, blood vessels, nerves, etc. This is the basic structure, but above this is the soul. There are thousands of spirits inside of us and outside of us which form our spiritual being. I also know that the 'soul' consists of thousands of spirits of all levels. The integration of this multitude of spirits can be attained and a higher integration achieved. I still need further confirmation of this through self-proof and achievement to contact them as my internal parts which form one important section of my life being."

The teacher said, "Your understanding is much deeper than before, so today I will tell you a number of things.

"I need to point out to you now that immortality comes naturally. When you learn the serious immortal practice, do not push yourself to achieve it in one day. You open up, and just allow things to happen; allow the transformation to happen internally. The internal sublimation simply happens; you only maintain the basic laws or rules of how to project your physical, mental and spiritual energy, or you do not project at all. In your case, you are in a situation in which you need to achieve immortality in a certain amount of time. Immortal achievement has no deadline, but you need to set up a period of time for your achievement, because there are a number of things you must accomplish before you can independently practice and teach the Way to the world.

"Anything that you do that is hurried, anything that you do from strong motivation will meet with a strong obstacle as the response from the world. This is natural law; this is the law of T'ai Chi. Your internal strength will always find strong external resistance. Therefore, it is necessary that you experience demons as well as satan. Strong desire and motivation will make it necessary for you to experience internal conflict.

"On the one hand, you wish to go upward to Heaven, but on the other, there is a force inside of you trying to pull you down to Earth. If you follow the normal way and set no deadline for yourself, then surely you will reduce the internal and external resistance. Your achievement will come naturally and you will feel almost nothing. That is called the principle of non-doing or doing nothing. It is not that you are doing nothing; you accomplish a lot, but you do not feel the internal and external changes.

"If at one period of time you wish to accomplish a certain thing, dualistic confrontation is established. First of all, you need to understand that your life pattern is different. It is unusual, but accept it as it is. Then you do not need to worry about resistance or inertia or possible hostility. You need to overcome all these possible problems. Spiritual achievement is a war. It is a battle, but there is only survival, triumphant survival. Do not yield to the negativity inside yourself. Do not yield to negative thoughts from the lower or middle sphere. Beware of the middle sphere which can create an external situation which looks exactly like something you thought.

"Surely you remember a number of years ago when you were a newcomer. The first thing I taught you was to be fearless. If you are serious in your spiritual cultivation and you have some fear, the thing you fear will necessarily happen to you. If you are worried about anything, the thing will happen. If there is anything you are nervous about, the thing will happen. Just focus upon what needs to be accomplished, without fear or worry. Sometimes the consequence happens on the physical level, but it will happen at least in the spiritual realm. It is hard to handle the demonic force of your own sexual energy, but it is precisely that energy which is the main part of your energy force, your capital, to achieve immortality.

"Now you need to know about all the possible resistance from your mind. People who are achieved to a certain level can hear subtle voices, see subtle images, and experience different fragrances. In your spiritual cultivation, contact with the spiritual world is more complicated than contact with the physical world. You will hear voices which suggest that you kill yourself or someone else. They are subtle voices. If you listen to them, you will fall into the trap of the devil. You will see images, demons, beautiful women, many attractions, everything that you desire. If you become confused by these, you will fall in the trap of Satan.

"Always command your mind to stay in your spiritual center. Ignore whatever negative voices you hear and only pay heed to the positive voices. Ignore whatever negative images or smells you experience."

At this moment, the mentor took out a roll of stringed pieces of bamboo slips which he spread out. "I need to explain some things to you. In each human person, there are two types of spirits. One type is called Hun. The other type is called Po. Now I am going to explain the basic foundation that will help you win the battle and achieve your immortal life.

"I will quote different achieved ones of ancient times who explained Hun and Po, and how we handle those forces. For your understanding, I will not add my personal words to this.

"Po belongs to yin. It perches on the body, and that is where it can find a place to stay. If the Po stays with the body, the body looks strong and healthy.

"Hun belongs to yang. Its subtle energy level can go anywhere. This is why the Hun is always on a trip.

"The achieved one uses the conscious mind to govern the shape of the body. In other words, he uses the Hun to control or cooperate with the Po. When I say 'govern the shape' I am talking about controlling one's own life and the activities of life. The conscious mind always needs to conduct the Po, but not be conducted by the Po. If you can do this, you will be spiritually healthy. Otherwise, you become materially oriented, having only a material interest in life. If you do not set the internal order right, it is like putting the cart in front of the horse.

"If you look at the energy of the weather, you can see the changes of the four seasons. Warmth comes, cold goes. Cold weather comes, warm weather goes. Our soul energy does not stay the same either but keeps moving. The Hun lives with the body, but it also can be outside the body; it likes a trip. Thus, it lives with the world and also can travel far away from the body. The Hun is hard to keep in the body; though it helps keep the heart and mind from being encaged. However, if you let your mind stay in a state of wandering, the conscious mind will not stay together with the Po.

"Life on earth began with watery energy. In our bodies, water energy is the sexual fluid, semen or eggs. Fiery energy helped give the nature of life on earth. In the body, fire energy is the conscious mind. We sometimes call the fire energy *sen* (spirit) and the water energy *ching* (essence). Whatever terms you use, sexual energy and mental energy are both productive in a normal way of life. The cooperation of these two types of energy can be either worldly or spiritual. If they are worldly, there will be worldly achievement. If they are spiritual, there will be immortality of the soul, which brings about the higher evolution of life.

"The substance of the conscious mind comes from the subtle source. The body comes from water - here, water means the physical essence. The one who learns to be immortal first needs to keep the water energy united with the fire energy. Once the water and fire energy are united and do not leave each other, then your physical essence can gather spiritual essence. Spiritual essence lives with the form; the form nurtures the spirits. If you damage the physical essence, the situation will be different, so it is important to maintain the physical essence well and not exhaust it so that you will not be worn out physically or spiritually. You need to be like the sun and moon shining brightly in the fine sky, with your life like the flowers, trees and vegetation flourishing on the ground.

The mentor paused here and then suggested, "You need to digest what we have discussed today. I will continue our conversation where we left it." The young one was a careful student, so he agreed.

Chapter 17

The Basic Spiritual Unity of an Individual

The young one tried to move some small stones on the flat surface of a boulder by projecting his energy through his eyes. He kept moving a number of small stones left to right and right to left. He almost exhausted himself before closing his eyes to rest. When he opened his eyes, he saw his local friend approaching with a big smile in his face. In one of his palms, he carried a number of small stones. The young one immediately looked at the boulder and found that there were no longer any stones on it. To his surprise, the stones his friend played with in his hand were those exact stones. How could they have so quickly appeared on his friend's palm? He was still over 50 yards away. The young one could not help but ask, "How did you do it?"

His friend grinned and answered, "I did it the same way you moved them."

The young one felt somewhat embarrassed.

His friend continued, "Keep doing it. Keep your concentration. There is no other secret. That is the Way."

The young man felt encouraged and after his friend put the stones back on the boulder, he started practicing again.

They played with the stones for a while in this way, then his friend suggested, "Now, stop doing it. Power needs practice, but it comes naturally. You cannot push it and make it happen. It is not safe to overdo something." The young one stopped. His friend continued, "I heard that a king whose kingdom is about two hundred miles away from here is now searching for a great magician to be his top adviser in his court. Are you interested?"

The young one said, "You know, I have not achieved anything high. Even so, I will not use my magic to please a king or lord, or to entertain anyone, unless I use it to attract people in order to teach the Way."

His friend said, "I knew that you wouldn't be interested; I was just kidding. Aside from military force, magic is the only thing that can make one distinguished in the world."

The young one smiled and said, "We do not look to be distinguished in the worldly way. We would look for spiritual distinguishing by our own discipline and cultivation."

The friend applauded him.   "You are truly my good brother," and they laughed and parted. The young one went to see the teacher.

The teacher smiled when he saw him and said, "Let us start where we left off last time. Although the learning of the Way can be allowed to happen spontaneously, when people reach adulthood, the internal physical essence can gather the spirits. By this cooperation, a man or woman can produce positive, creative work. This is the way to reach God, but the foolish people of the world are enslaved by their overbearing material interests. They lose their spiritual nature by their heavy worldly interests. They do not spend a moment's time to maintain their spirit. All the time, the spirit is rushing around, searching outside like a wild horse. Therefore, they lose their Hun because they have made Po the boss of their life, and is concerned with only the short material sphere of physical existence.

"Your first taste of this may give you a little difficulty, but do not worry; learning the Way needs patience. I would like to quote another sage to help explain it. You shall find each achieved one offers a different vision to help you differently.

"People of the Immortal Way called the yang energy or yang spirits Hun. Hun energy is happy to live, happy to enjoy life. The yin spirits are called Po. Po energy likes to kill others or kill the yang spirits. Hun makes you active, Po makes you inert. Remember the description: Hun is the essence of the being, Po is the effective spirits of the body. You need to know this division.

"You also need to know that sexual energy does not like to stay in your body, it likes to go away. Immortal practice has a way to teach you to keep it inside the body. When your own spirits within float up to your brain, they make you bewildered or perplexed by dreams. There is a practice for subduing them.

"The principle of life always makes your body carry the yang energy and makes the yin energy hold the great harmony within. This causes the unity of yin and yang so that there is no separation between them. Unity is how a person attains immortality. A person of the Way likes to embrace oneness.

"The spiritual energy of the mind is like a mirror which has the function of reflection. If it should happen to lose the reflective function, would you still call it a mirror? The mirror is a metaphor. Achieved ones nurture the spirits of the mind to help the health of the bodily spirits.

"I see you still cannot answer me positively that you understand well. I can refer to the words of other sages.

"The difference between a wise spiritual person and a vulgar worldly person is that the spirit of the spiritual person is calm. His nature is calm and his spirits are converged. He is not changed by external stimulation. Although he makes the Po as his house attendants, any time the Hun decides to act, the Po always follow. This is how the Hun carry the Po. Within unachieved people, the spiritual order is opposite. They choose Po as the boss of their life, thus material things enslave their spiritual nature and their spirits are confused and ungoverned. Their spirits listen to the Po, so their ears listen to lower stimulating music, their eyes are entrapped by lower stimulating colors, and their nostrils and mouth are attached to lower stimulating tastes and smells. The desire of the Po is to make the spirits follow it, so in the case of an unachieved person, the Po is above and the Hun is underneath. The normal, correct way is the other way around. From this you can know how to be a spiritual person. Do you understand a little better?"

The young student then said, "You are talking about internal Tai Chi. The two forces of life being in the right order is beneficial to eternal life. When they are in the wrong order, the life being is like a kingdom in which a corrupt tyrant is the ruler of the life force."

"Your understanding is quick, yet sometimes a teacher will keep teaching the same theme until the student is totally able to use the knowledge. Let us learn from another of the ancient teachers.

"The Po is the staff or workers, not the lord and master of the formed life. The Hun is its associate in the good spiritual function of life, yet it is constantly on a trip because of its nature. It brings about cooperation between all the bodily faculties. If the Hun is bound by the Po for physical interests, the spirits are caged within the body. If the spirits are encaged within the body, a person's vision will be narrow, and his understanding becomes rigid.

"The one who learns the Way first needs to clearly set his or her internal spiritual world in order, which is not a form of external worship, but to be determined to move in the direction of internal spiritual integration. It means not to be burdened by desires or the unreasonable needs of the body. Always allow the spirits to have freedom from worldly troubles. Carry the Po during all important necessary activities, but do not be held by the Po.

"In the matter of death, there are two ways that the soul of a person can go: one way is to rise upward, and other way is to sink. Ordinary people are mortals. The one who sinks sacrifices the health of the spirit for the sake of the form. That person makes the spiritual essence follow the Po. The one who rises does so by nurturing the health of the spirits; the health and strength of Hun includes the Po. When the Hun is not pulled down by the heavy interest of Po, the internal physical and spiritual essence are harmoniously united until the time of exuviation, when the soul leaves the body."

The student said, "At this point, I totally understand what you have explained, but please continue to tell me more of what is written on the bamboo slips."

"There is a lot more," replied the mentor. "They are all different ways to explain the same thing. What I would like you to remember is that Hun belongs to yang. Yang means uprising. Po belongs to yin. Yin means downsinking and stagnancy. These two forces are in each individual. A normal person maintains a balance of the two forces within one life. To materialize one's life is the direction of the Po. Po is connected with sexual energy. It can disappear but does not change. A bad life hastens the disintegration and causes the main soul to sink with the Po.

"To spiritualize one's life is the direction of Hun. Cultivation brings about oneness between the Hun and Po so that they are not separate from each other but unite to produce the high essence of immortality. For the immortal pursuit, Hun helps the gathering of various spiritual agents and entities. They are refined instead of scattered. Immortality is a higher integration of Hun and Po.

"Integration at the normal level produces what we know as life, while ordinary death is the result of disintegration of Hun and Po. This is the basic spiritual reality of life that needs to be understood."

Chapter 18

The Interpretation
of the Precious, Wordless Teaching
Is Found Within Your Developed Spirit

The mentor let some time pass so that the young man could absorb everything he had said and achieve some degree of preparation in the practice. The young man thought about the important learning he had received.

Then the mentor spoke. "In the last meeting, we talked about how in immortal practice, the mind is the key to reach success or failure. In general, a spiritual student needs to keep his mind as clear as that of a child before any formal learning or schooling. Before education, a child's life function is complete because he follows his natural instinct. Once a child is educated, the separation between originality and intellectual activity gradually grows stronger and stronger. This can damage one's natural intuitive capability.

"Life is nature. Life does not need experimentation. Yet intellectual knowledge is obtained by experiment. Each individual life can move in the direction of avoiding waste and unnecessary trouble through healthy intuition. The capability for internal knowledge can help a person live a peaceful, smooth life which is problemless or at least has fewer problems. Only the untouched originality, with the help of intuitive capability, enables a person to live with great content.

"In spiritual practice, originality and internal oneness are both important. Making life decisions does not always need to depend upon searching through one's thoughts or looking around at the experience of others in order to find what is right. Maintaining internal oneness, like a child before complicated learning, serves life more directly and is of great benefit in accomplishing life in a simple way.

"When the mind extends itself intellectually and emotionally, it engages in multiple conceptual activities. People become ideologic and idealistic and perceive their life as far more complicated than it needs to be. It is to say, when people's minds diverge from their originality to extend intellectually and spiritually, emotionally and materially, the multiplicity of conceptual activities that are created as a consequence causes people to become ideologic and idealistic, which complicates their taste and fulfillment. The multiplication or fragmentation of the oneness of the spirits damages the power of a life. Thus, when you learn a spiritual path, you can still have intellectual development, but you need to be sure to purify yourself by doing a special cultivation that reunites the originality of life's simplicity with your newly complicated intellectual being. To return to simplicity, unify the mind with the body and spirit without extending it to become subnormal, imbalanced or an awkward intellectual monster.

"For example, in general, each person needs to bathe every day or every few days. How about your mind? Your mind also needs to be cleansed and refreshed, but of course this is not done with water. This is an important part of practicing spiritual cultivation; purification is the reunification of the mind and body. The function of the mind is restored to be whole-hearted and whole-minded, even to its original wholeness before the separation of mind and heart.

"A child's mind is always related with its heart. When people reach adulthood, they subordinate their heart to their mind because of the tensions of daily life.

"The benefit of having a physical life is that if we think wrongly or if our mental and spiritual projection is wrong, we still can escape, correct or remedy the corresponding action by the solidity of the physical being. The physical body moves slower than the mind and spirit and is more controllable. Thus, spiritual crises can be saved. In immortal practice, however, you project your spirit on a different level; you bring your subtle being into action. At that time, no physical shape can cover you or slow you down. You are active only by the mind. Whatever thoughts are in your mind set the direction of your new being, which is an integration of the astral being and the conscious mind. Danger can result from your fear. Great fright or terror can come from your negative imagination. You may lose the ability to come back to the physical being simply by issuing a bad thought. Therefore, in preparing for immortal practice, the mind must be trained.

"For example, in your sleep, you dream. All dreams indicate life activity in a different sphere. Usually you experience a trip, and you do not even know where you went, but you always come back safely. However, children are unlearned or uneducated and their dreams can verily easy cause the projection of their astral body. On some occasions, because the child did not reach maturity of spirit, it loses the path and ability to come back to the body. When a young child loses its association with the body, an early death can happen. Fortunately, children's tender spiritual projection is limited.

"Adults can have stronger spiritual projections, yet the adult's physical structure is strong enough to act as a link between the physical and the astral. When they become older, this tie is loosened At the same time, the spirit is also weak. There is no danger in normal situations but they may suffer from physical degeneration. They may also suffer from the loss of some mental capacity.

"Spiritual learning is putting all this knowledge into use. For example, before you go on a trip, you equip yourself with all the right things, including the basic knowledge of the route. Surely not all details can be known before you leave, but you learn as much as possible.

"Most people have experienced dreams. During normal sleep, the activity of the spiritual and mental faculties from the head needs to become loose so one can rest. However, not all spiritual or mental agents become loose, because the body and life are still guarded. Dreams are incomplete mental activity or mental activity at different levels. They reflect the activities of spiritual agents that are swimming inside the physical body. Usually this does not attract the attention or tension of the astral partner. Occasionally, however, the dream will be unconsciously associated with the projection of the astral partner. Some years later, he may suddenly find himself in a place or being with some people that he never met on the physical plane, but has known in dreams or visions.

"In general, you need to nurture your spirits within yourself. Dreams can be a form of internal communication between the spiritual agents and the mind. Whether or not the mind can pick up the message depends upon the development of the mind. Dreams can also be nonsense, because sometimes they happen on a different level. Dreams can be healthy, or they can show signs of an unhealthy condition of the total being or the physical being.

"Usually the three partners, body, mind and spirit, are always connected. Cultivating and nurturing your spirits helps you recognize your internal faculties. Internally you do not have language, only the memory of past experience as intuition. When internal communication is made, such as in dreams or visions, you see reruns of pictures of past experiences. This can sometimes be a premonition of a new, similar experience which will happen, but with different people, location, etc.

"Learn to nurture your spirit in preparation for projection of the yang energy, the new baby which is formed by the intercourse of Hun and Po within. The practice of the quest of soul lays the foundation for this endeavor.

"At all moments, I would like you to be careful and remember the guidelines I give to you. Prepare yourself to produce yang energy, which is also called the Light Body, or the Body of Light, which can penetrate stone, sit in fire, and stay in water without suffering any damage. It will be your life partner; some day, you will need the help of this practice. I shall instruct you separately.[1] Most people should be able to produce the Light Body. The immortal body, the immortal being, happens naturally, step by step.

"In my personal room in the rock, I have a special collection of ancient books. Your physical being cannot enter my room. However, I am preparing you to take the first step toward learning the spiritual trip. When you can enter my study, I will authorize you to understand all the scrolls made of cloth. If you try to read them, you will not succeed because you do not know the language, but you do not need to learn the language, because your mind will interpret each picture for you. That capability is installed in each developed person."

---

[1]See Master Ni's book, *Quest of Soul.*

Chapter 19

The Yin and Yang Pattern
Of Internal and External Nature

The young one had heard about the *I Ching* or *Book of Changes and the Unchanging Truth.* It seemed to be the essential foundation of the Way. He was not prepared to do scholastic study, but he wished to grasp the essence of this important development of human spirituality. In the local market, he had seen people doing *I Ching* readings, using sticks to get the answer. They seemed to trust their hands more than their minds. The *I Ching* tells how the hand can receive special energy from an internal or external source and answer the question of their life stage when they are looking for guidance. This book had been in his mind for some time, so he presented himself to the teacher and asked, "You have mentioned the book called the *I Ching* several times. Should I also learn the *I Ching*?"

The mentor replied, "The *I Ching* describes the principles of interchange between yin and yang. This is the basic structure of the cosmos that can be found in the smallest substance of nature as well as the big universe or multi-universe. This principle is unfolding in all levels of existence. Especially at the surface level of nature, nothing can be beyond yin, the hidden, and yang, the apparent. I would like to make it easy for you to escape a word-for-word study of the book by explaining the useful principles to you.

"First we come to what is called yang and yin. Then we need to understand their sphere and application.

Yang:
Heaven or sky
the sun
the side of anything that faces the sun (tree, mountain, house, etc.)
male and masculine
apparent
the head of the human body
the back of the human body
the creative energy of life

the giver
the upper part of anything
the leader
father
brother
husband
the positive

yin:
Earth
the moon
the side of anything with its back to the sun or facing the shade
female and feminine
the hidden
the belly of the human body
the front of the human body
the receptive energy of life
the lower part of anything
the supporter
mother
sister
wife
the negative

The above mentioned classifications are the basic differences of yang and yin. In reality, anything including an event or any type of affair, and including the recognition capability of the human mind, has a basic dualistic or relative nature. In the depth of a phenomenon or real event, the *I Ching* is applicable. It describes almost all situations and provides useful knowledge and understanding. For example, in a group of people, if the leader is a woman, she is the yang energy of the group as a function of nature. In a family, if the wife or the mother is the main financial provider, then she is the yang energy of the family. In most circumstances, yin and yang are interchangeable and interdependent. The *I Ching* is the deep understanding of the co-existence and interdependency of all differences.

"For example, in a work team, the members might be all male, all female or mixed, yet it is easy to see that in the accomplishment of a task, especially for bigger things, each member provides a different function. Sometimes one becomes yang energy, sometimes one needs to be yin energy. The interweaving of the basic two types of energy accomplishes the goal.

"In another example, a family relationship, the husband and the wife are a relationship of male and female. Sometimes a female may contain more energy of yang nature, such as being creative. A male also may contain yin energy and be more receptive. However, in general, it does not matter whether one is female or male in different types of work or activity, it is the work, the situation, and the nature of one's energy which brings about fulfillment. It means, in some things, a person, whether male or female, physically can have more yang type of energy in one thing and more yin type of energy in another. Such an individual, whether male or female, needs to exercise both types of functions in order to accomplish something. Such an individual supplements the insufficiency of one type of energy in order to attain the dual function.

"Sometimes people are a team in earning a living, accomplishing a bigger task or operating a business. By nature or by the need of two types of mentality, cooperation is achieved when the basic two types of energy are interwoven. Similarly, in an individual life, the interweaving of multiple energies can be recognized.

"The principle of yang and yin is the simplest illustration of the fact of natural interdependence. On the surface, the function of nature is plural and dualistic. This interesting dualism is not only expressed as mutual opposition but also mutual assistance. Each side simultaneously accomplishes and assists the other. Within each side, there are still smaller levels of self-contradiction. In the bigger picture, the two energies are always interdependent.

"To know this is to know that all types of conflict are unavoidable. The fact of interdependence is also unavoidable. This is nature. Spiritual growth can help people know that when interrelations present a harmonious situation, there is creativity. When the interrelation presents a disharmonious situation, there is destruction. Creation can be for good and bad, destruction also can be for good and bad. From this, you can see that the dualistic nature of the surface of universal nature and the human mind does not need to be eliminated. Differences should be allowed to exist. The desire to put everything in order is an extension of yang energy. If overly extended, it only creates strong competition between yin and yang.

"The ancient wise ones left the world alone to allow people to see the importance of interdependence and co-existence for themselves. The same principle can be used to govern one's life. Harmony can be brought about by ceasing the use of external interference. This is the secret of everlasting life. Because people are so caught up in external pursuits and busy-minded, they forget the internal reality that it is better not to apply any external interference such as medication, artificial ideology or false faith.

"In human life, the body and mind are a duality. The Po (the spirits of the body) and the Hun (the spirits of mind) are a duality. The Po comes from physical life. It does not like to stay in a body that has high spiritual intention. The Hun comes from the mind. It does not relate with Po too long, because it likes new experience. Thus, each tends to go its own way.

"The high condition of natural life is like the early young life. Both types of spirits - Hun and Po - have not divided yet. They are whole. Divergence of the life spirits comes after worldly attraction becomes a strong desire in life. If one's desire is less and one's ambition is modest, an acute confrontation of the two types of internal spirits will not be established.

"The highest developed individuals live with high integration of the life spirit. They have health by enjoying simplicity, and allow everlasting life to happen to them with no particular effort. Effortlessness is how they achieve themselves.

"Worldly people are different once they lose the vision of the naturalness of life. Their society is built differently. It is full of conflict between the different interests of various classes and groups, racial differences and cultural differences. The selfishness of each group is extended. Short term remedies can be found by compromise between different interest groups. An overall remedy cannot be reached except by changing this type of life and correcting social and cultural corruption.

"If we define the spiritual-natured spirits as holy and the physical-natured spirits as unholy, a conflict between the holy spirits and unholy spirits is created on the surface of the mind and life is punished. Life is burned by sin, which is unnatural desire. Moral understanding among people is forsaken. Ethics are abandoned by people who forsake their spiritual nature. God - the spiritual energy - in such an individual sadly allows the fires of hell to burn the life.   God in such a society or individual is dethroned, and instead the devil is crowned master of their life."

"Then, what is the best way to apply the *I Ching*?" queried the young one.

His mentor replied, "'*I Ching*' means the principle of change.   Change is created by movement.   Movement is the reality of change.   The universe is always moving.   The things of the universe do not only need to cope with the big movement of the universe, but a thing itself also has its own movement; thus, changes are expressed.

"When a big thing happens, we call it change.   When a small change happens, we call it fluctuation.   All changes express the movement of a wave.   When any changes that are observed are understood as a wave movement, then the difference between the peak and the valley of the wave is seen. These are respectively titled as yang and yin.   We recognize yang and yin from the movement that expresses them.

"Nature itself is created by the movement of yang and yin. The movement of yang and yin also expresses itself through the duality of dynamic and static, active and passive, mobile and still.   All movement contains stillness.   All stillness contains movement.   Nature is self-contradictory in that each thing contains its opposite.   Changes happen to changing circum-stances.   Changing circumstances are built up for a change to happen.   It is a mutual relationship which brings about the different side.

"By observing the water in the ocean, it is known that the low tide builds the high tide and the high tide builds the low tide.   In people's emotion, when one remains idle for a long time, one would think of making a move in life. If a person has been already overactive, one might think of slowing oneself down. So, everything, internally or externally, is brought about by duality. Sameness builds differences; differences build sameness.

"Most important is what the Ageless Teacher told us: 'Fortune depends on alertness in misfortune. Misfortune is produced by negligence after fortune.' From the above reality, the law of causality is expressed. If we recognize one factor as a cause, we can then recognize another, related factor as the effect. Yet, the affect can become the cause of a new effect. The new effect becomes the new cause of a new event. In depth, one could give up knowing cause or effect; we might distinguish between them as primary and secondary causes. However, in the next run of an event, the primary causes become secondary, and the secondary causes become primary. They are merely expressed as a chain of cause and effect.

"Because changes happen according to changing circumstances, changing circumstances happen according to change. From the continuity of change, the antecedent and the consequence replace each other. It means from the antecedents, the consequence is reached; then the consequences become the antecedents of a new change. Sometimes we consider that something is the immediate cause of an event, but the immediate cause becomes the distant cause of a new event. This happens to human history or in the activity of a society."

The young one asked, "The ancient developed ones knew how to apply that to their lives, didn't they?"

"From this foundation of the external world and internal world, the ancient developed ones applied two good principles in their lives. The first one was to follow the normalcy of nature because the normalcy of nature is a rhythm. It is not as mechanical as the pendulum of the ancient type of clock[2] which can illustrate change by swinging to the left or swinging to the right. Once the rhythmical swinging of life does not go outside the bounds of normalcy, internally and externally, harmony exists, and safety is present. This is a mechanical metaphor; the real range of life is much wider than the distance in which a pendulum is allowed to move. From this observation, we know that the use of personal force, violence, brutality

---

[2]The clock illustration is given by the author.

or a radical approach does not express the normalcy of nature, because they are all extreme. Contrarily, they express the subnormalcy of nature; therefore, it is easy to perceive that doing those things does not follow the Way. The Way is normalcy or the Way is to learn to live with normalcy.

"The second principle is to be spiritually centered. Once you are centered, you form the axis of all your movements and activities, so you experience less polarity. You do not overly polarize your energy, because you are centered. To remain in one's center means not to polarize oneself. To extend one's self over to one direction is to create the opposite swing back either stronger or too far away from center. Surely difficulty or trouble will be caused by this.

"The law of yin and yang interprets nature - both internal nature and external nature. It was yin and yang that inspired the ancient spiritually developed ones. Yin and yang are expressed as the Way. This means that we cannot avoid or abolish the practical, contradictory nature of physical nature or the nature of life. Following the Way is to discover the middle range of swinging from right to left and back again, which causes no problem. One learns to enjoy this safety zone. Because the contradictory nature of the universe or individual life is unavoidable, we cannot do anything about it. The only thing we can do is find out the Way of nature, internally or externally.

"We do not need to be sentimental about ourselves. People become over-sentimental because they lose themselves in extreme or radical experiences of life. However, one's self-treatment in life is changeable, depending upon how you manage the scope of your safety. From the knowledge of the pattern of the outside world and the pattern of the inside world, becoming sentimental about your life is not the Way. To become too pessimistic or too optimistic is also not an objective attitude toward natural reality. Practically, spiritual calmness and composure of mind in life is the direct benefit above all. This is the straight light from the wisdom of God."

The young one exclaimed, "Ah! This message is clear for me to see: it is an important personal spiritual duty to help other people to know this truth."

The mentor smiled and approved by saying, "This is why I am interested in helping you. You have such a high divine nature that you always think of other people."

The young one said, "Now I would like to know the normal function of Po and Hun in a life."

The mentor answered, "First I will tell you about the Po.

Positive:
1. *Helps the normal function of the body and all the organs.*
2. *Sustains the wellness of the physical being.*
3. *In dreams, is the impression of external stimulation. It is not a clear picture but is interpretable. Thus it serves as the passive receiver in spiritual function.*
4. *It enhances sexual energy.*

Negative:
1. *Physical interest that is too strong causes the loss of natural balance of life.*
2. *Activity in dreams disturbs the peace of mind.*
3. *Selfish, cruel and destructive to the life of others, if over-extended.*
4. *Brutal.*
5. *Over-sexed.*

Now I will tell you about the Hun:

Positive:
1. *Helps the healthy function of the mind*
2. *Enhances the memory*
3. *A great reminder of setting a schedule or certain things to do*
4. *Is a transmitter which can issue energy to another person*
5. *It enhances higher spiritual energy.*

Negative:
1. *Unearthly or unrealistic inclinations*
2. *Mental activity replaces real action in life*
3. *Its strong memory causes the association of a thought and makes the conscious flow unstoppable.*
4. *Overly sensitive*
5. *It would tend toward the ascetic type of spiritual discipline.*

The discipline for the two is as follows:

To Po: Avoid the unconscious suggestion of day dreams when one engages in life activities

To Hun: Learn clean thinking to stop the wandering nature of the Hun. Once unconscious thought is stopped, there is no new mental activity by association with any old memories of the unimportant past.

To both: Midnight is the time for the intercourse of yin and yang energy without and within. Thus, meditation at this time can help the stronger integration of yin and yang or of Hun and Po, and create new spiritual energy. Meditation of the sedated, thoughtless mind at this time is suitable for both men and women. When they become older, such practice is even more important. This is the only important life ritual one needs in older age. Until then, people may be too busy and neglect the internal balance and harmony.

Chapter 20

From the Dualistic World, Know the One Truth

The young one was instructed to get up early, before sunrise. Then, he was to do some special exercises which could help his growth so that he would be in good health. Yet he was not to over do it and become too physical, or it could hinder his spiritual growth. He learned the five-to-one breathing and did it whenever he had time, particularly in the morning, in order to take in the natural life energy. The five-to-one breathing is five inhales and one exhale. The mentor had told him, "According to the experience of the immortal spirits, there are three treasures on earth for human survival. They are water, fire and wind (air). The wise use of these elements will affect the length of years people live. The five-to-one breathing tonifies one's life energy, increasing the power of immunity and helping people tolerate hunger or have less reliance on food."

Other similar practices were taught to the young one. It took a great deal of time to learn and practice them. Spiritual discussion took the smallest portion of the time that the young one spent in that high rural land. He understood that the minds of people who learn the Way in depth accept Heaven, Earth and mankind as equals. It is not that people must obey God or Heaven, but people's growth is for attaining spiritual independence. With this independence they extend their spiritual responsibility to take care of their own lives and all other lives while at the same time doing nothing to damage the support from Heaven and Earth.

Intuitively, the young one very much agreed with the new type of life. Occasionally, the habitual dependence on an external God would stir his mind, but he knew he had to achieve himself above that type of reliance. The practice of five-to-one was helpful at a different level to his old psychological being to be reborn to the broad and profound truth of life.

One morning, the young one requested: "I was brought up in an environment where people believed that there is only one God with one name. When I started traveling with my cousin, I saw that different people have different customs and different types of temples to worship different gods with different names. All of these aroused the question: what is right?"

The mentor smiled and answered, "Right or wrong is installed in your question."

The young one looked startled, and asked, "How?"

The mentor smiled and answered, "God can be one, and God also can be many. If you believe God is the most powerful being, then God can have many transformations. Although there are many transformations, God still is one. The one needs to be recognized, just as the multi-transformations. The human mind should not limit the free will of God, but allow God to exercise his own free will to be one and to be many.

"The question of one God or many gods is not God's problem, it is the problem of the human mind which lacks sufficient growth. One or many is not the question."

The young one kept quiet for a moment, then sighed and said, "So are the different spiritual customs and different names the transformation of the one God? If I knew this earlier, my cousin and I would have enjoyed our trip together more."

The mentor smiled and answered, "I have just given the answer to relieve the tightness of your emotion which was built up by your childhood customs. I have not answered the deeper question. Since you are one who will help many people's souls, we must take enough time this morning to show the truth of God.

"Your original beliefs have been challenged by the experience of your trip. I can see that challenges from the trip built the openness of your mind and reduced the emotional difficulty of searching for the deeper reality."

The young one said, "My cousin and I were instructed by our uncle who is an elder priest. He had seen our ancestors' good faith dying among our people. He also supported our learning trip so that we could learn the best, then return to help our own people."

The mentor smiled and said, "He must be a wise person. However, the people of the east side of the city like to have a fine day and the people of the west side like to have rain. What usually happens is that the east side has rain and the west side has a fine, dry day. We can only concentrate on what we can do. Right? My job is to pass the teaching of the Ageless

One to you, so let us go through the teaching and reach the Way.

"If God is one, then it does not need a name. If there are two similar things, they each need a name in order to know one from the other. If God is recognized as one, name or no name is irrelevant. If God has a greater power than the human mind, no human mind should do the business of God.

"Let God choose whether to be one or many. Both conceptions have the same fundamental problem. As Chuang Tzu said,

"'Using the human mind to interfere with Heaven is to go against Heaven and Nature; not using the human mind to interfere with Heaven or nature is to be with Heaven and Nature.'"

The young one carefully received this teaching. After a pause of some time, he raised his head and said, "In my deep heart, I am clear that the nature of God is not a human complication. The nature of God is easy, smooth and joyful. The nature of God does not fight, but is peaceful. The nature of God is life giving and does not create steep cliffs for jumping. I have received the word of the Ageless One which expresses the health of the Godly Way. I deeply accept it, as I truly believe that the Godly Way offers happiness. There need never be the bitter struggle of one generation after another. Faith in a name-claiming religion does not increase internal peace or the peace of the world. It has not elevated the quality of people. External suppression cannot replace people's own enlightenment. External culture or a social religion is a false flower. Intuitively, after experiencing external faith, people know there must be something wrong with it. Since I was young, I have not been able to get along well or agree with the accepted customs."

The mentor nodded his head to show his understanding of what the boy told him, and said, "The fundamental mistake of such artificial bondage which is put over the true nature of life is to not accept what God is, but create a God out of a partial vision and out of the psychology of one society or person. This basic fault goes against the nature of God instead of obeying the nature of God.

"The Ageless One said,

'The unnamed is the beginning of the universe;
the named is the mother of all things.'

"The spirit of God is the universal conscience. It is not one society or one race. God is universal faith. Reducing God to a mental creation is degrading to the human spirit. The human mind did not participate in the beginning of the universe; no such experience is available to the human mind, so any name or concept for the formation of the world is nonsense. The beginning of the universe is beyond concept. It can only be known by indescribable intuition.

"The mind developed long after the human form of life was obtained. All things at the nameable level are different conceptions of the mind. It is not that the mind is the mother of everything; the mind is only the mother of all concepts related to things."

The young one asked, "Then what is the position of God?"

"If the mind witnessed the beginning of the universe," replied his teacher, "then who is qualified to describe the beginning of the universe and to give a reliable testimony of the work of God? Only God, unless duality existed in the first place. Then here comes the first paired duality, like this:

"It became the pattern of Tai Chi, the ultimate law.

"If God said to someone, 'I made everything out of my own being,' then he created something different from himself. This still follows the pattern of yin and yang.

"If God said, 'I have done nothing,' then it becomes

and God is not expressed. Then, no one knows the existence of God and God does not need to be known unless duality existed in the first place. This would be the pattern of the human mind. This system of interpretation cannot present the absolute and unique truth of the deep world."

The young one said, "Must there be God?"

"Right," said the mentor, smiling. "There must be God. God can be known through the cognitive capability of mind. Cognition must have an object. God is not a thing. God is associated with the self-cognition of the mind, so it is correct for the one who breaks through the dualistic pattern of mind to say 'I am God.' Saying this, however, has no particular purpose, except to give strength to oneself. Faith in God is needed by people who lose the internal God, the spirit of responsibility. To determine whether a faith is healthy still needs another part of cognition to examine it. If the faith is examined, then the faith is mental not spiritual."

The young one hurriedly said, "Then for most people, God is only the mind of people; thus it becomes relative. God is not spiritual as God should be. External faith is wrong."

The mentor saw that he was able to follow closely and continued, "God is more than the mind. God is above the conceptual level of mind. God does not need description from the mind. God can be proven through spiritual intuition.

"The dualistic T'ai Chi pattern cannot be avoided by any level of things or beings. Anything that is made to be falls from the absolute to the relative sphere. Any attempt to describe God or spirit pulls God down to the level of myriad things and beings.

"Many times I asked my teacher about God. My teacher sometimes raised his hand, sometimes pointed to a tree or sometimes shouted. I was confused until I received the enlightenment that it was his great kindness to have never used language to tell me. I suffered through living in my own darkness for many years. Suddenly, one day, I heard the singing of a little bird standing on a branch of flowers, and I came to know that God is something that cannot be put under one's conceptual grasp and put into language. I suddenly understood what been clearly revealed in the first few lines of the teaching of the Ageless Master:

'The Way cannot be told.
If it can be told,
*   it is just an ordinary way.*
The high essence cannot be named.
If it can be named,
*   it is just an ordinary thing.'*

"Then, I was so happy that my own darkness disappeared and I knew the Way of knowing God, and the true name of God. So I went back to see my teacher and to tell him my enlightenment. At the very moment I opened my mouth to put it into language, my teacher suddenly, unexpectedly, raised his palm to cover my mouth. I struggled in an effort to say it, but my teacher made his other hand into a fist and hit me on my side. I suddenly became enlightened that it was wrong to habitually use words or language to describe the absolute. What was left for me was to embrace God and realize God in my life all the time."

The young one said, "You have made this so crystal clear. Right now, I have received your precious experience as transferred to me directly."

The mentor smiled and asked, "What is God?"

The young one wanted to answer, and as he opened his mouth, he found he could not say anything because the mentor's palm covered his mouth.

The young one understood right away that using words to explain the absolute reality with the mind is only relative struggling. The young one straightened up his emotional being and mental being and thanked the mentor for the day's meeting. After he walked ten paces, he turned back to the mentor and yelled, "I am God," to express his young immortal spirit.

The mentor laughed loudly and nodded his head in approval.

Chapter 21

Being the One-Headed Nature of Life

Sometimes the young one talked about religion with his local friend. The friend always gave his short and simple comment that religion was like installing a head over one's head. The young one did not understand what he meant.

One day, the two were chatting together. This time, the friend mentioned something about the religious activity of people. Then, the young one made the same comment about installing a head over one's head. His friend thus discovered the breakthrough of the young one and said, "Our teacher must have helped you remove the stone head which was placed over your real head."

The young one said, "No. It was not a stone head, it was stone tablets."

The friend did not totally understand this but the two of them started to laugh and kept on laughing for a long time. The friend asked, "It took a long time for someone to put a false head over your real head. It also takes a long time to remove it. What are you going to do next?"

The young one answered, "When people think that they have two heads, God and themselves, they make the other head responsible for their life. When I know I have only one head, I must be responsible for everything in life now. That is the price and prize of spiritual freedom and independence. I wish I knew that long ago; I would have saved myself so much struggle. Now, brother, I am born again. It is a new life, a new life of self-responsibility and a new life of responsibility for taking care of other people's spiritual lives. That is what I am going to do."

After being quiet for a while, they started to do some practices together.

After several months, the mentor came to see to the young one.

In the meeting, the difference in the young one was conspicuous. The mentor noticed that he was more high-spirited and happy because he was enlightened.

The mentor started by saying, "I know you have been enjoying your Godhood. However, you will go to the masses to do your work. Your learning of the absolute truth through service to the relative world should be continued now. Usually, a student is sent away to live simply and earnestly, but it is the instruction of the Ageless One that a spiritual person cannot do good for oneself alone, he needs to help others. It is your spiritual mission to do so, thus today we need to learn more.

"Last time, you heard that the Ageless One said,

'The unnamed is the beginning of the universe.
The named is the mother of all things.'

"We learned that the mind is the source of cognition. Names are given by the mind to all things by formalizing different concepts for them. Different conception is reflected in the cognition. Then there are already two parts: the conception and the cognition. Thus, cognition is the function of mind, and conception is the product of mind. What then is mind itself?

"What do you call the stage before the function of cognition of mind or the function of cognition is stirred? You cannot call it anything or put any image of the mind upon it. It is just like salt in water, until an object appears to it. At this point, you are in the yin/yang pattern of universal structure, so the range to which cognition is able to be applied is limited. It cannot extend itself to something unformed and uncreated.

"Yet, there is something that is known by the intuitive spirit. The existence of that something cannot be perceived by cognition. Cognition of this something is the limitation of the perceptive mind. It is knowledge beyond the capability of the perceptive mind. That type of knowledge comes by intuition. Thus, intuition is a higher and more subtle function of the mind; intuition is direct knowledge by mind. Cognition is knowledge filtered through different sensory organs, thus the mind cannot establish cognition without first associating with the sensory organs. In contrast, the highest intuition needs to be totally free from interference by the sensory functions which work only at the perceptible level.

"Correct cognition exists on a comparable plane where a thing can be known by you and a thing can also be known by another. Intuition is not like cognition; it is individual. People always ask, how do you know something? Usually you reply, 'I saw it, I heard it,' etc. However, intuitive knowledge cannot be proven unless one sees the consequence of a certain event.

Some intuitive knowledge has no relationship with the consequence, such as the knowledge of spiritual matters. Spiritual
enlightenment is only produced in the scope of intuitive
capability. It has no need for verification by others, unless you
wish the opinion of one higher than yourself. Thus, enlightenment directly serves the individual self. When enlightenment
needs to be transferred to others, if it is treated as a thought,
then it falls into the scope or the range of cognition.

"Cognition and intuition are not on the same level of mind.
The different sensitivities of the mind need to be nurtured and
developed in order to reach direct perception. At the higher
sphere of cognition and intuition, there is enlightenment.

"The enlightenment of reaching Godhood is of use only to
the individual. It also can do great service through the
individual. However, my purpose is to guide you to see the
different levels of sensitivity which express different levels of
energy. The energy of mind is more sensitive than the physical
level of energy. The power of cognition is a little more sensitive
than the general function of mind. The power of spiritual
discernment is higher than the general capability of cognition.
The power of intuition is even higher, yet there are even higher
powers in the mind. Enlightenment and conscience tell you
what should and should not be done.

"Enlightenment is not God, but God can be known only
through enlightenment. Each step of sensitivity of the mind
ascends until the most exquisite energy, the true essence is
reached. This exquisite energy is the most subtle and sensitive, thus it knows all. It is all-able and all-knowing, thus it is
God. It is inside of us, and it is also outside of us.

"The mind of an individual is good at some things at some
times. The mind can be not good at some things all the time.
The mind is just the vehicle that carries the exquisite energy,
even a little. No individual is filled with exquisite energy all the
time. This is why sometimes we are smart about things and at
other times we are stupid.

"In the development of human life, we have been equipped
with all possible good capabilities, thus we are able to do many
things. The image of a creative God can almost emerge from a
capable human individual, yet what human life needs most is
the wisdom of God."

When the mentor said this, he rose from the stone where he was sitting and looked up at the sky. He said, "The Ageless Master is the name for the exquisite energy of the universe. This energy can be passed to anyone who learns and follows the Way. The Way is wisdom. Wisdom is the Way. It is the body of the exquisite universal energy or subtle energy. It reveals itself by the writings of the Way.

"There is no other possibility for salvation. The only saving power is the wisdom of God.

"In the world, there are always two forces, good and bad, which struggle and war on a large scale and a small scale. Each side thinks it is right. Human destiny is always involved in the battle of right and wrong, good and bad, unless the wisdom of God is seen.

"All men and women were born with purity. Because they turn away from the wisdom of God they fall into the blind pursuit of worldly expansion. Only those who choose the wisdom of God can be saved from inescapable suffering and misery. To follow the wisdom of God is to attain the capability of making the right choice. Following the Way is interpreted as following the wisdom of God.

"In a complicated human life, people need to make choices every day. What people choose becomes their fate. God has not decided each person's destiny, but God is the power of choice available to all people. God offers his divine energy for people in choice making. It is the wisdom of God to guide people to improve and correct themselves."

The young one asked, "Does the wisdom of God have a different name?"

The mentor smiled. He sat down on the stone and said, "The wisdom of God can be anywhere at any time. It is still the wisdom of God no matter where it is. How would you name it? Naming has been a problem of people, it has never been a problem of God.

"God is the exquisite energy of the universe. It has been through the process of transformation

from chaotic to clear
from messy to refined
from confused to clean
from coarse to neat

from rough to essential
from turbid to pure
from mixed up to well-ordered
from dark to bright
from noisy to tranquil
from tumultuous to sober
from low based to upward moving.

God is another name for universal spiritual nature.

"All lives and all movements, including momentary stillness, are expressions of universal nature. God is the awake and sober power of universal nature. God leads universal evolution toward upwardness and forwardness.

"God is the exquisite energy in the universe and human life. This energy was called 'sen' or the extendable energy in human life and nature. In external religions, they call sen God. Yet, there is no other God than this universal extendable exquisite energy.

"You can follow God by nurturing the exquisite energy within oneself. God is power of making choices. God is beyond relative opposites of good or bad, right or wrong, bright or dark, etc. God uplifts the relative mind which confuses itself in dualistic situations and doesn't know to choose good from bad, right from wrong, true from untrue, etc. No one is born bad; it is a matter of failing to develop the subtle, exquisite energy within and using it to make right choices.

"In order to achieve the growth of the God within, it is necessary for people to discard lower desires and worries from the mind. By purging the mind of lower desires and ambition, the exquisite energy becomes strong within and can help them make important choices in life. Reaching Heaven or reaching hell resides in one's own choice. All people are born good, all people know to choose what is nice, wonderful, beautiful, graceful and resonant. Yet they use impulse instead of the Ageless Truth of life when they make choices. They see momentary need, not the long term disaster or great trouble that will result from their impulsive choice. Rather than be impulsive, it is better to be receptive and let what is yours come to you.

"People may know to choose the wisdom of God, yet they do not know God or how to nurture the exquisite energy within them which serves their life best. Exquisite energy comes to a person who lives with a sober and awakened mind.

The young one responded, "Now I know it is important to nurture the exquisite energy, the light inside by living correctly and practicing self-cultivation. External belief in God only pulls people away from the spiritual center of their own natural life being and causes them to behave strangely. I appreciate this guidance."

Chapter 22

New Hope

The young one knew after the last instruction that there would be more serious revelation or practical assignments for him to carry out. He was ready for this spiritually but he was not totally ready to return to the world.

The mentor continued, "All good things in the world were brought about by God, the exquisite energy of the universe. Useful inventions, beautiful music, efficient systems, stunning paintings, superior literature, artful sculpture, deep religious theology, profound spiritual discussion of all different schools, etc., all exhibit this unselfish, exquisite universal energy when it is expressed through the human mind.

"Why then has the world become so unbearable and unlivable? We must know the root of its troubles. Originally, the exquisite energy of the nature was almost everywhere on earth. When it first entered the world, the early human race was united in mind and spirit. Later, the mind split itself from the spirit of life. Culture competes against the true spiritual nature of life. Alongside the harmonious creation of life, there developed the misapplication of exquisite energy in disharmonious creations that diverged from the pure nature of life.

"The earth was the paradise of ancient people. People are children of the physical and spiritual nature of the universe. When referring to the spiritual nature of the universe, we say that people are children of God. As time passed, in order to find new stimulation for the mind, people did not stay with the original nature of healthy life which produces pure energy and brings out useful creations which in turn support the naturalness of life.

"The new approach to life was developed with impure things. With the purpose of searching for God, poisonous plants were eaten to create hallucination. Alcohol was created for celebration or experiencing the Earth God. In the end, this could be called original sin. God did not decide to punish people; people do. Punishment comes through poor health or unhappiness. Mostly people let other people do what they wanted to spread the harmful influence.

"Sin is the inability to make choices. Salvation is merely the power to make the right choice. Using too much alcohol or hallucinogenic plants or any other way in searching for the experience of ecstacy resulted in the formation of a new fashion in external religious worship. Then people became addicted to using poisonous stimulants all the time. The extreme pursuit of brain stimulation became the next step beyond external religious worship. When people are born into the world, they receive the sins of their parents, and each generation has more trouble than the previous one.

"I would like to give an illustration of this. At the beginning of time, all people in a community had pure energy. Then, one small portion of people's energy became turbid. As the population increased, the power of this confused energy also increased among a small percent of people. Gradually its influence grew bigger and bigger. The world's energy changed from being simple and manageable to become unmanageable. In another two thousand years along the road of development, the problem will have increased almost beyond measure. People will wonder, "What will become of the world? Total destruction is the destination of the human race. That will be doomsday."

The young one asked, "What can I do to help the world?"

The mentor smiled and said, "Teach the masses. When you do so, straight language is less attractive than parables and metaphors. The crisis of total destruction is waiting at the end of the road unless people learn to respect everlasting life. This teaching was given through the Ageless One; now it will be through you. Teaching is not a matter of establishing a religion for racism or egotistic self-aggrandizement, but from universal moral responsibility. Even giving one's precious life to save people halfway approaching doomsday is still worth doing. If one person dies then many people can be saved. It is the work of God."

The young replied, "What is a practical approach to help the people of the world? Am I allowed to start working with my own people?"

The mentor said calmly, "The way of everlasting life should be taught to all people.

"The secret of the Kingdom of God has been given to you. The warning of doomsday should be known by all people."

The young one said, "I am carefully remembering and taking heed of all you have said. But what hope is there?"

The mentor said calmly, "The hope will be in your teaching to the masses. At least it can slow down the time of total destruction of human race. If the trend toward self-destruction is continued, doomsday will happen of necessity.

"However, if people straighten out their lives and worship only the most pure, exquisite energy in the entire universe, then the Kingdom of God prevails and doomsday as a most unnatural happening will not be the direction human society moves in.

"You could call the great one God by the names of its attributes: the God of Wisdom, God of Purity, God of All Wonderful Creation, God of Unruling Rule, God of Granting Eternal Life, God of Good Deeds, God of Subtly Helping. God can be realized by one person whose spiritual awareness equals the universal conscience.   God can also be realized by all people who nurture the exquisite energy within themselves and make use of it in their personal and public lives."

The young one asked again, "What hope is there in making this effort?"

The mentor said, "When people live the everlasting way of life, they will be awake and sober in their spirit.   At least the exquisite energy will remain within their life beings.

"The key point which will bring about the prosperity of humankind can be found simply in the relationship between men and women.   Salvation from doomsday also starts by straightening out this basic behavior.

"Correct behavior that will strengthen the human race is as follows.   People will not have excessive sex, thus human seeds will not be weakened.   Parents will not have all types of stimulation in their lives such as alcohol and drugs and they will surely not use these things before mating.   Thus children will not be born already addicted to drugs and alcohol. Parents will not go to bed with emotion.   They will choose a bright moonlit night to engender the coming of new life.   They will find well-matched partners instead of being oblivious to the suitability of their choice.

"By following all these important practices, the pure energy of the human race can be improved and maintained. No confused people will be brought into the world.

"No mixed up or muddle-headed people with blocked minds, no violent population, no people of low morality and irresponsibility will become the main or dominant force of the world. When this is the case, the Heavenly Kingdom will return to be enjoyed on Earth again.

"Spiritual work should start from the point of organic consideration of the development of the human society. In the long run, spiritual teaching is more responsible to the world than negative preaching about escaping the wrath of God. God is not in a rage, ever. God is saddened by leaving the self-destructive human life."

The young one asked for confirmation of what he understood by saying, "Am I correct in saying that the fruit of spiritual teaching is people following the Way of life to attain the health of the individual and society, and the health of all future generations? And that to help teach this, whether I have a family or live singly, I need to set a model for the whole world and all generations?"

The mentor smiled and said, "I am so happy with your quick understanding and absorption of what we have discussed. Because the universal exquisite energy manifests through the human mind and spirit, it is the energy of deathlessness. The Ageless Truth is passed down to us. The work of teaching the Ageless Truth of life continues the spiritual service of previous teachers, so the Ageless Teaching never dies. It continues and is continued by all new life.

"The Ageless Teacher will appear in the world in you. You will come back again in people of the same spirit of love and kindness and work to turn around the self-destructive trend of the human race."

The young one gladly received this explanation of his mission.

Chapter 23

The Childlike Heart
is the Pass to Enter Heaven

The young one was instructed to place particular value upon the morning hours. His mentor described the importance of morning by saying, "Youth is a time for preparation of one's entire lifetime. Springtime prepares for the entire year. Morning prepares the whole day. Thus, morning hours should not be disturbed in order to have the whole day be good."

"Prepare yourself for the day in the open air of morning by intaking the sweet energy and watching the gold chariot of God carry the healthful energy for all good souls and good spirits. No spiritual individual can afford to miss this heavenly nourishment. Gently use the breathing system and the nervous system under the command of the prime minister (the mind) to intake the Godly golden energy by gathering the white light particles on the eastern sky during the time before the sun rises and when the young sun is still on the horizon. It is preferable not to do it after the sun is higher than 30 degrees over the horizon. If the sun has already risen too high, do not look directly at the sun, but divert your eyes away from it; the focus can be to the left or right of the sun, which would make an angle around 30 degrees. If your foundation of yang energy is not strong enough, it can harm your vision. Be aware of this. Doing this in the morning is enough.

"If you do it in the evening, during and after the sunset, the same practice can be done, but the effect is different. The sunset lasts longer. The quality of solar energy is stronger than that of the rising morning sun. That will cause you to separate from the body by internally burning it during the time of your leaving the flesh body. It is the preparation for self-explosion materially; you might leave nothing of the body behind.

"Meditation can be done from the hours of midnight to noon. Because meditation should not interfere with one's daytime schedule, most people do it between 11:00 p.m. to 7:00 a.m., using the same technique whether one closes or opens the eyes in the darkness: look at the light particles and gently gather them to the deep center of the eyebrows. When your mind becomes strong, these particles will follow the wish of the mind and form the shape one wishes. It is recommended to use the symbol

as the subtle form. It pronounced "Shuan."[1] Project this image as a magnet to the sky to collect the tiny small white light particles, and then gather this back to the center. The secret gate is the location of the boneless opening in a baby's skull (the fontanel). It is also the gate where the flying soul travels in and out.

"Moon energy intake can be done, too. During the first quarter of the moon, a similar practice to the sun energy intake can be done. This should be done less than the sun practice. A few times a year will be enough, because the moon is reflecting light and its energy quality is different. Human life does not need much reflecting light. The variation of moonlight influences the liquid bodily energy strongly, and if one's nervous system is too highly charged with lunar energy, one's mental control will be affected.

"The North Star and the Great Dipper are the energy throne of nature. Doing a similar practice to the intake of sun and moon energy is beneficial, because it will help longevity and immortality. Bare eyes can see a double star in the Great Dipper, proving the strength of one's spirit.

"The important instruction for this practice says,

"'There are three treasures in the sky:
sun, moon and stars.
There are three treasures on the earth:
water, fire and wind (air).
There are three treasures in the individual self:
Tsing[2] which is sexual essence,
Chi which is semi physical power and
Sen which is spirits.

---

[1]This is the Chinese symbol for infinity. For detailed explanation, please refer to the book, *Mysticism: Empowering the Spirit Within.*

[2]Sometimes written as jing or ching.

*The integration of all nine energies
is how to attain everlasting life.'*

"Attaining everlasting life is not hard, but your internal enemy
is usually stronger than the will of healthy life. Thus, there are
few who achieve themselves without self-discipline."

After doing his morning practice, and after eating a simple
and easily digested breakfast and a short rest, the young one
saw his teacher for that day.

In this day's meeting, the mentor started by saying,

"Let the Way, truth and life follow 'me;' no one except 'I'
can be close to God. 'I' am completely filled with all three.'
Now repeat this!"

The young one repeated:

"Let the Way, truth and life follow 'me,' no one except 'I'
can be close to God. 'I' am completely filled with all three."

The mentor smiled with satisfaction.

The young one asked, "Why did you ask me to repeat
that?"

The mentor smiled and said, "I am confirming your
spiritual attainment because, the Way, truth, life and God can
be conceptions. However, they are also subtle reality; you need
to maintain your life firmly at this level of attainment and
frequently remind yourself by repeating this statement."

The young one said, "When I have realized the Way, the
truth and the light, they become non-verbal."

The mentor smiled and said, "They can also be verbal, just
as you and I have said them. There is the need for clarity, not
only to know but also to be them, to embody all of them.

"Today, we are going to continue the verbal exploration of
spiritual reality connected with the destiny of the human
individual and society."

The young one said, "I welcome this because I need it. I
would also like to ask a few questions to clarify my own
understanding; I am asking these questions for the benefit of
others."

The mentor nodded his head in agreement. The young one
was thus encouraged to ask, "The world is full of good and evil.
It is easy to attribute all good to God, but who is responsible for

the evil? If the creator is responsible for evil, then where does the creator's virtue of goodness and righteousness go?"

The mentor smiled and answered, "What is known through the senses as good or bad is not definite, although it can be true at its own level.

"At another, different level of understanding, the strong force and weak force of nature are interdependent by intersecting each other as a network which lays down the frame of life in the world. This invisible energy network is more real than the surface of visible forms. The pattern of this invisible network is perceived by the relative and subjective human mind. It is not always in a balanced situation. In an individual or a society, harm can be brought about by the imbalance (too weak or too strong) of a relationship so that it becomes internecine or interlinking. The remedy for internal disharmony can be found in the subjective human mind: it is the subtle power of choice.

"The naturally endowed power of free will is responsible for all that happens. Free will is a precious gift from God if correctly used as an extension of Godly energy. Free will does not mean doing what one pleases. Surely one can do whatever he or she pleases without restraint or inhibition, but when it comes to evolution of the soul, different practices bring different results. Uncertainty and unsafety is not the wisdom of God.

"Therefore, good and evil in the world cannot be considered as the original spirits. They are like twin sisters that reflect each other in thought and action, although they do not wish to be so. They are the frame of the world; mostly they are mechanical and have no life. People need to avoid internecine relationship in society or in private life. The wise choose the righteous and the foolish · choose evil. The choice of right endows people with the power to create life, and the choice of evil endows them with the power to create death. In the end, the followers of lies, hatred and downfall eat their own fruit, and the people who choose righteousness find everlasting life. People of truth accept the equality of man and woman, which is the equilibrium of opposites. Good laws, good knowledge, non-discrimination, love, fidelity, sincere service, spiritual piety, filial duty, non-glittery perfection and everlasting life empower them.

"Your choice is what determines whether you meet with success or failure in life. Hypocrisy leads to a lifetime of punishment. Honesty leads to abundance. Good fortune is the outcome of good thought, positive language and appropriate behavior. Material life can be improved by ordinary education. Spiritual life can be improved by the self-realization of honesty, earnestness, simplicity, righteousness, sympathy, kindness to others and selfless service, plus doing no harm to the land.

"The human race has the freedom to choose whether or not to do right or wrong. It is inalterable that reward or retribution are the consequences of one's choices. The Way to stop punishment is to stop doing evil, because in the end, evil deeds cannot be covered up by money or power. It is wise to not even think of doing evil. Spiritual damage to oneself cannot be fixed by soliciting a favor or asking for mercy on behalf of yourself or someone else. No prayer or sacrificial offering to God can alter the result of one's behavior. People can freely choose their lifestyle, and they are also completely responsible for their lives.

"The human race is endowed with rational power. This makes it possible to choose what is good and right. True enjoyment is for a good soul to accomplish purity. The piety of a pure life is the power of happiness. All healthy happinesses of life are stored in an upright character, earnest work and simple living. These are the keys to turn one's destiny around. All it takes is determination to move toward the light. It is to say that any person who is upright and applies oneself to hard, effective work can turn his destiny around from bad to good. A sincere soul can bring the ones who live in the dusty world to the regretless range of highest enjoyment. Remember to guide people to pursue good thought, speech and behavior. Healthy thought, clean and kind speech, and upright behavior are their own benefit. They are real benefit.

The young one asked, "May I know what role God plays in people's lives?"

The mentor answered, "Some human ancestors defined God as the creator in order to reply to the external question of how the world came into existence. Just as the universe is in continual expansion, so is the human intellectual mind, and it was not the time for the ancient ancestors to offer an authoritative conclusion of how the world was made. We are questing for the solution to the problem of confrontation between the two forces. Ethically, we define or call those forces good and evil.

"So far, human intellectual knowledge has not moved in the positive direction of improving the internal quality of human survival. The spiritual response from some human ancestors can be seen as a contribution. The life spirit of the human race may be the best source to offer its own remedy to control the obsessive growth of human culture and society. The wisdom of God does not extend in the same direction as the intellectual mind. In the teaching of the Way, it takes what general people think of as smart to be foolish, and takes what is foolish to be smart. From this, one can understand the difference between the Kingdom of Heaven and the Kingdom of Earth.

"If one does not carefully study the Ageless Teaching, the wisdom of God will be twisted by the human mind for the sake of expedience. The wisdom of the Kingdom of God is only known by sincere-hearted people who take an honest approach to life. It cannot be understood by the false culture. All people have the same human foundation of free will as the most important element of their life, yet some become victims of the confused worldly culture which is the way of the lost."

The young one said, "I can appreciate that, but what immediate help is there?"

The mentor replied, "It takes a long time for most people to develop their own spiritual awareness. You can only apply the most truthful spiritual teaching, but the effect is not immediately seen. Thus, a devoted teacher can make it shorter and possible by showing the Way.

"In human life, rationality is not more trustworthy than good knowledge and broad vision, yet rationality guides people to the objective search for the best. Rationality could be said to be the eye that sees what is momentarily right in the present life situation. Spiritual truth is objective and also subjective. The vision of truth is the outcome of subjective growth. True objective prophecy does not exist in any of the religions. Religions are hardly the pure expression of the universal conscience. The only correct prophecy exists with the harmony of all religions which offer help to people of all regions.

"In the world, there is only one God. The true name of God is wisdom. God is not the creator of chaos. God has nothing to do with that type of irresponsible creation. God is the creator of all truth, all beauty and all good. The responsible creation of God leaves all other things behind as the dregs, sediment and discarded useless material. God does not create fear or evil intent. God does not provide people with prejudice and hatred. God does not guide people to separation and war, but to unity and cooperation. God is the spiritual function of universal conscience.

"Universal life always exists. Its nature contains only forwardness and upwardness. Universal life extends its own nature to all lives.

"The life of true God does not choose to be the beginning or end, but God chooses to live with the infinite as the whole.

"God knows to do creation subtly and gently because then no opposite thing will be created. Trouble is created by suddenness and strong willed ambition. Thus, the way of God is gentle, easy and smooth. The creation of God has the infinite potential to be all. God likes simple, direct communication. God does not like people deliberately arranging grand ceremonies. This type of worship and ritual does not express the truth of God."

The young one asked, "Did God create infinity or did God create the world?"

The mentor smiled and said, "The Way is infinite. It is the great energy flow and time flow of the universe. The universe is with the Way. The Way is wisdom. The Way is inexhaustible. If human achievements do not serve the world or people correctly, they will only accelerate that the world and people will be washed away by the energy flow of the universe.

"The strongest building will always fall. The most reliable knowledge will always need to be replaced. Fortunes will always be lost. The sharp sword of a great conqueror will become dull. Yet, the sublime and gentle Way of God is always there despite the changes of forms. It is wrong for any powerful individual to fight the Way of God; it is right to search for it."

The young one said, "Why do all individuals need to search for the Way?"

The mentor smiled and said, "Because the Way is the wisdom of God, the Way slows down their impulsive actions, their pride, their violence. All individuals need to search for the Way. Those who search for the Way will find it. Those who knock at the door will find that the door of subtle truth will open."

The young one asked, "What is the direct benefit to those who find the Way?"

The mentor smiled and said, "The Way is the wisdom of God and the subtle reality of the God of Wisdom. People who learn the Way live a simple, peaceful life. They cherish the knowledge that achievement which comes from strife will not last. Thus, they do not fight, but let achievement happen along side their main goal of everlasting life.

"The Way of life is simple. Life is found in sincerity and earnestness. External religious beliefs kill one's life energy; they do not truly nurture life. All people can learn to live the Way of life, which is fair, proper, just, appropriate, sure, steady and peaceful and therefore creates no accident or mishap. It extends no great attraction or extraordinary attraction, but is smooth, even and mild, enjoying the ride of equilibrium and balance. The Way expresses itself through wise individuals who are orderly, quiet and calm. There is no tricking or chicanery in the Way. It is easy to go and easy to get along with, and most agreeable. Most of all, God is found in earnest thought, speech and behavior. That is the Way.

"God does not exist in books or secret doctrines. God exists in the pure piety of an earnest life."

The young one responded, "Many people live with the Way. Vanity, empty glory and undeserved gain are not the pursuit of people of the Way. These things are the root of trouble that causes conflict among people. If people are content with the fulfillment of their simple needs by the power of their developed mind, they will not expect to outdo others, and their lives can be more harmonious and happy. The good guiding strength of people is intuition which appears only in a quiet and calm mind. Pride is not encouraged in living with the Way. People's pride draws harm to them. The tallest trees in the forest are cut down first.

"It is important to maintain a childlike heart and mind in most stages of life. A fresh heart and mind is ready for growth; it is ready to receive new light. You are always making room to grow if you do so. You are perfection in spirit, like a child before being abused by oneself or twisted by the world."

Chapter 24

It is the Nature of Life to Love Life

The young one asked, "How shall I teach people what I have learned from you?"

The mentor answered, "Most people have to earn a living and thus do not need to go into all the details. It is sometimes more effective to teach spiritual truth through the use of metaphors and parables than by direct presentation. For the purpose of effectiveness, the Ageless One said, 'People can be guided to know how; people do not need to search for the answer to why.'

"The learning of a full-time spiritual student who is preparing to be a teacher or developing a specific skill is different from the learning of the masses.

"Particularly, the Ageless One's way of teaching does not emphasize talking. It stresses setting an example. All parents, fathers and mothers, are teachers of their children. Their model of life and behavior has the strongest influence on the behavior of their sons and daughters. Spiritual teaching cannot be mere lip service. If so, then it is shallow and does not achieve its purpose. This is why the Ageless One emphasized setting oneself up as a model of natural spiritual truth.

"In spiritual understanding, it is not constructive to squander energy in the discussion of secondary ideological differences; one can learn to serve one's life. Spiritual learning is not about learning to argue. Spiritual teaching is accomplished by being a living example for one's own children and fellow people.

"Non-declared spiritual teachers are the great leaders of people. Surely, spiritual teaching or leadership is not meant for the expansion of ego. Spiritual teachers or leaders need to serve the world by their living example."

The young one asked, "I feel that in the teaching of the Way there is a lot of talk about retiring, retreating and withdrawing. How do I apply this in my life?"

"All people know to go forward for their own interest," replied the great man. "Few people know to withdraw. This is one important point of teaching the Way. It is important to withdraw from a situation of possible over-expansion. People tend to over-extend themselves in pursuit of their worldly interests. It is a loss rather than a gain if one damages one's life essence by spreading oneself too thin. It does not serve life."

The young one asked, "Is there a doomsday for the world, a day when it will end itself?"

The mentor answered, "All natural things of any size have a natural span of life. If the world dies, a new world will be born. This is not a problem. The problem is that the world has become unnatural and that it accelerates its own death. Whenever anything unnatural happens, it increases a critical situation. Thus, it is important to prepare oneself spiritually and help the world turn back around or at least slow down the destruction."

The young one asked, "Does God pass a last judgement on all souls?"

The mentor answered, "There is a last judgement in each person's life. The self-judgment is made by dying people on themselves, whether to go upward to enjoy the light and be free, or to sink and suffer from darkness and bondage. In general, if there is nothing in one's life to damage one's spiritual energy by disturbing the conscience, the judgement is positive. This is usually the case with someone who has frequently judged oneself during his or her lifetime in order to maintain spiritual responsibility. The conscience is the spiritual life within. One can enjoy everlasting spiritual life, even if the physical body is still alive. Death will be a natural transformation.

"If the person did not judge oneself frequently, there is no spiritual growth, and life is taken by one's own destructive manner of life. Who else should accept the judgement? Each individual is responsible for one's own life at all levels, particularly the spiritual level."

The young one asked, "Will the everlasting soul come back to the world again?"

The mentor said, "Yes, it will. As you know, each individual has three selves: the physical self, the mental self and the spiritual self. The physical self will die. The mental self will die also, but the spiritual self will not die; it is the root of eternal life. It comes back again to be newly fleshed and equipped with a better mind."

The young one asked, "Is it really good to come back again?"

The mentor answered, "That depends upon the refinement of one's soul. If the enjoyment of life is totally external, there is only exhaustion of the internal essence. If the enjoyment of life is internal, it is much greater than external pursuit of all types of fun.

"Reincarnation, whether it is good or bad, is decided by the condition of how well balanced a person is. The enjoyment of eternal life is more internal spirit than external fashion."

"You have mentioned the three selves," echoed the young one. "What do the selves do in my life?"

The mentor smiled at him and answered, "You already have the answer. In the kingdom of undeveloped people, the mind is the usurper which identifies as 'I' with possession, subordinates and belongings.

"In the kingdom of the usurping mind, the "I" is egotistic expansion.

"However, in the Kingdom of God, the upright life authority (the mind assisting the spiritual self in harmonious order) sits steadily on the throne. The spiritual "I" identifies with God, Heaven, the Way, the truth and the light.

"In the Kingdom of God, the "I" has been uplifted to the level of selflessness. The "I" is used to express the unity of internal and external spirits as the achieved and attained Godhood."

The young one asked again, "I clearly understand my spiritual mission and what will happen to my physical life if I challenge society, but I would like to know if I will come back to enjoy my next life."

The mentor smiled and answered, "Life comes back to itself; the new life will not necessarily be of the same race, same figure and complexion, or the same name. Yet, one's spiritual nature and temperament is carried to the new life. Usually, spiritual nature and temperament is not known to oneself. Because of the sudden jump into the strong energy whirlpool of different levels of natural life energy, the memory is washed out. However, an achieved one with strong spiritual volition is different. If volition is the reason for the soul to re-enter the flow of life, it will come back to make the similar endeavor which comes from a great love for all people. This type of spirit is the indestructible Godly quality which is forever living in the universe. The possibility of an indestructible being only exists for the one who identifies one's virtue as God or Heaven."

The young one asked, "Where does the soul go between lifetimes?"

The mentor smiled and answered, "Universal nature will take care of all good souls by the subtle law. The subtle law does not operate by any externally established authority, it extends itself to the individual soul. Yet, an individual still needs the development of internal knowledge to attain the necessary concordance with the subtle law. Thus salvation is the self-selection of one's own life. The developed spiritual self automatically and continually cleanses and weeds itself during the lifetime as a spiritual preparation.

"All souls are swimming in the subtle light of the universe. Some ascend, some sink, and some maintain their swimming or bathing in a middle range. They are all nurtured by the subtle divine light. When one reaches the highest nature, there is no more need of reorganizing oneself. Reorganizing is only necessary in physical life when one is associated with the three levels.

"The spiritual life of achieved immortals is completed by the higher integration of yin and yang from the lifetime. Achieved immortals are the holy spirit or God continuing the spiritual function of helping good individuals whose vibration is closer to them than that of other people. In life, there is a difference between carrying the physical life to receive the limitation or carrying the spirit to receive no limitation. Yet, even achieved ones are still bound by their own volition.

"The nature of life is to love life; may there be endless life for all people!"

Chapter 25

The Wild Man

Around two thirds of a day's trip from the village, was a mountain called the Mountain of Wild Man. On the top of the mountain was a natural cave where someone lived who had long hair and a beard so long it covered his body. He wore nothing, and nobody knew how he lived. Needless to say, he was the wild man.

There were many legends about him among the neighboring villages. Someone said he had lived there for 300 years. Someone else said he had lived there for at least 500 years. A few believed that he came from the far South, but some had a story about how he came from the far East. Actually, nobody knew for sure because he was not social and he did not come down to the villages. It was also told that several times, along the main road, a group of bandits ambushed some travellers. When the bandits attacked, the wild one appeared like a winged swallow, diving from the mountain top to the rescue the defenseless ones by shouting loudly. All the bandits became scared and scattered when that happened. He did not wait for thanks but disappeared before the frightened travelers had recovered from the shock.

Sometimes he rested on a high, open spot where people could see him from far away. Some elder villagers used him for divination; from the movements of his body or position, or from the direction he faced, they decided whether a certain thing should be done or not. They found this to be effective. Thus, people respected his spiritual being, but at the same time, they were afraid of his physical being.

The local boy had heard many of the legends about the wild man and had a secret wish to meet him in person. However, this plan has not been realized for one unimportant reason or another. One day, he told the young one about the wild man and his wish to see him. The young one felt that they should ask for approval from their teacher before attempting to see this person, but the local friend maintained that their teacher was open for students to have their own experiences in order to receive better growth. The principle of teaching a student is the same as teaching a child; no one can grow well if they are over-protected.

Thus, the local boy was not worried about the teacher, but he suggested that his father be the one they consult. Their reason for meeting the wild man was not mere curiosity but for possible learning. The two boys therefore went to see the father and described their plan to him.

The father mentioned that years ago, he himself had the same wish to see the wild one in person, but he was always occupied, so he did not do it. Therefore, he did not discourage them but said, "It is the time for both of you to test yourselves. To know people is the most difficult thing. True achievement is not decided by looking. Wise advice does not please the ears. Spiritual discernment is subtle. Do not deny people too quickly nor recognize them too quickly. Both are the root of mistakes. You may go."

Both of them took some dry food and went on their way. They left very early the next morning and traveled until the middle of the afternoon, when they reached the mountain and came closer to where the wild one lived. To their surprise, they felt that it became rather difficult to move as they came closer to the spot where the old man was known to live. The closer they went, the more difficult it was to push forward. Finally, they felt the invisible wall around the mountain ridge. Somewhat exhausted, they reached a point where they could not move any further.

Then the local friend said, "It must be the magic of the bearded one. Let me use my holy water to defeat his magic." He untied his belt and was about to go to the toilet there. Just at that moment, a loud shout with laughter said, "You mischievous boy, do not contaminate my energy wall!"

The local friend shouted back, "Grandpa, you do not need a wall. All four sides of the cliff around your place are ninety degrees. Nobody can approach you."

The wild man shouted back, "My doorway is flat and easy to enter for people who have a heart as big as the sky. Both of you have such a heart, so you can come in. I already knew your intention. I will give you no more difficulty. You can climb up here by using the vines and bushes."

Finally, they made it to the cave. The wild old man had a radiant, fiery energy aura around him. He was bearing a big smile of welcome and said, "I have been here many years, but

I have not seen or spoken with anyone. This is exceptional. It is nice to see you boys!

"Before I came here, I traveled many places. The place I stayed the longest was the South. It was there that I gave my service to people. Soon it will be your turn. Now I would like to talk to you randomly."

Both of the young men said, "Please, grandpa, teach us."

The wild sage opened his eyelids widely to give out a strong blue light before his talk. Then he gathered himself back to his inner center and voiced his spiritual energy:

"Life is universal nature expressing itself.
Life and death are the universal spirit
in and out of the physical shell.
Death is like taking off worn-out clothes.
Birth is like putting on a new robe.

This life spirit of the universe never dies.
It cannot be cut by a knife,
burned by fire
made wet by water
or dehydrated like fruit in the wind.
Yet it renews itself constantly.

"The universe displays itself in all directions with only the infinite. The infinite is known to all types of life after having been produced. Before that, the subtle reality of the universe has already been active in creation. It expands itself North, South, East and West. The infinite is immeasurable. It has no limitation. There is no deduction that can be made by the human mind about the beginning of the world. It is totally natural and incredible! The supreme self has made the infinite as itself.

"Then came two lords, the Lord of the False Form and the Lord of Ignorance. With the cooperation of both, the life of the world was covered up.

"Nobody knew how long these two lords had ruled before human culture was created. Religion was developed by people who thought the sky could give them extra help by making sacrificial offerings. Few people knew the truth that help comes only from the improvement of people's internal situation.

People were divided by their spiritual vision. Some said, 'God is one' and others said 'God is many.' Some said 'God is a man.' Others said 'God is a woman.' There were always two groups. One group worshipped the Lord of False Form (physical interest). The other worshipped the Lord of Ignorance (spiritual ignorance and religious dogma). Because of these divisions, it became difficult for people to get along with one another. There was always someone who proclaimed: My lord, or my way, is more powerful than yours.

"Later, people come to fight over the different worship and wars were started. Life was lost by the devotion to either the Lord of False Form or Lord of Ignorance.

"Much later, by the success of the example of the Lord of False Form and the Lord of Ignorance, newer and stronger religions were organized. The Lord of Confusion, the Lord of Contorted Vision, the Lord of Illusory Vision and the Lord of Spiritual Weakness joined together to create the religion of polytheism.

"Lord Egomania, Lord Dependency, Lord Monomania and Lord Conquering joined to create the religion of monotheism.

"Lord Monopolizer invented a new product, the chain of karma, to sell to people. People who were born from the spirits of the head of the great God became the priests. People who were born from the spirits of the trunk of the great God became the kings, officials and scholars. People who were born from the spirits of arms of the great God became the people of all occupations and businesses. People who were born from the spirits of the legs of the great God became the slaves. Thus, social ranks were fixed to all people by what type of parents and family they were born into. The social rank of the lifetime can not be changed because that is karma.

"The dissolution of karma could only happen by constantly making offerings to God. Only the helpers of Lord Monopolizer could conduct the offering of people to be received by God through their participation and prayer. This service is performed by the Lord Monopolizer to collect the offering and payment.

"Monopolized business found its challenge later from Master Self-Mistreatment. He announced that pleasing God was not the way to liberate karma. He focused on an ascetic way of life as the only way to create no karmic responsibility and eventually break the chain. His followers could be found meditating in the forest, living a life of extreme austerity and giving up normal life. They chained themselves with heavy metal chains or slept on beds made of nails arranged with the sharp tips pointing upward, etc.

"A young student of this practice spent six or seven years in the forest and gave up all the things that most people appreciated. However, he believed that reaching the truth was higher than all other tangible things, thus he gave up his crown, the enjoyment of a royal life, a young wife and son, to live in the forest and meditate under the trees. Early one morning, after a long night of meditation, the light stimulated his mind. The hungry man suddenly understood that if one does not debauch in life, there is no need for extreme ascetic practice in order to remove the bonds of karma. What one needs to follow is the middle way between debauchery and austerity.

"After having had this important enlightenment, he should have gone back to live a normal life. However, he had already gone too far to return to a well balanced life and he converted his faith from animism to spiritual pessimism. In his teaching, he became the Master of Half-Price. His new way was to reduce the severe austerity practiced and promoted by the Master of Self-Mistreatment but still reject an earnest, worldly life of labor. Although the extreme was decreased, this was still far from the golden mean.

"Once he said,

'Love no one or anything,
  because pain comes when you leave them.
If you do not have love or hatred,
  you are not bound!'

This expresses the disappointment of experiencing trouble and pain. Thus, he decided to shun the main road of life, like someone who finds satisfaction from the twilight of the stars at night rather than enjoy the bright light of the sun at daytime. All religions have this inclination.

"All spiritual students need to know that inspiration and enlightenment cannot be achieved once and for all. If one does not hurry to assert the conclusion one has reached, one will continue to achieve still higher stages.

"He concluded years of his concentrated pursuit with these lines:

'*1.   No external God is of any importance in personal liberation from karma.*
2.   There is no necessity to worship or make offerings to any external authority for personal liberation.
3.   Liberation can be accomplished by oneself.'

"After he passed away, new teachers made him into a new type of God to worship and a new teaching was established with a further reduced practice.   At the time of monopolized business, people needed to pay priests to remove their chains of karma.   Then at the time of Master Self-Mistreatment, people were taught to do it by themselves but to pay the whole price by living an ascetic life with all kinds of self-persecuting disciplines.   Then during the time of Master Half-Price, people were taught to do half of the severe discipline in order to be delivered from their karma, which was a better deal.   Now, I prophesize that after the ascetic practice of the Hinayana or lesser vehicle will come the great vehicle, Mahayana, which will be an improvement and further reduce the ascetic practice of the Hinayana.

"At this stage in the teaching of the Master of Half Price, new religious leaders began the wholesale promotion of delivery from one's karma and people were divided even further.   Some people still went to the monopolized store.   Some still went to the Master of Self-Mistreatment.   Some still went to the Master of Half-Price.   Some went to the Masters of Wholesale for Delivery.

"To start with, when the idea of karma was invented, priests were busy establishing the classes of society.   The religionists stole the fruit of the ordeal of life of the masses by treating religions as commerce.

"When the Masters of Self-Mistreatment arose, one of the important disciplines was to ask no help from other people.   It was a good discipline, yet the whole teaching was too far from the mainstream of life.

"When the Master of Half-Priced Delivery appeared, he set an example of going to a village to receive one meal a day. His teaching was for the small exchange.

"When the Master of Wholesale Delivery arose, priests had much food and lived like royal nobles. Their religion was totally commercialized."

"All four types of religious promotion came about from the notion of karma. This theory damaged people's perception of natural life by rationalizing the emotions of those who struggled with a troubled life and expected a happy one.

"The difficulty of life is commonly recognized by most people. Difficulties can be improved by individual effort, better education and especially the improvement of the structure of human society. If karma is true, these religious teachings are not the only possible way to defeat and unchain such bondage.

"Above all, there is the development of human wisdom to not overdo anything. It is the Way. However, karma has become an excuse for a non-productive life and a stagnant society. It expresses the dark side of life. Acceptance of karma is a passive attitude. The Lord of Laziness was behind its invention and he continues to help the sale of the product.

"Reincarnation is the subtle operation of the spiritual nature of the universe. It has nothing to do with cultural or conceptual attitudes; it is closely connected to one's individual personality and development in this lifetime. Spiritual cultivation can restore and improve one's life."

The young one sighed and said, "It seems that the world is not easily fixed. First one needs to climb very high to the top of the world spiritually in order to see clearly what has happened. Then, you still need to take all the inconvenience to come back down to the world in order to help people in trouble.

The wild man laughed and said, "In all of human religions, although God or the universal spiritual realm was exalted, God remains pure and innocent and has nothing to do with human mischief. The name of God as a religious promotion is only a ruse created by the immature mentality and spirituality of mankind.

"All religions were mostly created or based on an uneasy feeling about life and the expectation of external help. Religious teachers never reached the true spiritual knowledge of life. Now religions are developing faster than the learning of natural spiritual truth. The masses cannot wait for their own maturity; they set up leaders who are at their own level and it is a situation of the blind leading the blind. This type of spiritual leadership goes nowhere."

The young one said, ""May I request to know the natural spiritual truth?"

The old sage laughed and said, "You have great heart. To answer your request, the truth can be divided into two parts: the big scale of the universe and the small scale of individual human life. Natural spiritual truth is all within the experience of immortal spirits. It is not beyond the knowledge of the highly evolved immortal spirits. Thus, it can be learned from them."

The young one said, "I would first like to learn the natural spiritual truth on the big scale."

The wild one laughed and said, "The infinity of universal nature cannot be obstructed by anyone who intends to cover it up. Spiritual development brings good knowledge about the spiritual sphere of nature. The Lord of False Form means the manifest spheres of the universe, the formed world. All forms are subject to transformation; no form can stay the same or live in the world forever. At this level, forms are both real and at the same time unreal, but people think they are real. It is false human perception to stay at the level of form. No knowledge of permanent usefulness can be established from this level.

"The local friend asked, "Grandpa, I know you speak metaphorically. Please correct me if I am wrong. The Lord of Ignorance is the state of spiritual ignorance of people. For human people, is it not a shame to be ignorant? Is it not shameful to insist on knowledge established by perceptions of the unreliable level of false forms?

"The chain of karma is based on the law of cause and effect, which is one way of interpreting the pattern of yin and yang when it is applied to human life. It is the incomplete perception of the relative yin and yang pattern of life. This level is shallow and mechanical. The Lord of Karma has no feeling toward what you do; you cannot either please or displease him. Karma is only one description of the level of nature; thus, it treats everyone the same. Karma is merely an expression of the sentimental quality of the human mind. The teaching of the Ageless One and the sages are not sentimental. The whole thing can be surpassed by one's own spiritual development. On one hand, the achieved ones calmly accept the dualistic pattern of life. On the other, by being gentle and doing things with gentleness, they can avoid stirring up any sudden reaction which would be like strong waves which could create difficult life experiences.

"Since the Ageless Master said that on the human sphere, misfortune is antecedent to good fortune and good fortune can be a hidden cause of misfortune, this simple line can explain the whole truth and the deep fact of karma. It is exemplified by the development of human history and individuals. In everyday behavior, especially big events, we have to watch ourself no matter what situation we face."

The wild one laughed and replied, "I am glad for your quick understanding of all this. Your learning has made you my guests. In my words, nobody who lives on the relative plane of life can totally expect the special treatment of being left alone. However, most yo-yo patterns of rise and fall can be restructured and modified by oneself. This is to live with the Way and to closely follow the God of Wisdom. Self-salvation and delivery will truly reduce the problem installed in anyone's radical action, thought and behavior.

"On the level of mind, finding peace of mind was considered as delivery from karma, which is, directly speaking, the troubled mind itself. However, few can realize that pain or peace are relative, because life is based on the relative plane. Yet the spirit of life is far behind the surface; it belongs to the infinite.

"The practice of the later three religious promotions all stress sitting meditation. If the spirits of life wish to free themselves from the alternation of life and death, then meditation is unnecessary. Few know that meditation cannot shake off life and death. Meditation or no meditation, what is truly needed in life is to find a compromise between the pride of the spirit of life and the toil of undertakings of life. All people need to pay attention to the importance of the compromise. The concession making does not happen all at once, but over a lifetime. How much concession one needs to make in the bargain of life depends upon your development in making attunements to a life situation by conducting yourself along the middle line between what you can avoid and what possible problems you will run into.

"Universal nature cannot be expressed by anything other than things of nature, such as the sun, moon, stars, earth, mountains, water and people themselves. Temples, houses of worship, etc., are not direct expressions of universal nature. A symbol of universal divinity could be a bowl of fresh water, a lamp of light or a bunch of flowers, etc. When natural energy is felt and presented, it can be considered a suitable shrine or altar for the great infinite.

"All things and people are equal in the embrace of the great infinite. The nature of truth is unique but not monotonous. The variety of all types of inventions increases the fun of life and is allowed to express the artful mind; it is one of the products of the refined mind.

"On the big scale, the universe is an infinite energy ocean. On the small scale, each individual's bodily life is also a small energy ocean. Life has nothing to do with karma; karma is related to mind. Although there is no karma in life, there is a dualistic energy pattern. If you move to the left, then you must move to the right; if you move high then you must move low; if you move to the front then you must move to the back, if something flows strongly then it must flow softly, etc. All movements express the polarity of energy: solar-type energy is called yang, and lunar-type energy is called yin. The interdependence of these two types of energy is called Tai Chi or the ultimate law."

The local friend said, "Grandpa, your wisdom covers at least three thousand years of the life experience of mankind. Your teaching can save us at least a ten-year burden of study. We appreciate this greatly."

The wild one laughed and answered, "I do not have the wisdom to know this much. It all comes from the immortal spirits to inspire me on an occasion like this.

The young one requested, "May we have your trust in our worthiness to know your practice?"

The wild one replied, "My art of life is called the Correspondence of the Sun and Moon. It was what I simplified from my own learning from the achieved ones. It includes the art of maintaining life, movement, choice of food, cleansing the body, fasting, breathing, meditation and most of all, sun worship."

The local one requested, "Would you show us your arts, Grandpa?"

The respectable wild one laughed and said, "According to your own level of achievement, as I see, not including the use of your holy water, it will take one hour or two for me to teach it to you. I am interested in having you to continue my teaching in the South, so I will help you to learn the art and forget about karma. If you decide to learn it now, I will show you everything once and I will not repeat anything."

The local one said, "We are glad."

The wild man said, "Now I am going to show you the movement of energy conducting. Numerous ancient arts are based upon the principle of yin and yang. To face down is yin, and to face up is yang. To breathe in is yang, to breathe out is yin. To move left is yang and to move right is yin. You watch."

Then the respectable wild one laid down on the slippery surface of the flat stone. He started doing all types of postures exactly according to the yin and yang rhythm. According to his explanation, yin and yang cannot be disordered. One yang move must be followed by a yin move, and vice versa.

After doing this, the moon was already shining in the sky. The respectable wild sage suggested that the two young men stay there overnight.

The youths took out their dry food and respectfully offered some to the wild one. He laughed and stopped them from eating it. Suddenly, in a snap of time, many delicious dishes of food and drink were displayed in front of them.

The wild one assured them, "These are all real food. I took them from the royal kitchen of the Emperor thousands of miles away. Both of you enjoy them. I myself have no interest in these foods."

Because these great foods reminded the young one of the good eating experiences in his home town, the image of a smoked fish appeared in his mind. Then, a real smoked fish was brought in front to him, with fresh bread and curds.

So the young ones enjoyed their meal wholeheartedly, bathing in the great friendly warmth of the old wild man, as he was called.

They departed the next morning.

Chapter 26

Reaching the Universal, Infinite Source of Life

On the way home, both of the young gentlemen felt they needed time to digest what the respectable old hermit had said to them. His suggested life attitude was different from the approach of social religions. It was definitely not a monopolized promotion, nor did it demand a high payment as the price of life or offer a diluted means of paying half-price or much less than wholesale in order to deliver the soul.

His way was to change one's internal energy flow and to live a pure life. Although it was not the mainstream of life, his vision of religious teaching was deep. His offering and his practices were useful. The boy's local friend saw that the simple system of reorganized practice had its value. He thought it could be a tool for teaching people the nonverbal subtle truth and helping them to realize it in life. The young one's mind was focused on teaching the people in the mainstream, and after they returned home, he continued to concentrate upon the knowledge of internal life.

Because there was something unanswered by the wild sage, the young one went to see the mentor.

The young one asked, "When people reach the natural spiritual truth on the scale that is related to their individual lives, deeper understanding from their own life could verify the truth. Then, they might make better use of broader guidance."

The mentor answered, "The small scale of individual life *is* the simple spiritual truth. Human life is the integration of two types of spirits with different natures: heavenly spirits and earthly spirits. The spirit of Heaven or sky, once embodied in an earthly life, expresses nature. The spirits of the sky have been swimming in the energy flow of the vast sky for a long time. Their natural tendency is to roam around where there are no obligations or boundaries.

"After they enter physical life, they meet a new group of earthly spirits in the body they inhabit. This new integration brings the joy of life only in the short stage of youth. As the life continues, the number of different unbearable life situations increase. Thus, the wish and hope of escaping is cherished from the first moment they meet things they do not like to face.

"It is the spiritual nature of the sky spirit to like what is light and reject heaviness; to like freedom and refuse the bondage of responsibility; to like travel and different experiences; and to loathe the boredom of routine; to like things of an imaginary or illusory nature and to dislike things that are real or concrete; to like the touch and silhouette of things and to dislike the details, etc. These are the spiritual tendencies of sky spirits. When those spirits are weak in the body, then these inclinations become stronger because the person cannot stand the pressure of worldly life. If the physical condition is not well matched to the condition of internal spirits, the same inclination is also seen. Such a person risks the possibility of losing the balance of life."

The young one asked, "What are the earthly spirits like?"

The mentor answered, "Just the opposite. The earthly spirits grew up in one spot. They are used to not moving around; they are not afraid of being heavy or being associated with things of a heavy nature. They do not mind being tied to one thing or another. They do not like things of imaginary or illusory nature; they like things that are physical or real. They do not mind entering disputes. They do not mind arguing or fighting to win anything, even minor things to do with emotional territory. They like to have power to secure their own existence. They like money; the more money the better. They also like emotional security. They are selfish and cruel and will even deny all human relationships but exaggerate the importance of their own emotional needs, etc.

"With this foundation of an individual life, you face possible battles which develop from the natural conflict of sky and earth spirits within you. This has been reviewed in the preceding discussion. Externally, you face each person whose internal reality is the same as yours. All undeveloped people are too ready to become involved in conflict, which may develop into a fight or war. From this reality, spiritual condition and teaching is necessary for the attunement of one's human relationships.

"We cannot consider one side more important than the other. Also, at different stages of life, the balance is not always the same.   Poise in life is greater than any type of external education or religion."

The young one asked, "What is the principal guidance of life?"

The mentor smiled and answered, "The Ageless Teaching is totally aware of the numerous conflicts in life.   Thus, the Ageless One instructed us as follows:

"It is wise for people in public office and personal affairs to learn
to love but not possess
to give but not take
to do a job but not take credit for it
to render service, but not overcharge for it
to take what is disfavorable, and not argue about it.

On all occasions, remain moderate.
On occasions where balance can not be achieved,
*   practice yielding.*
Be soft and gentle in normal situations.
In a situation where all other choice is gone,
*   it is always right to keep the option*
*   to withdraw from conflict.*
In the long run, and on a bigger scale,
*   you will find yourself still*
*   on the winning side of life*
*   without the need to raise one's voice or finger."'*

The young one said, "It seems to me one must devote oneself to the wisdom of God to be the wise simpleton who practices indiscriminative mindedness.   There is no other choice."

The mentor smiled and said, "The religions of the masses know nothing of the necessary poise of life.   They developed something to increase the imbalance of life because they neglected their internal reality, but the material foundation of life is still half of the partnership.   Thus, religion is one-sided. In the end, all mass religions must be corrected by the individual.   One must turn away from the partial tendency of different types of spirits and learn to find a balance between what is spiritual and what is material.

"Typically, these religions: 1) cause separation among people, 2) manipulate the masses, 3) amass a great fortune for their own security, 4) become overly commercialized, 5) remain on the shallow surface of life, 6) function as a cosmetic for human life without working on its practical improvement, 7) offer tranquilizers to numb the feeling of life, 8) become pitfalls for the developing mind, 9) shift people's minds from finding a realistic solution to unrealistic imaginary consolations, 10) take advantage of people's ignorance and foolishness by adopting false creation, 11) gather people without offering a positive direction of society, because a healthy society cannot go together with artificial beliefs and superstition, 12) become a cover up for of spiritual weakness, 13) reduce the temporal suffering of people without giving back the natural healthy strength of life, but make people dependent upon an untruthful spiritual structure, 14) are supported by the masses without having guided the masses to their own spiritual center of life, 15) cheat the masses by useless rituals and inappropriate spiritual service, 16) become social monsters that are sources of negativity in human society.

"I will remember all of these large shortcomings," declared the young one.

The mentor smiled and said, "True and useful spiritual teaching respects natural life. The nature of life is universal nature itself. Natural spiritual life is the enjoyment of the infinite, where there are no more boundaries, only the fullness of freedom.

"When establishing a spiritual teaching in the human world, the first and most important thing is to teach people to respect their own lives; what they are, where they are, and how to live a decent life. If people lack this, they need to restore their respect for life.

"In other words, you first learn to respect life. Life is the expression of Godly energy. Life is the integration of all spirits and gods. The body is the temple. From this point, you need to learn to attune the mood of life; are you too tight, too nervous, or too serious? If you are, it is because there is too much fighting you need to do. Therefore, adjust yourself to be less tight, less nervous and less serious, because a good life cannot be carried out by being excessively tight, nervous or serious. If you are not relaxed, you need a retreat, a turning around. Then you can come back to life with a refreshed and readjusted mood which will serve your life better.

"Are you too loose in your life? Are you self-indulgent in your emotions? Do you wish to escape all the necessary duties of life? Do you think that life is unworthy? If you answer yes to these questions, you need stronger self-discipline. It is wrong to set up a self-designed hibernation for yourself with all kinds of 'ordeals.' This will lead you to lose the totality of your life strength. By ordeals I mean things such as negative fasting. Life itself is a school. Life itself is a system of education. Life needs to be learned more than anything. A good life can be self-achieved. A good life can be helped by apprenticeship with someone; your parents, uncle or teachers.

"Parents who escape the responsibility of tutoring their children in the real education of a livelihood may as well not have brought a life into this world. Even a good boss or employer should correctly and unselfishly guide and help all the people he employs."

When it came to this point, the young one looked for confirmation from the mentor by saying, "Then being correctly spiritual is living a balanced, well-poised life. Being spiritual also means being morally responsible without relying upon the discipline or restraint of any type of external force. Being spiritual is neither finding escape from worldly life nor being attached to physical expansion. Being spiritual is being spiritually centered within one's own life being and, at the same time, opening the broad access to the indescribable and undefinable infinite, which provides the power of life." The mentor confirmed his statements and the meeting was fruitfully accomplished.

Chapter 27

A Thousand Mile Trip Within One Step

In the next meeting, the mentor said to the young one, "Today you will go back early to your quarters and eat less. After finishing your evening practice, lay on your back to do breathing. Put a light covering over your body."

The young one responded, "That would be like making a suggestion to myself to go to sleep."

The mentor smiled and said, "Just go ahead and do as I said."

The young one obeyed. He felt nothing but slept all night long. He continued to experience the same deep sleep for a couple of nights, until one night when his active mind slid to one side and became inactive. In his sleep, he felt like a reflecting mirror was used by someone to shine upon the third eye of his forehead. He was irritated by the light.

He felt that the light came from the octagon, a symbol of spiritual protection carved on the wooden door of the cottages. Its eight sides formed an octahedron. The empty central space was inlaid with a round reflecting stone symbolizing the Tai Chi with its white and black sides. The whole symbol of the octahedron with the stone and energy symbols presents the highest spiritual power which comes from the integration of eight natural energies: sky, earth, water, fire, thunder, rain, wind and mountain.

At first, he felt that the light was shining on his forehead. The symbol seemed to keep turning around, but it could have been the slight dizzy feeling of the young one himself. The symbol turned around, alternately of light and then dark. Then he felt himself go out and travel through the center space of the octahedron. His personal motivation was to examine what had happened outside that became the source of light which had disturbed him or intentionally attracted him out of his hut. He felt he was guided somewhere, a place sort of like a terrace or a high mountain top. People with light bodies were there, in a gathering of inspiration, peace and gaiety.

On a higher stone cloud were three respectful figures sitting in a triangle. The center one was bathed in purple light, the left one in blue light and the right in yellow light. They were sitting peacefully and quietly. They were not introduced to the young one by anyone, because they were known by all. They were the leaders of the immortal world, representing the highest trinity: the pure origin, the subtle law and the subtle power.

Then, he saw that a baby was being carried into the gathering to be shown to everyone there. That was the happiest moment of the meeting and in his personal feeling.

However, after a while, the scene changed. He felt that he was in the stone chambers of the mentor. It seemed like he was holding a regular class meeting. They were alone.

Then, suddenly, he woke up. He could not sleep any more because of the vision of his dream. He was instructed by his teacher that it is okay to be awake at nighttime, but to remain without mental activity. That does not harm our energy. If you transfer the mind from the waking stage to engage in lots of thinking activity, that is called insomnia. By doing so, you create anxiety about going back to sleep. Then the internal disharmony becomes even more aggravated by mishandling.

When people of spiritual cultivation wake up during the night, they practice meditation or some other type of gentle spiritual practice. Some cultivators follow special instruction to do vigorous but rhythmic and methodic exercise which can conduct the sexual energy to be peaceful. This can usually be done by practicing sitting meditation in a relaxed sitting position. The sexual energy internally will start its own transformation. If you are wise, this simple sitting, straight and still, breathing evenly, is good enough to allow all benign spiritual phenomena to happen naturally. If nothing is seen or experienced, there is nothing wrong. If there are any obstacles to meditation, the wrong flow of energy is usually caused by the boss (the mind) being too smart and too active.

So the younger one was in a situation where he could not sleep. It was a time for him to experience the naturalness of his bodily life being. He had learned many practices which had specific purposes, so he was able to use them to fill the blank during this weak stage of nighttime.

When he saw his mentor several days later, he asked him about the phenomena in his dream. The mentor answered, "It was a vision, not an ordinary dream. The octagon symbol is for general spiritual people. In your case, you need to learn spiritual independence and rely on nothing else, but allow your spiritual energy to function freely."

The young one asked, "Why did I feel the light shining upon my third eye?"

"That really happened to you," answered the mentor, "It was done by the spirits outside of you who were carrying out the order to summon your soul to see the vision. The meaning of your vision needs no further interpretation.

"By the way, sometimes dreams are the activity of your soul in a different sphere of your bodily life or in a different sphere of nature. All young people go through a stage of intensified dreams which are related to their sexual energy. Remember that the strength of spiritual energy is truly related with the sexual energy of the person. This is why in immortal cultivation, sexual energy must not be damaged, but needs to be nurtured and sublimated. Then you see the light. For young people who do not damage their sexual energy, if everything is in order, the cultivation and achievement of immortality is as easy as eating a piece of cake. During the stage of youth, this energy needs to be conducted to be internal wisdom. A young person has not yet fulfilled any important, meaningful life creation. Why should a young person think about hurrying to give up this new house - the young, bodily life - and rush to the uncertainty of the next run of life.

The young one said, "You didn't finish telling me about the dream yet."

The mentor smiled and said, "I have lots to tell you. Because a strong dream vision is connected with one's sexual energy generation, sometimes you are helped by the light which causes sexual energy sublimation, then you see the respected one or the spiritual model you respect in your vision. When the sexual energy is pulled down to the organ, then the good vision is twisted into a useless dream. If one has too many useless but vivid dreams, they consume one's good energy. Therefore, it is important for an immortal student or any student who is learning to become spiritual to avoid two things:

1) Spiritual vision can be obtained by the sublimation of sexual energy, so it is important not to be carried away by your sexual energy, especially in the stage of trance-type of mind. If you do, you mix up your life experience and create stories.

It is a waste. If you truly insist upon believing that this dream or vision is true, then you only increase the loss.

2) You already know that spiritual immortality is new life. The worst disturbance to the spiritual being is old memories. Old memories, good or bad, begin a chain of uncontrolled mental associations; this is particularly true when a person is kind of in a trance or stupor. Then new stories are created, your mind becomes further confused and you might truly believe that that is a valuable spiritual experience. It could not be further from the truth.

"So in immortal spiritual cultivation or general spiritual cultivation for spiritual health, mental health and physical health, it is important to reach dreamless sleep, which means you might have light dreams, but you have no memory of them. Such light dreams do not affect your mental health, just like a child does not try to establish what is real and what is unreal. The experience of dreams is at the level of false form.

"The other important thing is to be thoughtless. It means you might have your thoughts, but the thoughts do not draw any specific attention. They do not create a disturbance to your spiritual center.

"The new spiritual life is disassociated from the old mind which is deeply associated with life experience at the level of form. These two things, dreamless sleep and no disturbing thought are fundamental and essential. Other small techniques may have a certain value, but they are not as fundamental as these two. The experience of people who achieved themselves by their spiritual cultivation is that achieving immortality is not hard. To appease disturbance from the mind is truly hard.

"For most people, the mind has acted as the authority of life for too long. To learn spiritually is to put the spiritual essence back on the throne of life and allow the natural flow to become the creation for you. If you achieve this, whether you live with the body or without the body, you become the rider of universal energy waves; this enjoyment is much greater than that of those who are struggling between the two peaks of the energy waves in their earthly life experience. If you achieve centeredness, you do not need to go anywhere. A thousand mile trip is within reach of your first step."

Chapter 28

Harmony With the Subtle Law

Since the last meeting, the young one realized that if you wish to do right, you need to have the right energy. Skepticism is a stage of experimentation before reaching the truthful knowledge of energy. The truthful knowledge of immortality has already been completed by the ancient achieved ones; any experimental attempt to rediscover it is too costly to any individual and would only be a waste of life. It is important, therefore, in immortal learning to first attain truthful knowledge of all aspects of immortality. Proof can then be gathered in the step-by-step progress of one's own spiritual cultivation.

The young man asked his mentor, "What do people do when they have achieved the practice of spiritual immortality, but have not yet exuviated from the body?"

The mentor replied, "There are three ways to fulfill or achieve immortal power. The first is to become a hermit; a small hermit stays in the mountains. A great hermit keeps a low profile in an ordinary occupation, living an ordinary life and practicing moderation and offering service in an unnoticeable way that cannot be known or recognized. In their whole lifetime, they keep quiet and do not talk about spiritual immortality. This one will achieve highly and maintain a childlike heart by playing the simpleton who knows nothing about anything. Because he practices indiscriminative mindedness, he does not extend himself into what is good and bad or right and wrong in the human world. Such people shield themselves from things that would damage their sensitivity. They do not think they need to put themselves in any position other than one of service given by living an immortal life.

"The second way is that of people who have achieved spiritual power. They practice spiritual knighthood or spiritual swordsmanship. If they have a chance, they assist victims of evil who are caught in a helpless situation. They extend their spiritual power to help a good person or to punish a wrongdoer without asking anything in return or looking for recognition. If an evil force is known by a spiritual knight, even if the evil one has the protection of thousands of guards, his head can be taken by the knight as easily as taking something out of his pocket. However, warning is always given first. Some spiritual knights travel in general society looking for opportunities to render their knight service. Others live in the world for six months and then return to live in their mountain huts for another six months.

"These people have sharp tempers and strong feelings toward what is good and bad, right and evil. The punishment they mete out is quick and thorough, but no mistakes are made, because they take careful measure of the truth of a situation. These people first achieved themselves highly in martial arts and swordsmanship. Some of them were taught by their teachers to accomplish their virtuous fulfillment for a length of years, then they become hermits and live an ordinary life.

"The third way is that of people who attain healing power or the power of foreknowledge as they achieve immortal power. They either become healers, fortune tellers or both. Those are not highly positioned professions, but real service can be given to the right people.

"The above three ways are general descriptions of the lifestyle of those who achieve immortal power. Occasionally there are spiritual heroes who become historically influential people. For example, about 450 years ago, there was a man who achieved immortal power who could be considered a third generation student of the Ageless Master. He helped a king restore dominion over his own land after it had been taken by a neighboring king. He declined any reward and became a hermit who engaged in commerce, shipping goods from one place and selling them at another. Many times he amassed great amounts of money, which he kept giving away to poor people.

"Surely history has recorded many spiritually achieved people who made special achievements in critical political situations or were great healers or great advisors who rendered important service. If they were advisors, they always chose the right people and the right reasons for their giving help. In all, the one who will be the greatest is the one who has his own real spiritual achievement but is still willing to go to the ignorant masses to teach them good behavior and a good life. However, that is like using one's body to feed a pack of beasts."

The young one said with great courage, "I know that is my choice."

After several moments of silence, the boy asked, "May I have your confirmation of the value and meaning of going to the masses to teach?"

The mentor said, "I have mentioned that culturally, spirituality needs to be somewhat externalized as has been done by all religions in different times and places. Because individual and universal spiritual energy is subtle and formless, a certain approach is made through pictures, sculpture, temples, books and all types of religious practices which give form to the unformable for developing people. Otherwise, they do not know there is an important subtle root to individual subtle reality. Unfortunately, those cultural and religious creations do not convey the subtle message. Instead, they create prejudice and separation among people."

The young one then asked, "Then, you are saying that personal spiritual cultivation is still important."

The mentor replied, "That is true, and this is why I point out the importance of self cultivation and self-discipline.

"All generations have testified to the truth of the need for spiritual self cultivation. The spiritual development of achieved ones depends upon spiritual cultivation, especially for immortal achievement. All masters were once students. Most masters were tested for a long time before their teachers really gave them important instruction. Yet even if important instruction is given, the determination of the person to achieve oneself must be unshakable. Even so, that person still needs to accomplish each step in the right order to receive the true achievement. Other immortals may receive no direct test, but the many years of unyielding, disappointing search often results in the fulfillment or good answer to their test.

"Spiritual immortality is not something that can be inherited or bestowed: if you are the son of the king, you are higher than all others and are assured of receiving the throne at a certain time. In spiritual learning, without going through the learning process of cultivation, there will be no guaranteed achievement.

"General religions present the spiritual condition of their promoters as having a special purpose and good intention. Religions are the externalized spiritual knowledge of their promoter. Sometimes they lack accuracy or the promoters set up an overly rigid teaching or model. Frequently, religions create bias or dependence because their followers do not do anything by themselves. A person who joins them only becomes controlled by the leaders.

"People of spiritual interest oftentimes go to the wilderness and travel through several countries. Even with their special spiritual quality, they still need to learn, to be trained and to have their own personal achievement. Being a son or a daughter of a sage does not mean that you do not need to learn or have achievement through your own self-cultivation.

"Religions create bias and discrimination. Yet, once you ascend to the immortal world (kingdom), you give help indiscriminatively. You listen to and answer people's prayers no matter what religion they belong to and regardless of whether they are a believer or a non-believer. The Ageless Teacher has given an important message: 'Although the Heavenly Way is not partial to anyone, it first reaches sincere people.'

"From what he said, we know that even if people do not engage in serious cultivation to achieve themselves, moral health is the key to reach the Heavenly Way. Yet it is still necessary that the masses be taught. This is why all achieved ones must offer themselves to do some amount of service to the masses.

"Spiritually responsible people know how to engage in spiritual self-discipline and self-cultivation in order to develop themselves spiritually. People who are willing to make changes by sacrificing some of their unhealthy actions or habits can learn from people of spiritual discipline. It is like people who are ill who need a doctor. Spiritual teaching is also spiritual healing."

Then the young man asked, "What about the achieved ones who have already left their bodies?"

"As I described before, they become immortal spirits who respond to prayers indiscriminately," responded his teacher. "Their spiritual response is not according to race, gender, age, religion position, etc. of the person who requests it, but to the spiritual sincerity. However, most people have too much blockage from their intellectual attitudes which become spiritual obstacles to sincerity, thus they cannot reach the immortal spirits. Yet most people's sincerity still has enough power to remove even the biggest blockages and spiritual contaminants such as hatred, prejudice, etc.

"Only those who fulfill their spiritual duty as immortal beings have an opportunity to continue their spiritual evolution without needing to be reborn in the world after a certain number of years. Otherwise, there is the need to maintain the life energy by re-incarnation. However, if an immortal being is reborn again, because of staying in the womb of an ordinary or even an extraordinary woman, the immortal might lose his sense of purpose and desire to strengthen his spiritual position and achievement. Especially after being born into the world, the life experience is so vastly different that it is difficult for many immortals to remember why they were born. I am not sure if they still know clearly or remember who they were, what they were, the purpose of their new life or what they need to do in order to achieve themselves again and better. Perhaps one needs to learn everything again. It is also necessary that the right teaching and the right teacher are available in the new lifetime.

"The great immortals recognize that life is just like the universe itself. It keeps moving harmoniously in concordance with the subtle law. Keep moving harmoniously in concordance with the subtle law of individual life, because each individual life is a small universe."

Chapter 29

Higher Achievement is Known
to the One Close to It

At this time, the young one grew tremendously in his learning about the spiritual truth, and from his own practice he truly proved that through spiritual cultivation or meditation, sexual energy can be transformed into light energy. At the beginning, the light was just like a beam, which he saw several times on the ground in his dark room at night. At first, he mistook it for some moonlight coming into the room through a small hole in the wall or roof of the cottage, and then he tried to imagine that it was a piece of frost shining in the moonlight. Yet every time he tried to put his hand in the beam of light to block it from lighting the ground, he could not do it; the light stayed there, and he could not catch it on his hand. He consulted his mentor, who gave him some special instructions. He was to continue to live normally. He did not command the light to grow stronger but he continued to learn different spiritual practices.

One night, as he got up from the bed, he suddenly felt that he was enveloped by a strong golden light. He had received the instruction that during this moment he should just be relaxed and calm, and to gently gather his spiritual light back to be re-embodied safely within.

His mentor had told him that there was differing instruction from two schools about what to do next. One school taught that after you fully release the golden light, you gently put it back in the top of your head and conduct it down to the solar plexus, which is located around the spine approximately at the level of the stomach. Then you just need to live a normal life as described in the *Tao Teh Ching*. You do well to live in coherence with the inner nature, as the *Tao Teh Ching* says, so you do not need to do anything else. You do not even need to think about your longevity or anything else, because you have it. This is a once and for all achievement.

His mentor also told him that a different school suggests that one, two or three days later, each night you conduct the golden light out of the body for short distance and each night send it out a little longer and farther. In a number of days, it can reach thousands of miles and go and come back in the time it takes to snap your fingers. It can gather information, examine a situation or become a healing power. To some people this power becomes merely instrumental practice. Yet if one overuses its special gift and does something against spiritual nature, then one falls. This is the Heavenly law.

The mentor also said that it is the precious guidance from the Ageless One to let the knowledge of something you need to know to come to you, it is better not to go searching for the knowledge. Even if the knowledge comes to you, you still need to live as ordinary a life as possible. Do not make use of such knowledge to take advantage of other lives that cannot achieve it. The Ageless One's own words were, "Make no use of wisdom. Remain as a dumb person, because on the level of the world, if you resort to the wisdom you have attained, it will create your reentrance into the energy net of yin and yang which will lead to conflict. It is so beautiful to be like a dummy who knows nothing and worries abut nothing, and totally dissolves oneself with heavenly light.

After experiencing all the important stages of spiritual proof and experience, the confidence of the young one was almost complete. Thus, he went to the mentor to request some other, deeper knowledge of spiritual immortality.

The young one asked, "Are there different levels of spiritual immortality?"

The mentor answered, "Throughout ancient times, the pursuit of spiritual achievement and immortality was known to have three levels. The first achievement is the earthly level. If a person, through diligent cultivation, even once gathers personal spiritual energy, and has good moral strength which expresses that he or she is moral enough to be known as a spiritual being, this person shall attain the earthly level of spiritual immortality.

"The second level is the heavenly level of spiritual immortality. The difference between the earthly and heavenly levels is that the earthly level of spiritual immortals are usually still active around the earth. Their activities are more or less still related to the world's dualistic pattern. The heavenly level of spiritual immortals are active above the Great Dipper and North Star. Their activities are expressions of universal spiritual vitality.

"All levels of spiritual immortality are achieved by the individual who for many lifetimes sets the personal life goal to break away from or be above physical law, and also to break out of the dualistic pattern of life and the individual mind. In other words, the cultivation aims to attain freedom from physical law and from the mental law of the relative sphere.

"Both the earthly and heavenly immortal spirits live in the relative sphere. However, the heavenly level of immortal spirit achieves greater than the earthly level when the person has dissolved the sense of self. That one exercises his spiritual energy to help others reach the possibility of breaking away from physical law and mental law to attain freedom.

"We speak about these things as laws, but they are not laws, they are patterns. For example, worldly things always have two sides. Everybody has to face conflicts which are brought about by the dualistic nature of life. Immortal achievement is a breakthrough from the stronger and heavier energy net to a lighter and less restraining one in which there are no obstacles.

"The heavenly level of immortal spirits are those who achieve themselves to be heavenly immortals. When in the world, they break away from the pattern of confrontation, conflict, different types of battles, war and engagements. Those people not only attain spiritual wholeness, but they also help others. Helping others makes them different from earthly immortal spirits.

"As I mentioned, after a good length of years, the earthly level of immortal spirits must come back to experience the same old pattern of worldly life and mentality. I do not know if the person can still achieve himself in the new opportunity.

"Heavenly spirits were achieved by teaching many people and helping them to dissolve and resolve the dualistic pattern of physical law and mental law. This is a higher level of spiritual immortality, which can also be directly called 'spiritual immortality,' or 'the spiritual level or Godly level of immortality.' Those who have achieved the Godly level put everything under their care. Those highly achieved ones are the subtle law. For them, there is nothing to call physical law or mental law. They can distinguish between different levels of natural beings, and they experience great smoothness and harmony between all levels of existence. That is the great achievement which is attained by great spiritual merit. It is achieved by someone who has been in the real world, working as a leader or just a worker. This is a dutiful person who benefits other lives. He or she lives like the heavenly level of immortal spirit, who sometimes forgets their achievement, but still helps other people.

"Teaching can help people spiritually. The high achievement of immortality comes from practical spiritual merit. Spiritual merit means you have been in a position of leadership or any position that brings lots of goodness and important help to worldly people and other lives. By this spiritual merit, Godly immortality is achieved. There is no law that binds you, because you are a person who has completely achieved freedom from physical law, mental law and spiritual law.

"The third type of spiritual immortality is to achieve the Immortality of the Integral Life. In this achievement, the achieved one practices no discrimination while in worldly life and makes no division in spiritual achievement. One works to achieve oneself regardless of whether he becomes an earthly or heavenly immortal, but does all the discipline of both levels. One learns not to create any special opportunity to do good, and one avoids all possible occasions that might result in doing bad or harm. One does not put one's mind over the spirit. One does not allow one's mind to project itself onto the net of the worldly pattern of life, which is full of contradiction. One dissolves the pattern of the mind which is marooned in worldly conflict. One will not sharpen one's senses or thoughts which express conflict and contradiction with the life nature.

"The Immortals of Integral Life join the immortality of the universal life. They do nothing against anything, but only offer to benefit all people. They continue the life of universal life; they are the life of the universe.

"This is the ancient classification of the three levels of spiritual achievement.

"Some immortal teachers added two additional levels. They included the ghost level and the human level. If a human individual is achieved to the extent that he or she can break away from or not be totally controlled by physical or mental law, and can exercise free choice by virtue of practical achievement, there is a certain amount of achievement and the ability to know the possibility for higher achievement. Such people still have the physical shape of life and will eventually experience death, which is part of physical law. This is why they are called human-level immortals. It is not a necessary level because all immortals must achieve themselves from the human level. The difference between being nature and supernature is the achievement of dissolving the low sphere of natural bondage.

"Truthfully, no human is immortal. The reason why there is a classification called human immortals is because some individuals are engaged in cultivation and are learning to challenge physical law. They wish to attain freedom, so they are students of the immortal realm. They create the possibility of achieving that special development.

"Beneath the human level of immortals is the ghost-level immortals. They are not capable of exercising much of an influence over human society. However, they have friends and relatives, and they do whatever they can to help people living in the world move toward a good direction. Worldly religions classify many levels of ghost spirits. Some of them are respected as 'holy ghosts.' In truth, they are the high level of ghosts of general human ancestors who wish to see positive progress in human society and in individuals. They are mostly interested in certain individuals to whom they are related. Those ghost immortals usually have a good opportunity to be reborn into the world with a spiritual inclination to achieve themselves in that lifetime. This is why we call them the ghost level of spiritual immortal. It is also unnecessary to name levels; basically, all are in one of two levels: those who attain spiritual achievement, and those of unachievement. The ghostly immortals are in the unachieved level; their inclination is to continue to relate to their own family and race."

The young one said, "It is easier for me to understand the simple classification of the three levels. Now, I would like to know another important fact. Is a person a single soul or single spirit? I mean, is there more than one?"

The mentor smiled and answered, "You are intuitively aware that there are a number of spirits which constitute the soul. There are three levels of spirits: the spirits of spiritual realm of the individual life, numerous chi spirits of the body, and the spirits of the mind. The number of spiritual and mental spirits that a person contains in one's soul at any time depends upon the person's ability to stay open and absorb the high spirits.   Thus, their number is not as fixed as is the number of physical spirits (chi spirits).

"There are also spiritual level spirits. This is the level of one's own personal god; it is the godly or divine energy in a person.   This energy is always respected by the other two levels, the body and mental spirits.

"A highly achieved divine immortal can be summoned by prayer. The spiritual response to the prayer cannot be accomplished by the main spirit of the divine immortal, but by associated spirits. God is one, but how does God respond to millions of people's prayers? It is like there is one torch which lights many unlit torches; then there are many torches giving light, but the light itself shines as one light.

"Another way of saying this is that there is only one moon in the sky, yet in each lake, pond and river you can see a moon. God responds to people's prayers in the same way. All universal spirits are part of the One.

"Also, an achieved being is not the achievement of a single being. The attainment is the achievement of many associated spiritual beings. It is the spiritual reality of the universe that when a spiritual agent responds to the world, that response is equal to having come from the wholeness of God, because in spiritual truth, one is all and all is one. That means that any one single spirit which responds to a prayer to God is God, yet the totality of universal spirits constitutes one God.

"Knowing the spiritual world is like tasting the water of the ocean; if you taste one drop of it, you have tasted the whole ocean. It means if you contact one spirit, you have contacted all spirits.   This expresses the undiscriminating universal spirituality. No wars or conflicts over spiritual differences have any meaning, although people can still express the spiritual world differently by their type of mentality.

"Sometimes a godly level immortal has the mission of helping the world and will reincarnate in the shape of physical life. However, it might not be his main spirit which reincarnates, but one of the bodily and mental spirits from a previous lifetime. It is to say, in the lifetime of an achieved person, some of the spirits like body spirits or mental spirits are not achieved as highly as the spiritual spirits in the subtle realm of the individual life. Thus they later receive the life opportunity for independent spiritual development. They had been apprenticed to the individual's spirits of the higher sphere. In this new life, the being recruits scattered spiritual energy in the world too. This is how lower level spirits achieve themselves. Although they were integrated with the main spirit of an achieved person, after exuviation they have the opportunity to be born in a life by themselves as the main soul, which is a promotion. Because they come from the same source - an achieved individual - you can still consider these spirits the reincarnation of someone, although it is not a totally accurate description. This is to say that independence is possible for all associated spirits.

"Practically, each individual body spirit or mental spirit is one spirit in a big spiritual company or order. Therefore, their reincarnation can be considered as the incarnation of someone, because the spiritual law is 'one is all and all is one.' There is no difference between one spirit and another; each is part of the spiritual self.

"From this fact, one can also know that even in one spiritual body, the level of evolution of each individual entity or agent is different. Some are higher and some are lower, but total achievement means that ascension or progress becomes possible.

"The higher level of spiritual immortals, the Immortals of the Integral Life, once achieved, are less known to people as individuals but are recognized as individuals who once lived in the world. The highest godly level of immortal spirits can hardly be recognized as having lived as a human person because they have achieved themselves above personality and individuality and have thus broken totally away from the dualistic, relative net of life. In the net, there is the existence of opposites of happiness and pain. On the dualistic level, if one does not feel tired, then one does not rest. If one does not feel hungry, then one does not feel satisfied eating a meal. This is all dualistic. Because of many years of cultivation, the highly achieved ones have broken away from the law of opposites which only knows happiness after suffering pain, and only knows the value of normalcy after suffering trouble. To them, happiness and joy are as natural as the essence of their beings.

"The more subtle and higher something is, the less knowable it is. The lower levels of subtlety can still connect with the world and be known. The existence of a higher level is known to the level next to it. However, the fulfillment and realization of reducing the importance of individuality and personal style is more important than all personal achievement. It does not create opportunities to be or do good. To let opportunity come to you means to live with nature. It is also suitable to give help without personally being pulled down to the level of the person who comes to you."

Chapter 30

All Life is One Life Spirit

The young man was close to accomplishing the important learning of immortality. Now, he quieted down himself to review what he had learned and how he had proved the immortal truth with the help of his mentor.

He truly knew that there are two types of spiritual projection. One type is the projection of the yin spirit, which is also called the yin sen. It operates primarily by the power of the mind. When a person projects the yin spirit, he has an experience and clear memory about what was experienced, but no power.

The other type of projection is the projection of the yang spirit, which is also called the yang sen. The yang spirit has power. It is just like a beam of light from a flashlight; it illuminates quickly. It can cover a whole range of space or it can be small and enter the tiniest hole. An immortal being, therefore, is flexible and has absolute freedom.

The first type of projection, that of yin sen or yin spirit, is too related with the suggestion of the mind to be influenced. It is similar to the scatteredness of one's pure energy. An artificial experience can be created by the subconscious mind, but that is not the fruit wanted by immortal cultivation.

In immortal cultivation, there are still differences between the yang sen and the intellectual spirit. The projection of the intellectual spirit carries the purpose of knowing. The projection of yang sen is to be the universal immortal life.

The young one was clear about this knowledge. He particularly bore in mind to have no fear of life and no worry. He remembered his mentor told him that the Ageless Master once said that to achieve oneself spiritually, calm yourself down. Keep very quiet. Then you can witness that all lives are pushing themselves to grow fast. When things reach their full growth, they suddenly return to the deep and indistinguishable root and all becomes quiet again. To preserve the root of life is to change from being active to being inactive. One is able to be active again. Changing from activity to inactivity and back again is the constant cycle of life. It is wise to know the cycle and to accept the return to a quiet life. The one who does not know this law of constant cyclical change and pushes against its normalcy shall find himself in danger.

Normalcy is valued in the teachings of the Ageless Master. The Ageless One taught the everlasting life of universal spiritual nature. The Ageless One taught to embrace the unity of Hun and Po within one's life. From this union, the nurturing of spirit produces new yang energy. Once this union is achieved, it can shape itself into the infant form of the spiritual person. It can even achieve a life that is independent from the spiritual person's physical life. This independent life is called the spiritual baby or spiritual angel.

Because the spiritual baby or angel is made of light energy, it moves fast. If we use the word 'projection' or 'traveling out' to describe the dispatch of this essence, we would say that it is the projection of the yang spirit. If the yang spirit responds to a specific spiritual function which ordinary spiritual energy cannot accomplish, projection is considered natural. The light experience is self-proof of one's spiritual cultivation. The Way to achieve oneself needs to be done step-by-step; this will fulfill one's immortal pursuit. Exuviation is the last moment when one gives up the bodily shell. It should be not a willful choice, but something that happens naturally. The independent new spiritual life is the spiritual fruit of cultivation. It is what is valued through all the trouble of life. Spiritual cultivation produces the higher essence to form the new spiritual life.

The young one asked his teacher, "Is the fruit or result of spiritual cultivation always the same?"

"No," was the reply of the mentor. "Some people who have achieved themselves partially only know the part that they have achieved. Although they have attained some capability, they could be pulled into worldly interests again. Some people, after achievement, immediately exuviate from the body. Because those spirits are achieved spirits, they then go on to fulfill their spiritual merit on the spiritual plane, especially by listening to people's prayers, responding to people's needs, giving help and curing people who are virtuous. They keep practicing such spiritual knighthood and respond whenever and wherever God is needed.

"In the universe, some people may not think there is a Heaven, but that is wrong. Even on Earth, some geographical locations have better energy than others. In some places, people attain better health, while in others, they have poor health. People who live in some locations become creative, and in others the inhabitants become lazy. This is not necessarily due to climate; there are energy reasons which were discovered by the practice of geomancy. Because the universe is so big, surely there is some place that has supportive energy. Is that not Heaven?"

The young one had discussed this with the father of the host family and received his instruction also. The father told him:

"In the universe, there is surely a Heaven with the exquisite energy to repair and rejuvenate souls. Heaven is a rich energy spot for achieved spirits. Early spirits were limited by their life experience, but after fulfilling extraordinary spiritual merit those earthly immortal spirits received the most precious invitation to go to Heaven by their refined energy.

"The immortal spirits who live on earth are still comparatively limited, so they must reincarnate again and use the new opportunity to be refreshed and recharged. Once they come back, their achievement may be totally lost during the nine months of pregnancy in the mother's womb, especially their mental achievement and good habits or good qualities. Universal immortals and heavenly immortals have much greater achievement."

Then the mentor wanted to know the young one's reaction, so he asked, "Is there a good purpose for projecting out one's yang sen?"

The young one replied, "As I learned from you, it must have a good purpose. It only needs to be projected once and then one can stop doing it. It does not need to be done again. I have proved the truth of yang sen for myself, so it is not a theory to me any more."

The mentor further queried, "You keep projecting it so that you can do good deeds, right?"

The young one answered his elder, "During the course of my physical lifetime, I can project again and again, and do good deeds, but I need to be careful, because then I am still partly worldly.

"Usually immortal practice can also lengthen one's physical life but that is not important. Some achieved masters do not choose to live long; they have the full freedom to choose whether to stay or go, but when choosing to go, one must know where to go afterwards. When I go[1] I must be the godly spirit who helps the world and helps people, then my achievement is much more than just living longer. Maintaining the physical being like a turtle, for hundreds of years, has no spiritual meaning."

Then the young man looked at his teacher and requested, "Can I project my spirit to visit you and observe the ancient books? I am asking your permission."

The teacher simply gave him further detailed instructions about what to do. He said, "I believe you have started practicing the projection. The spiritual baby is just like a human infant. It takes years to grow but it attains your full size much quicker than a physical baby. You have been instructed to project it step by step. On the first night, let it wander around only in your room. On the second night, you might let it go to the next room. On the third night, perhaps it could move around the whole cottage. Then maybe let it have a one or two mile range. That will be true and safe."

The young man asked, "How do I know I have really been somewhere with the yang sen? Maybe I will think I have been dreaming."

The teacher then instructed him to use a small piece of red cloth and make three flags from three triangles like tiny banners. The flag could be as small as one or two inches high with a stick on the side. "When you project yourself," instructed the teacher, "be sure to use the flag by inserting it at the farthest point you go."

The young one asked, "How do I carry them?"

The teacher smiled and said, "When you are out, you become the energy body, and what you wear is made by your thinking. These tiny flags are moved just by your thinking. It is accomplished as quickly as a snap of the fingers. Then, the next day when you are awake, go to look for it."

The young man followed this instruction step by step. When he felt the courage come to him, and he seemed to be strong, he decided to visit his teacher. He did not actually know how he got there, but after he thought about going to the

---

[1]"Die" is a word for ordinary people; for spiritually achieved ones, the end of physical life is a trip.

teacher's room, he was immediately there. The teacher greeted him with a big smile. Their communication was non-verbal, but everything was understood between them. The teacher guided him to roam around and look at many different types of books and scrolls, and he absorbed the book energy. One part was the collection of the Great Yu, one was of earlier human ancestors. Another part was the later collection in 'tadpole' characters of the early Chou Dynasty. He was especially interested in the system of tying knots in rope to express the stars and the connection in the form of different interesting figures. This knot-tying system served as the inspiration for the development of written characters.

When the young one went back to his cottage, he immediately thought, "Why don't I visit my family whom I have not seen for a long time?" This time, because he had total knowledge from his teacher's books, he knew that his spiritual body could travel a thousand miles in less than a second. Thus he projected his thought and was immediately home, but no one could see him. They were all very busy. He could not communicate with them, so he kissed his mother and father, and rubbed the backs of his brothers and then returned back to his body. He also felt enraged and sad that his people and their spiritual leaders promoted the culture of hypocrites.

From this trip, he also knew that his cousin, who had originally come on the voyage with him but had stayed in the south, had returned many years ago. He had already begun to work, asking people to repent their sins to help them cleanse their spiritual beings. Knowing this, the young man decided that it was time for him to return home and join the teaching work.

However, the next day, his host friend came around and said, "It is time for you to see our teacher." They walked down the path to the teacher's dwelling, but this time when they got to the stream, the friend took his hand and they both walked across the water together.

The teacher said, "I know it is time for you to return home. Before you go, I would like to tell you two things that you need to remember.

"One is that spiritual learning takes many years, but learning to be ordinary also takes years. After you reach the highest level of spiritual attainment, you need to come back to normalcy, which is the way of all ordinary people. A decent, ordinary life is the way to embody the high truth. It is not suitable to show off powers, unless it is for helping others. Would you do that?"

The young one promised that until the time came when he would release his power, he would be as ordinary as any other person.

"Second," the teacher said, "when you go back to the world, you must understand the ignorance of the masses. I need to prepare you for the danger. Take a stick and put an incantation on it. After 49 days of daily cultivation, in any bad circumstance, that stick will appear as your person, and will die for you. You do not really need to suffer any type of persecution or ill treatment from evil people or authorities. If you remember this, you will save the temple of your God and keep it safe so that you can reach immortality naturally.

"Also, during exuviation, keep your consciousness calm and clear. Do not be confused by what you see, because in the moment of your transformation you shall see many things. There will be good things and bad, friendly things and evil ones. Ignore all of them and maintain yourself in crystal clarity without confusing yourself. Those things you see are on a different level; they are illusions of the body or the mind. They should all be ignored. Be like a mother delivering a baby: concentrate only on the delivery without letting your attention drift away to anything else.

"When you meet the time of most difficulty, remember, face the East, the sun, and project yourself to the light. If the moment is critical, you can shout out with your whole strength and ride upon your own voice energy. This is another way that you can be out of a troubled body."

The young man received all of these important instructions. He bid farewell to his mentor with deep love, respect and emotion. However, he could not stay; according to the teaching and the practice, he must leave. Although he was still a young man, he must leave for his spiritual mission, for he was trained that power or no power, living in the world was the opportunity to fulfill one's natural virtue. Whether you could do a lot or a little, one needed to accomplish one's life decently and give help and convenience to other people when they are in need. He knew that the achievement of immortality depends upon how many great deeds were done toward others people.

Before he left, the boy mentioned to the teacher, "I shall always have deep appreciation for your teaching me this, because I clearly know my vision and the result of my type of life. This shall make me ready to courageously carry out my duty in this lifetime."

The mentor smiled. "All big events in the world," he said, "if they are healthy and beneficial, are always assisted by immortal spiritual beings. All great fulfillment is the fulfillment of the spiritual world. One is all, all is one; there is no discrimination. You can consider my teaching you as my spiritual fulfillment. What you learn and use to help other people is an extension of my spiritual fulfillment, but you must also know that I learned because I was taught by someone else. There is only one universal life; one is all, all is one.

"Do not worry, it is habitual for people who have lived in the world for many years to have a strong sense of individuality and neglect the spiritual level in which one is all and all is one. Before they come into the world, the life energy is forming. After they are born, the life energy is exhibited. You will be helped by the immortal spirits. Individually they are spirits, yet as a whole they are God."

Chapter 31

Conclusion:
The Evergreen Life

After he left his teacher, it was time to bid goodbye and express his deep gratitude to his host family and his friend. Both of them felt difficulty at parting from each other. The young one said, "I have never felt like an outsider in your family. Your mother is a great woman. I will always remember her as a virtuous model. She does not complain, but resolves important matters in tactful ways. Thus, she is usually quiet and attentive as she supports and assists your father in running the family and taking care of the business. This is like making Heaven appear in the family. Among your brother, sister and sister-in-law, no one competes with one another or becomes jealous of someone else, but each works to fulfill their duty and helps each other. Jobs are done by anyone who is capable or available and no one makes excuses for being incapable of doing anything. It seems that everything is done naturally and as a matter of course. I cannot find any other words to express my appreciation of the peaceful and happy life of your family."

The local friend said, "You can have a family like this of your own in the future."

The young one smiled and answered, "I never thought of that, but your family does impress me greatly."

The quiet and benevolent father of the host family said to the young one, "In spiritual learning, there are lots of bypaths. One can never clearly know which way is the main road. One may need to spend many lifetimes in order to find the true spiritual teaching worth knowing because it serves the life correctly. A truly spiritually achieved one goes through three stages: first to search for and find the right teacher; second, to find friends who are equally achieved; and third, to enjoy one's own maturity and enlighten future searchers.

"There are many teachers who can increase a student's interest in the by paths of life and distract him from the main Way by encouraging the imbalanced inclinations of the student. There are still many other teachers who build the darkness of prejudice in the mind of a student. There are few teachers who pull the searchers' minds and hearts away from the tendency toward imbalance and help students return to their own center; that is a truthful teacher. When their teaching is not appreciated or accepted, teachers sometimes feel that they have thrown pearls before swine.

"In the world of spiritual promotion, if you sell artificial pearls, there are a lot of buyers. If you have the real thing, it is not necessary to attract the right 'buyers.' A few people can really distinguish false from true. I am not discouraging you from teaching the people of your homeland; I am merely telling you about the typical situation of the unhealthy world. The illness of human society will become worse and worse. The world definitely needs light."

The kind father continued speaking. "The human world is made of people," he said, "and people are dominated by the desires of the majority. If the majority of people have confused energy, it is a bad time for the world. Confused energy means lack of spiritual vision. We can reluctantly classify people as having different types of energy; people of light energy, people of heavy energy and people of confused energy.

"During good times, people of light energy take the lead. During bad times, people of heavy energy take the lead. In times of confused energy, there are only bad or confused leaders or no leaders at all. During such times, violence, brutality, disorder, social turmoil, war, social epidemics and disease dominate worldly life. People of sensitivity and responsibility should not cooperate with the downfall of the majority and spare no effort to clean up their own lives.

"The trend of the world is set by its leadership and the quality of the majority of people. People of light energy find that it is hard to argue or fight with heavy people, especially because people of light do not argue or fight as a principle in their lives. In their individual private lives, the people of light energy should absolutely avoid the confusion of the world, including confused sexual behavior such as homosexual and violent sex or combining sex with alcohol and drugs; avoid confused means of livelihood such business that would enhance the unhealthy condition of others, and especially avoid participating in the promotion of violence and brutality.

"God and Heaven are the subtle sphere of nature. They are not as easily observed as the physical sphere of nature. Most people have no knowledge about or totally ignore the subtle sphere which is internal within their own lives, thus, they cannot be expected to be deep enough to have the knowledge of God and Heaven. People can live without the concepts of God and Heaven because the divine reality is spiritual and internal rather than external and material, but one principle can be applied to each individual's life; if you do anything against your own nature or damage the natural environment, you invite punishment from the spirits of life and the practical sphere of life. Also, whatever you do that goes in the positive direction of health and the subtle sphere will help your life spirit and the practical sphere of your life.

"It is not easy to guide people to know the subtle truth of life. It is still more difficult to teach them how to achieve harmony among their body, mind and spirit of their own life. People of light energy tend to avoid having too much involvement with the confused culture of the human world. If one cannot creatively guide people away from a destructive future, at least one can maintain self-discipline and reduce one's involvement in the world's downfall."

The young one said, "I am grateful for the years of support that have allowed me to live with your divine family. I have learned greatly from all of you. I clearly see that people must recognize their personal spiritual obligation in a family. In a family, it is holy to be a father and to have the spiritual responsibility to take care of all family members and form the good character of the younger ones you bring into the world. They are the offspring of your own body and spirit, just as we are the spiritual offspring of God. To be a mother is also a holy position to take care of the whole family and nurture young spirits so they will move in a constructive direction. She is the one who nurtures and practices the holy duty of the universal mother in the family. Children also need to recognize their holy duty to learn from their parents; they should forgive their mistakes, assist them in difficulty and take care of them when they are older. To learn to live as a human person in whatever position or work is to fulfill the holiness of one's decent work, helpful profession or honest business. Those who become leaders or work for the government accomplish their holy duty by taking care of all people. Godly love is fulfilled by their devotion. The holy duty of a spiritual teacher is to help people recognize their holy duty in their personal lives, family life and in society. The divine light shines from inside out. The divine light of all people shines together to eliminate darkness in the world. A good foundation is made from such families and spiritual teachers. All people conjointly come together to build the brightness of the world."

The local friend said, "I would like to live in a community like the Ageless One described: 'The big kingdom is downstream where the waters converge; it remains receptive. The small kingdom is also receptive. The cooperation of the two types of energies is attained by being receptive. To be receptive is to accept the other. The big kingdom accepts the small kingdom; thus it absorbs the small kingdom. The small kingdom accepts the big kingdom; thus, it absorbs the big kingdom. Each accepts the other. The big kingdom fulfills the function of serving more people. The small kingdom fulfills cooperation and receives the protection of the big kingdom. Each attains what it needs. The bigger kingdom particularly needs to be receptive in order to earn cooperation."

His father commented, "Each individual is a kingdom with one's own independence and individual dignity. Thus, I was instructed that receptivity and cooperation are also the way to fulfill relationships with other people in a family, workplace or community. Cooperation is needed in all walks of life. Cooperation is attained by being receptive and accepting each other's differences. Being receptive and cooperative is how a man and a woman can build a good family life.

"By the same principle, all independent people can get along with one another. If they choose to live without having a family, then the community can be their extended family life. Some individuals live alone because they do not enjoy the life of family or have personal reasons such as spiritual cultivation and development.

"In any relationship, each person should do what he or she is good at. Each person also assists the other, thus each accomplishes the other as they work together or independently to help other people. In community life, one works for all others while at the same time taking care of one's growth."

The young one said, "I will remember what you have said and I will always remember your help."

The local friend said, "Before you leave, I would like you to meet a woman of spiritual nature who lives in one of our neighboring tribes. For years she has shared the feeling of supporting your spiritual learning. She lives an even more simple life and is a straight-mannered person."

The young one said, "I have seen many spiritual women here: your mother, sisters and sisters-in-law, plus the old women I have helped. They are all spiritual and have all been supportive in one way or another. They can all be teachers for other people. I did not know there was a particular woman who had helped me."

The local friend said, "She does not like to be mentioned. If you agree, this should be like an ordinary visit. You have visited neighboring tribes, so you know how much we lose by making our own lives more complicated. I enjoy visiting them. This woman, who is in her middle years, is different from other women. She sometimes plays music or sings to people. People who have listened to her felt enlightened. You have achieved yourself, but that is not why I suggest we see her."

The young one said, "I will gladly go with you. As your father says, one of spiritual achievement enjoys friends of spiritual achievement."

The friend said, "If you do not mind, she speaks mostly in her tribal language."

The young one said, "I know a few words, too."

They went to visit the tribal woman. She received them warmly and offered them warm milk tea. After enjoying the beverage, they chatted. The woman offered to play her simple musical instrument and sing a song about the story of a tribal hero to their delight. Only the local friend could understand the lyrics, but they both enjoyed the singing. The song was long, and the local friend only remembered a few lines:

Song of the Tribal Hero

1

Is this always true?
Great love is not appreciated.
Faithful friendly advice is considered offensive.
Great help is not understood.
Generous grace is not appreciated or accepted.

2

The people are enslaved by enemies.
Expecting a hero to come to rescue them,
    they wanted to change their luck.
They did not want to change
    their own deceiving habits.

3

The hero entered the city of sins.
He raised his sword high.
He shouted out,
    "All people are my brothers;
    only evil is the true enemy."

4

Disappointment changes into hatred.
Truth cannot go through ears of stone.
Righteousness is recognized as the enemy.
The evil ones kill the conscience.

5

Heavenly law is inescapable.
Self-created punishment is unavoidable.
Pride kills righteousness.
People of prejudice kill their own soul.

6

The war is being fought.
The battle has never been won.
The wish of the hero is not achieved.
Yet, clear direction has been given.

7

No war has ever been fought
    for what is truly right or truly wrong.
People fight for their own darkness.
They come together and invite the suicide of mankind.

8

The essence of life is peace and normalcy.
All creations of life move toward
        the enjoyment of one's pure nature.
External attraction causes one
        to become lost and fight.
The Way is to return to the true
        from what is untrue.

9

The Way is easy and smooth.
Life is simple and pure.
True achievement is internal;
        no one needs to conquer the world.

10

Lightning and thunder were active
        in the eastern sky,
        yet the rain came down on the western land.
Lions' roars quiet down the active wolves,
        yet were no warning to the deceivers of humankind.
Years come and years go.
People keep murmuring
        the name of a great immortal.

After singing, the woman brought out some dry food as a gift for the young one.

After they left, the young one was ready to go on his way. He had deepest gratitude for his friend. The young one had lots of friendship and love for all the years that he had helped him across the water.

"Do not worry," said the local friend, "I heard our teacher say that maybe in several years we will meet again." The young man could not respond because he did not know what that meant. Then he asked his friend, "You have been here so long with the teacher. What else did the teacher teach you, or what did he teach you differently from me?"

His friend responded, "My own understanding of the worldly mission of all young teachers is that our spiritual work is to carry the light of God to people who have not completely overcome their animal nature.

"It is easy to be a false prophet and enjoy prosperity. It is hard to be a true prophet and suffer difficulty.

"A true prophet is one who has achieved liberation from personal spiritual confusion, contorted vision, illusory vision and spiritual weakness. Surely, he is not a model of egomania, monomania, conquering-mania or the mania of creating dependency in order to enslave people.

"As for my personal cultivation, I am working upon living up to the six questions set up by the Ageless One. They are:

1. Can you embrace spiritual unity and guide the bodily life toward complete integration of the opposing spiritual energies, Hun and Po?

2. Can you nurture the budding energy of a newborn baby to be your goal in life?

3. Can you clear the distortion and confusion of your spiritual focus to become spotless?

4. Can you love your life and the lives of other people, and not use your mind to govern or disturb the healthy natural life condition of yourself and other people?

5. Can you be brave in the face of big changes, such as life and death?

6. Can you keep crystal clear without allowing the mind to create clouds and smoke?

"This is what our teacher shared with me. About you, our teacher said that you have all the qualities to be a high God. Your growth is different from mine. As I see it, you have a better opportunity; you might learn to not take the world too seriously."

The young man asked, "What does that mean?"

"In our learning, everybody knows that in life there is nothing worth dying for, and there also is nothing worth living for. I have learned to be prudent in everyday life by avoiding slipping to one side or other. If you can remember that, maybe you can also live like me. If you do so, you shall enjoy more from your life. However, anytime you need help, it seems that the teacher will send me to you. Farewell now, friend."

This is how the young man ended his formal learning. Then he started on his way home.

Full of spiritual energy, after some time he returned to his homeland. He started to heal and teach people and pushed himself to correct a world of hypocrisy and swindling. In a short three years, the respectful young life which carried the conscience of mankind was nailed to a cross by the force of darkness. He was too earnest to use magic to help himself and escape death. Before the time his body needed to give up its spirit, someone in the crowd offered him a drink to quench his thirst. It was wine which had been boiled with an herb called the 'flower of drunken sheep' which was used to make a person unconscious for three days. This would have saved him the pain of the external injuries and keep the soul from leaving the body. However, the young teacher refused to drink the beverage which numbed one's feeling because he wanted to be fully conscious at the time of death.

Afterwards, a man in the crowd kept trying to attract the attention of the young teacher who was nailed to the cross by yelling profanities to disguise his real relationship from the persecutors. The young one finally recognized him as someone of great friendly affection from the mountain land thousands of miles away. He had come to rescue the young one. After the young one recognized his friend, he yelled for something to drink. This time, his friend gave him a less potent mixture of wine vinegar boiled with the same herb on a sponge, the only way the drink could be given. The young teacher took some of it for his thirst and then there was no more reaction from him.

A year later, the two young friends lived in the northern part of the southern land. They taught the correspondence of the sun and moon to people and fulfilled the promise that they had given to the wild sage to teach others. The young one married and became a hermit there to enjoy the universal divine life in simplicity without social glamour. He practiced carpentry to support the life of his family. This is the end of the story, with the story teller's comment:

The evil force is like a poisonous flower
     which gives its dazzling colors.
Yet it enjoys only momentary glory.
Moral strength is lonely
     and attracts no admiration.
Like the pine and the cypress in the mountains,
     moral strength remains evergreen all the time.

Afterword

It is a great joy to work with those who value their own life as a great religion by uniting their intellect with their spirit as well as supporting the spiritual integration of East and West and live the immortal life beyond arguments and quarrels.

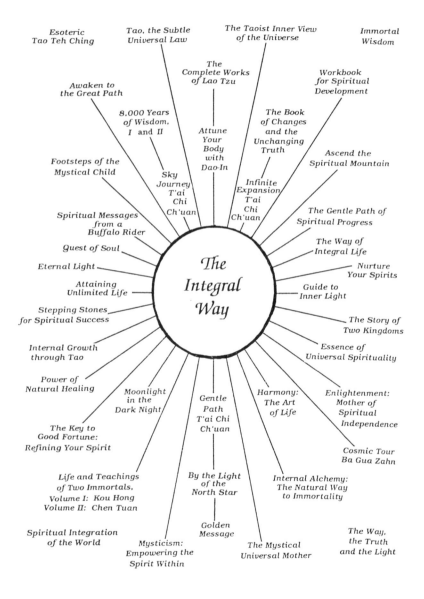

Esoteric
Tao Teh Ching

Tao, the Subtle
Universal Law

The Taoist Inner View
of the Universe

Immortal
Wisdom

The
Complete Works
of Lao Tzu

Awaken to
the Great Path

Workbook
for Spiritual
Development

8,000 Years
of Wisdom,
I and II

The Book
of Changes
and the
Unchanging
Truth

Attune
Your
Body
with
Dao-In

Footsteps of the
Mystical Child

Ascend the
Spiritual Mountain

Sky
Journey
T'ai
Chi
Ch'uan

Infinite
Expansion
T'ai
Chi
Ch'uan

Spiritual Messages
from a
Buffalo Rider

The Gentle Path of
Spiritual Progress

Quest of Soul

The Way of
Integral Life

Eternal Light

The
Integral
Way

Nurture
Your Spirits

Attaining
Unlimited Life

Guide to
Inner Light

Stepping Stones
for Spiritual Success

The Story of
Two Kingdoms

Internal Growth
through Tao

Essence of
Universal Spirituality

Power of
Natural Healing

Moonlight
in the
Dark Night

Gentle
Path
T'ai Chi
Ch'uan

Harmony:
The Art
of Life

Enlightenment:
Mother of
Spiritual
Independence

The Key to
Good Fortune:
Refining Your Spirit

Cosmic Tour
Ba Gua Zahn

Life and Teachings
of Two Immortals,
Volume I: Kou Hong
Volume II: Chen Tuan

By the Light
of the
North Star

Internal Alchemy:
The Natural Way
to Immortality

Spiritual Integration
of the World

Golden
Message

The Way,
the Truth
and the Light

Mysticism:
Empowering the
Spirit Within

The Mystical
Universal Mother

This list is according to date of publication, and offers a way to study Master Ni's work in order of his spiritual revelation.

1979:   *The Complete Works of Lao Tzu*
        The Taoist Inner View of the Universe
        Tao, the Subtle Universal Law
1983:   *The Book of Changes and the Unchanging Truth*
        8,000 Years of Wisdom, I
        8,000 Years of Wisdom, II
1984:   *Workbook for Spiritual Development*
1985:   *The Uncharted Voyage Toward the Subtle Light* (reprinted as
            Awaken to the Great Path and
            Ascend the Spiritual Mountain)
1986:   *Footsteps of the Mystical Child*
1987:   *The Gentle Path of Spiritual Progress*
        Spiritual Messages from a Buffalo Rider (originally
            part of *Gentle Path of Spiritual Progress*)
1989:   *The Way of Integral Life*
        Enlightenment: Mother of Spiritual Independence
        Attaining Unlimited Life
        The Story of Two Kingdoms
1990:   *Stepping Stones for Spiritual Success*
        Guide to Inner Light
        Essence of Universal Spirituality
1991:   *Internal Growth through Tao*
        Nurture Your Spirits
        Quest of Soul
        Power of Natural Healing
        Eternal Light
        The Key to Good Fortune: Refining Your Spirit
1992:   *Attune Your Body with Dao-In*
        Harmony: The Art of Life
        Moonlight in the Dark Night
        Life and Teachings of Two Immortals, Volume I: Kou Hong
        The Mystical Universal Mother
        Ageless Counsel for Modern Times
        Mysticism: Empowering the Spirit Within
        The Time is Now for a Better Life and Better World
1993:   *Internal Alchemy: The Natural Way to Immortality*
        Golden Message (by Daoshing and Maoshing Ni, based on
            the works of Master Ni, Hua-Ching)
        Esoteric Tao Teh Ching
        The Way, the Truth and the Light
        From Diversity to Unity: Spiritual Integration of the World
        Life and Teachings of Two Immortals, Volume II: Chen Tuan

In addition, the forthcoming books will be compiled from his lecturing and teaching service:

Gentle Path T'ai Chi Ch'uan
Sky Journey T'ai Chi Ch'uan
Infinite Expansion T'ai Chi Ch'uan
Cosmic Tour Ba Gua Zahn
Immortal Wisdom
By the Light of the North Star: Cultivating Your Spiritual Life
Seeing the Unseen: The Reality of Universal Spiritual Beings

BOOKS IN ENGLISH BY MASTER NI

The Time is Now for a Better Life and a Better World - *New Publication*
What is the purpose of achievement? Is it just self-preservation or is it to exercise whatever you have attained from your spiritual cultivation to serve the public by improving the life of the majority of people? Master Ni offers his profound vision of our modern day spiritual dilemma to help us awaken to combine our personal necessity with the better survival of universal society. 136 pages, Softcover, Stock No. BTIME, $10.95

The Way, the Truth and the Light - *New Publication!*
Of all teachings by famous worldly sages, the teaching of this highly exalted sage in this book expresses the Way closest to that of Lao Tzu. The genuine life of this young sage links the spiritual achievement of east and west which highlights the subtle truth. 232 pages, Softcover, Stock No. BLIGH, $14.95

Life and Teaching of Two Immortals, Volume 2: Chen Tuan - *New Publication!*
The second emperor of the Sung Dynasty entitled Master Chen Tuan "Master of Subtle Reality." Master Ni describes his life and cultivation and gives in-depth commentaries which provide teaching and insight into the achievement of this highly respected Master. 192 pages, Softcover, Stock No. BLIF2, $12.95

Esoteric Tao Teh Ching - *New Publication!*
Tao Teh Ching has great profundity in philosophy and spiritual meaning, and can be understood in many ways and on many levels. In this new previously unreleased edition, Master Ni gives instruction for spiritual practices, which includes in-depth information and important techniques for spiritual benefit. 192 pages, Softcover, Stock No. BESOT, $12.95

Golden Message - A Guide to Spiritual Life with Self-Study Program for Learning the Integral Way - *New Publication!*
This volume begins with a traditional treatise by Master Ni's sons about the general nature of spiritual learning and its application for human life and behavior. It is followed by a message from Master Ni and an outline of the Spiritual Self-Study Program and Correspondence Course of the College of Tao. 160 pages, Softcover, Stock No. BGOLD, $11.95

Internal Alchemy: The Natural Way to Immortality - *New Publication!*
Ancient spiritually achieved ones used alchemical terminology metaphorically for human internal energy transformation. Internal alchemy intends for an individual to transform one's emotion and lower energy to be higher energy and to find the unity of life in order to reach the divine immortality. 288 pages, Softcover, Stock No. BALCH, $15.95

Mysticism: Empowering the Spirit Within - *New Publication!*
For more than 8,000 years, mystical knowledge has been passed down by sages. Master Ni introduces spiritual knowledge of the developed ones which does not use the senses or machines like scientific knowledge, yet can know both the entirety of the universe and the spirits. 200 pages, Softcover, Stock No. BMYST2, $13.95

Life and Teaching of Two Immortals, Volume 1: Kou Hong - *New Publication!*
Master Kou Hong was an achieved Master, a healer in Traditional Chinese Medicine and a specialist in the art of refining medicines who was born in 363 A.D. He laid the foundation of later cultural development in China. 176 pages, Softcover, Stock No. BLIF1, $12.95.

Ageless Counsel for Modern Life - *New Publication!*
These sixty-four writings, originally illustrative commentaries on the *I Ching*, are meaningful and useful spiritual guidance on various topics to enrich your life. Master Ni's delightful poetry and some teachings of esoteric Taoism can be found here as well. 256 pages, Softcover, Stock No. BAGEL, $15.95.

The Mystical Universal Mother
An understanding of both masculine and feminine energies are crucial to understanding oneself, in particular for people moving to higher spiritual evolution. Master Ni focuses upon the feminine through the examples of some ancient and modern women. 240 pages, Softcover, Stock No. BMYST, $14.95

Moonlight in the Dark Night
To attain inner clarity and freedom of the soul, you have to control your emotions. This book contains wisdom on balancing the emotions, including balancing love relationships, so that spiritual achievement becomes possible. 168 pages, Softcover, Stock No. BMOON, $12.95

Harmony - The Art of Life
Harmony occurs when two different things find the point at which they can link together. Master Ni shares valuable spiritual understanding and insight about the ability to bring harmony within one's own self, one's relationships and the world. 208 pages, Softcover, Stock No. BHARM, $14.95

Attune Your Body with Dao-In
The ancients discovered that Dao-In exercises solved problems of stagnant energy, increased their health and lengthened their years. The exercises are also used as practical support for cultivation and higher achievements of spiritual immortality. 144 pages, Softcover with photographs, Stock No. BDAOI, $14.95 Also on VHS, Stock No. VDAOI, $39.95

The Key to Good Fortune: Refining Your Spirit
Straighten Your Way *(Tai Shan Kan Yin Pien)* and The Silent Way of Blessing *(Yin Chia Wen)* are the main guidance for a mature, healthy life. Spiritual improvement can be an integral part of realizing a Heavenly life on earth. 144 pages, Softcover, Stock No. BKEYT, $12.95

Eternal Light
Master Ni presents the life and teachings of his father, Grandmaster Ni, Yo San, who was a spiritually achieved person, healer and teacher, and a source of inspiration to Master Ni. Some deeper teachings and understandings on living a spiritual life and higher achievement are given. 208 pages, Softcover, Stock No. BETER, $14.95

Quest of Soul
Master Ni addresses many concepts about the soul such as saving the soul, improving the soul's quality, the free soul, what happens at death and the universal soul. He guides and

inspires the reader into deeper self-knowledge and to move forward to increase personal happiness and spiritual depth. 152 pages, Softcover, Stock No. BQUES, $11.95

Nurture Your Spirits
Master Ni breaks some spiritual prohibitions and presents the spiritual truth he has studied and proven. This truth may help you develop and nurture your own spirits which are the truthful internal foundation of your life being. 176 pages, Softcover, Stock No. BNURT, $12.95

Internal Growth through Tao
Master Ni teaches the more subtle, much deeper sphere of the reality of life that is above the shallow sphere of external achievement. He also clears the confusion caused by some spiritual teachings and guides you in the direction of developing spiritually by growing internally. 208 pages, Softcover, Stock No. BINTE, $13.95

Power of Natural Healing
Master Ni discusses the natural capability of self-healing, information and practices which can assist any treatment method and presents methods of cultivation which promote a healthy life, longevity and spiritual achievement. 230 pages, Softcover, Stock No. BHEAL, $14.95

Essence of Universal Spirituality
In this volume, as an open-minded learner and achieved teacher of universal spirituality, Master Ni examines and discusses all levels and topics of religious and spiritual teaching to help you understand the ultimate truth and enjoy the achievement of all religions without becoming confused by them. 304 pages, Softcover, Stock No. BESSE, $19.95

Guide to Inner Light
Drawing inspiration from the experience of the ancient achieved ones, modern people looking for the true source and meaning of life can find great teachings to direct and benefit them. The invaluable ancient development can teach us to reach the attainable spiritual truth and point the way to the Inner Light. 192 pages, Softcover, Stock No. BGUID, $12.95

Stepping Stones for Spiritual Success
In this volume, Master Ni has taken the best of the traditional teachings and put them into contemporary language to make them more relevant to our time, culture and lives. 160 pages, Softcover, Stock No. BSTEP, $12.95.

The Complete Works of Lao Tzu
The *Tao Teh Ching* is one of the most widely translated and cherished works of literature. Its timeless wisdom provides a bridge to the subtle spiritual truth and aids harmonious and peaceful living. Also included is the *Hua Hu Ching*, a later work of Lao Tzu which was lost to the general public for a thousand years. 212 pages, Softcover, Stock No. BCOMP, $12.95

The Book of Changes and the Unchanging Truth
The legendary classic *I Ching* is recognized as the first written book of wisdom. Leaders and sages throughout history have consulted it as a trusted advisor which reveals the appropriate action in any circumstance. Includes over 200 pages of background material on natural energy cycles, instruction and commentaries. 669 pages, Stock No. BBOOK, Hardcover, $35.00

The Story of Two Kingdoms
This volume is the metaphoric tale of the conflict between the Kingdoms of Light and Darkness. Through this unique story, Master Ni transmits esoteric teachings of Taoism which have been carefully guarded secrets for over 5,000 years. This book is for those who are serious in achieving high spiritual goals. 122 pages, Stock No. BSTOR, Hardcover, $14.50

The Way of Integral Life
This book includes practical and applicable suggestions for daily life, philosophical thought, esoteric insight and guidelines for those aspiring to serve the world. The ancient sages' achievement can assist the growth of your own wisdom and balanced, reasonable life. 320 pages, Softcover, Stock No. BWAYS, $14.00. Hardcover, Stock No. BWAYH, $20.00.

Enlightenment: Mother of Spiritual Independence
The inspiring story and teachings of Master Hui Neng, the father of Zen Buddhism and Sixth Patriarch of the Buddhist tradition, highlight this volume. Hui Neng was a person of ordinary birth, intellectually unsophisticated, who achieved himself to become a spiritual leader. 264 pages, Softcover, Stock No. BENLS, $12.50 Hardcover, Stock No. BENLH, $22.00.

Attaining Unlimited Life
Chuang Tzu was perhaps the greatest philosopher and master of Tao. He touches the organic nature of human life more deeply and directly than do other great teachers. This volume also includes questions by students and answers by Master Ni. 467 pages, Softcover, Stock No. BATTS $18.00; Hardcover, Stock No. BATTH, $25.00.

The Gentle Path of Spiritual Progress
This book offers a glimpse into the dialogues between a Master and his students. In a relaxed, open manner, Master Ni, Hua-Ching explains to his students the fundamental practices that are the keys to experiencing enlightenment in everyday life. 290 pages, Softcover, Stock No. BGENT, $12.95.

Spiritual Messages from a Buffalo Rider, A Man of Tao
Our buffalo nature rides on us, whereas an achieved person rides the buffalo. Master Ni gives much helpful knowledge to those who are interested in improving their lives and deepening their cultivation so they too can develop beyond their mundane beings. 242 pages, Softcover, Stock No. BSPIR, $12.95.

8,000 Years of Wisdom, Volume I and II
This two-volume set contains a wealth of practical, down-to-earth advice given by Master Ni over a five-year period. Drawing on his training in Traditional Chinese Medicine, Herbology and Acupuncture, Master Ni gives candid answers to questions on many topics. Volume I includes dietary guidance; 236 pages; Stock No. BWIS1 Volume II includes sex and pregnancy guidance; 241 pages; Stock No. BWIS2. Softcover, each volume $12.50

Awaken to the Great Path
Originally the first half of the *Uncharted Voyage Toward the Subtle Light*, this volume offers a clear and direct vision of the spiritual truth of life. It explains many of the subtle truths which are obvious to some but unapparent to others. The Great Path is not the unique teaching, but it can show the way to the integral spiritual truth in every useful level of life. 248 pages, Softcover, Stock No. BAWAK, $14.95

Ascend the Spiritual Mountain
Originally the second half of the *Uncharted Voyage Toward the Subtle Light*, this book offers further spiritual understanding with many invaluable practices which may help you integrate your spiritual self with your daily life. In deep truth, at different times and places, people still have only one teacher: the universal spiritual self itself. 216 pages, Softcover, Stock No. BASCE, $14.95

Footsteps of the Mystical Child
This book poses and answers such questions as: What is a soul? What is wisdom? What is spiritual evolution? to enable readers to open themselves to new realms of understanding and personal growth. Includes true examples about people's internal and external struggles on the path of self-development and spiritual evolution. 166 pages, Softcover, Stock No. BFOOT, $9.50

The Heavenly Way
A translation of the classic Tai Shan Kan Yin Pien (Straighten Your Way) and Yin Chia Wen (The Silent Way of Blessing). The treatises in this booklet are the main guidance for a mature and healthy life. This truth can teach the perpetual Heavenly Way by which one reconnects oneself with the divine nature. 41 pages, Softcover, Stock No. BHEAV, $2.50

Workbook for Spiritual Development
This material summarizes thousands of years of traditional teachings and little-known practices for spiritual development. There are sections on ancient invocations, natural celibacy and postures for energy channeling. Master Ni explains basic attitudes and knowledge that supports spiritual practice. 240 pages, Softcover, Stock No. BWORK, $14.95

Poster of Master Lu
Color poster of Master Lu, Tung Ping (shown on cover of workbook), for use with the workbook or in one's shrine. 16" x 22"; Stock No. PMLTP. $10.95

The Taoist Inner View of the Universe
Master Ni has given all the opportunity to know the vast achievement of the ancient unspoiled mind and its transpiercing vision. This book offers a glimpse of the inner world and immortal realm known to achieved ones and makes it understandable for students aspiring to a more complete life. 218 pages, Softcover, Stock No. BTAOI, $14.95

Tao, the Subtle Universal Law
Most people are unaware that their thoughts and behavior evoke responses from the invisible net of universal energy. To lead a good stable life is to be aware of the universal subtle law in every moment of our lives. This book presents practical methods that have been successfully used for centuries to accomplish this. 165 pages, Softcover, Stock No. TAOS, $7.50

MATERIALS ON NATURAL HEALTH, ARTS AND SCIENCES

BOOKS

101 Vegetarian Delights - *New Publication!* by Lily Chuang and Cathy McNease
A vegetarian diet is a gentle way of life with both physical and spiritual benefits. The Oriental tradition provides helpful methods to assure that a vegetarian diet is well-balanced and nourishing. This book provides a variety of clear and precise recipes ranging from everyday nutrition to exotic and delicious feasts. 176 pages, Softcover, Stock No. B101V, $12.95

The Tao of Nutrition by Maoshing Ni, Ph.D., with Cathy McNease, B.S., M.H. - This book offers both a healing and a disease prevention system through eating habits. This volume contains 3 major sections: theories of Chinese nutrition and philosophy; descriptions of 100 common foods with energetic properties and therapeutic actions; and nutritional remedies for common ailments. 214 pages, Softcover, Stock No. BNUTR, $14.50

Chinese Vegetarian Delights by Lily Chuang
An extraordinary collection of recipes based on principles of traditional Chinese nutrition. For those who require restricted diets or who choose an optimal diet, this cookbook is a rare treasure. Meat, sugar, diary products and fried foods are excluded. 104 pages, Softcover, Stock No. BCHIV, $7.50

Chinese Herbology Made Easy - by Maoshing Ni, Ph.D.
This text provides an overview of Oriental medical theory, in-depth descriptions of each herb category, over 300 black and white photographs, extensive tables of individual herbs for easy reference and an index of pharmaceutical and Pin-Yin names. This book gives a clear, efficient focus to Chinese herbology. 202 pages, Softcover, Stock No. BCHIH, 14.50

Crane Style Chi Gong Book - By Daoshing Ni, Ph.D.
Chi Gong is a set of meditative exercises developed thousands of years ago in China and now practiced for healing purposes. It combines breathing techniques, body movements and mental imagery to guide the smooth flow of energy throughout the body. It may be used with or without the videotape. 55 pages. Stock No. BCRAN. Spiral-bound, $10.95

VIDEO TAPES

Attune Your Body with Dao-In (VHS) - by Master Ni. Dao-In is a series of movements traditionally used for conducting physical energy. The ancients discovered that Dao-In exercise solves problems of stagnant energy, increases health and lengthens one's years, providing support for cultivation and higher achievements of spiritual immortality. Stock No. VDAOI, VHS $39.95

T'ai Chi Ch'uan: An Appreciation (VHS) - by Master Ni.
Master Ni, Hua-Ching presents three styles of T'ai Chi handed down to him through generations of highly developed masters. "Gentle Path," "Sky Journey" and "Infinite Expansion" are presented uninterrupted in this unique videotape, set to music for observation and appreciation. Stock No. VAPPR. VHS 30 minutes $24.95

Crane Style Chi Gong (VHS) - by Dr. Daoshing Ni, Ph.D.
Chi Gong is a set of meditative exercises practiced for healing chronic diseases, strengthening the body and spiritual enlightenment. Correct and persistent practice will increase one's energy, relieve tension, improve concentration, release emotional stress and restore general well-being. 2 hours, Stock No. VCRAN. $39.95

Eight Treasures (VHS) - By Maoshing Ni, Ph.D.
These exercises help open blocks in your energy flow and strengthen your vitality. It is a complete exercise combining physical stretching, toning and energy-conducting movements coordinated with breathing. Patterned from nature, its 32 movements are an excellent foundation for T'ai Chi Ch'uan or martial arts. 1 hour, 45 minutes. Stock No. VEIGH. $39.95

T'ai Chi Ch'uan I & II (VHS) - By Maoshing Ni, Ph.D.
This exercise integrates the flow of physical movement with that of internal energy in the Taoist style of "Harmony," similar to the long form of Yang-style T'ai Chi Ch'uan. Tai Chi has been practiced for thousands of years to help both physical longevity and spiritual cultivation. 1 hour each. Each video tape $39.95. Order both for $69.95. Stock Nos: Part I, VTAI1; Part II, VTAI2; Set of two, VTAI3.

AUDIO CASSETTES

Invocations for Health, Longevity and Healing a Broken Heart - By Maoshing Ni, Ph.D.
This audio cassette guides the listener through a series of ancient invocations to channel and conduct one's own healing energy and vital force. "Thinking is louder than thunder. The mystical power which creates all miracles is your sincere practice of this principle." 30 minutes, Stock No. AINVO, $9.95

Stress Release with Chi Gong - By Maoshing Ni, Ph.D.
This audio cassette guides you through simple, ancient breathing exercises that enable you to release day-to-day stress and tension that are such a common cause of illness today. 30 minutes. Stock No. ACHIS. $9.95

Pain Management with Chi Gong - By Maoshing Ni, Ph.D.
Using easy visualization and deep-breathing techniques developed over thousands of years, this audio cassette offers methods for overcoming pain by invigorating your energy flow and unblocking obstructions that cause pain. 30 minutes, Stock No. ACHIP. $9.95

***Tao Teh Ching* Cassette Tapes**
This classic work of Lao Tzu has been recorded in this two-cassette set that is a companion to the book translated by Master Ni. Professionally recorded and read by Robert Rudelson. 120 minutes. Stock No. ATAOT. $12.95

Order Master Ni's book, *The Complete Works of Lao Tzu,* and *Tao Teh Ching* Cassette Tapes for only $23.00. Stock No. ABTAO.

How To Order

Name: _____

Address: _____

City: _____ State: _____ Zip: _____

Phone - Daytime: _____ Evening: _____

(We may telephone you if we have questions about your order.)

Qty.	Stock No.	Title/Description	Price Each	Total Price

Total amount for items ordered_____

Sales tax (CA residents only, 8-1/4%)_____

Shipping Charge (see below)_____

Total Amount Enclosed_____

Visa _____ Mastercard _____ Expiration Date _____

Card number:_____

Signature:_____

Shipping: Please give full street address or nearest crossroads. If shipping to more than one address, use separate shipping charges. Please allow 2 - 4 weeks for US delivery and 6 - 10 weeks for foreign surface mail.

By Mail: Complete this form with payment (US funds only, No Foreign Postal Money Orders, please) and mail to: Union of Tao and Man, 1314 Second St. #208, Santa Monica, CA 90401

Phone Orders: You may leave credit card orders anytime on our answering machine. Please speak clearly and remember to leave your full name and daytime phone number. Call (800) 578-9526 to order or (310) 576-1901 for information..

Shipping Charges:

Domestic Surface: First item $3.25, each additional, add $.50.
Canada Surface: First item $3.25, each additional, add $1.00.
Canada Air: First item $4.00, each additional, add $2.00
Foreign Surface: First Item $3.50, each additional, add $2.00.
Foreign Air: First item $12.00, each additional, add $7.00.

All foreign orders: Add 5% of your book total to shipping charges to cover insurance.

_____ Please send me your complete catalog.

Thank you for your order

Spiritual Study through the College of Tao

The College of Tao and the Union of Tao and Man were established formally in California in the 1970's. This tradition is a very old spiritual culture of mankind, holding long experience of human spiritual growth. Its central goal is to offer healthy spiritual education to all people of our society. This time-tested tradition values the spiritual development of each individual self and passes down its guidance and experience.

Master Ni carries his tradition from its country of origin to the west. He chooses to avoid making the mistake of old-style religions that have rigid establishments which resulted in fossilizing the delicacy of spiritual reality. He prefers to guide the teachings of his tradition as a school of no boundary rather than a religion with rigidity. Thus, the branches or centers of this Taoist school offer different programs of similar purpose. Each center extends its independent service, but all are unified in adopting Master Ni's work as the foundation of teaching to fulfill the mission of providing spiritual education to all people.

The centers offer their classes, teaching, guidance and practices on building the groundwork for cultivating a spiritually centered and well-balanced life. As a person obtains the correct knowledge with which to properly guide himself or herself, he or she can then become more skillful in handling the experiences of daily life. The assimilation of good guidance in one's practical life brings about different stages of spiritual development.

Any interested individual is welcome to join and learn to grow for yourself. Or you just might like to take a few classes in which you are interested. You might like to visit the center or take classes near where you live, or you may be interested in organizing a center or study group based on the model of existing centers. In that way, we all work together for the spiritual benefit of all people. We do not require any religious type of commitment.

The College of Tao also offers a Self-Study program based on Master Ni's books and videotapes. The course outline and details of how to participate are given in his book, *The Golden Message*. The Self-Study program gives people an opportunity to study the learning of Tao at their own speed, as a correspondence course, or for those who wish to study on their own or are too far from a center.

The learning is life. The development is yours. The connection of study may be helpful, useful and serviceable, directly to you.

- -

Mail to: Union of Tao and Man, 1314 Second Street #208, Santa Monica, CA 90401

_____ I wish to be put on the mailing list of the Union of Tao and Man to be notified of classes, educational activities and new publications.

Name:_____

Address:_____

City:_____State:_____Zip:_____

Herbs Used by Ancient Taoist Masters

The pursuit of everlasting youth or immortality throughout human history is an innate human desire. Long ago, Chinese esoteric Taoists went to the high mountains to contemplate nature, strengthen their bodies, empower their minds and develop their spirit. From their studies and cultivation, they gave China alchemy and chemistry, herbology and acupuncture, the I Ching, astrology, martial arts and T'ai Chi Ch'uan, Chi Gong and many other useful kinds of knowledge.

Most important, they handed down in secrecy methods for attaining longevity and spiritual immortality. There were different levels of approach; one was to use a collection of food herb formulas that were only available to highly achieved Taoist masters. They used these food herbs to increase energy and heighten vitality. This treasured collection of herbal formulas remained within the Ni family for centuries.

Now, through Traditions of Tao, the Ni family makes these foods available for you to use to assist the foundation of your own positive development. It is only with a strong foundation that expected results are produced from diligent cultivation.

As a further benefit, in concert with the Taoist principle of self-sufficiency, Traditions of Tao offers the food herbs along with the Union of Tao and Man's publications in a distribution opportunity for anyone serious about financial independence.

Send to: *Traditions of Tao*
1314 Second Street #208
Santa Monica, CA 90401

Please send me a Traditions of Tao brochure.

Name _____

Address _____

City _____ *State* _____ *Zip* _____

Phone (day) _____ *(night)* _____

Yo San University of Traditional Chinese Medicine

"Not just a medical career, but a life-time commitment to raising one's spiritual standard."

Thank you for your support and interest in our publications and services. It is by your patronage that we continue to offer you the practical knowledge and wisdom from this venerable Taoist tradition.

Because of your sustained interest in Taoism, in January 1989 we formed Yo San University of Traditional Chinese Medicine, a non-profit educational institution under the direction of founder Master Ni, Hua-Ching. Yo San University is the continuation of 38 generations of Ni family practitioners who handed down knowledge and wisdom from father to son. Its purpose is to train and graduate practitioners of the highest caliber in Traditional Chinese Medicine, which includes acupuncture, herbology and spiritual development.

We view Traditional Chinese Medicine as the application of spiritual development. Its foundation is the spiritual capability to know life, to diagnose a person's problem and how to cure it. We teach students how to care for themselves and other, emphasizing the integration of traditional knowledge and modern science. Yo San University offers a complete Master's degree program approved by the California State Department of Education that provides an excellent education in Traditional Chinese Medicine and meets all requirements for state licensure.

We invite you to inquire into our university for a creative and rewarding career as a holistic physician. Classes are also open to persons interested only in self-enrichment. For more information, please fill out the form below and send it to:

Yo San University
of Traditional Chinese Medicine
1314 Second Street
Santa Monica, CA 90401

☐ Please send me information on the Masters degree program in Traditional Chinese Medicine.

☐ Please send me information on health workshops and seminars.

☐ Please send me information on continuing education for acupuncturists and health professionals.

Name _____

Address_____

City_____State_____Zip_____

Phone(day)_____(evening)_____

Index of Some Topics

acupuncture 25, 27
Ageless Master 2, 3, 12, 32, 42, 46, 48-50, 52, 64, 70, 71, 73, 74, 75, 80, 85, 87, 88, 90, 93, 96-101, 131, 136, 163, 176, 188, 189
Ageless One 54, 74-76, 80, 82-86, 129, 134, 140, 151, 162, 168, 181, 189, 198, 202
alchemy 5
align your energy (practice) 55
angel 78, 81, 189
art 48, 89, 105, 164, 165
astral 115, 116
attitudes 161, 178
aura 4, 94, 156
awakening 3, 37, 59
baby 57, 58, 71, 93-95, 117, 144, 172, 189, 191, 193, 202
balance 13, 25, 49, 78, 79, 95, 96, 113, 125, 126, 150, 167, 168
bamboo 23, 26, 62, 108, 113
bandits 155
Big Dipper 102 (see also Great Dipper)
birth 52, 62-64, 76, 80, 94, 95, 104, 157
blessings 4, 80, 86
body spirit 185-186
Book of Changes 48, 52, 118
breathing 36, 52, 62, (practice) 64-66, 68, 127, 143, 164, 171, 172
bridge 36
calmness 124
cause and effect 123, 162
celibacy 27
centered 1, 21, 124, 170
centeredness 174
Chen 57
chi 40, 41, 56, 67, 107, 112, 130, 131, 144, 164, 171, 184, 185
chicken and the egg 77
childlike heart 143, 150, 175
ching 3, 48, 78, 95, 97, 109, 118, 119, 122, 144, 180
Chuang Tzu 129
clarity 42, 145, 193
composure 124
concentration 110
consciousness 193
constellations 102, 103
Correspondence of the Sun and Moon 164, 203
cousin 5, 127, 128, 192
crown 55, 159
cycle 65, 97, 102-105, 188
daily cycle (chart) 103
destiny 89, 136, 145, 147
devotion 105, 158, 197
diet 70
discipline 18, 28, 46, 59, 64, 72, 110, 125, 126, 145, 160, 170, 177, 178, 183, 197
doctor 25-27, 178
dream 4, 89, 111, 115, 116, 125-126, 172-174

earth energy 94
education 18, 93, 114, 147, 161, 168, 170
ego 83, 151
emotions 29, 38, 67, 70-72, 161, 170
enlightenment 41, 78-80, 129, 131, 132, 135, 159
ethics 78, 122
evolution 79, 94, 109, 137, 146, 179, 186
exercise 2, 18, 56, 65, 70, 120, 128, 172, 183, 184
exercises 127, 182
exuviation 113, 186, 189, 193
faith 29-35, 45, 71, 86, 91, 98, 121, 128-131, 159
fasting 164, 170
father iii, 4, 5, 29-31, 37, 52, 62, 63, 119, 156, 190, 192, 195, 196-199
fear 11-13, 19, 33, 43, 60, 62, 107, 108, 115, 149, 188
five elements 57, 61
five-to-one breathing (practice) 127
flexibility 16, 18, 72, 86
food 6, 23, 34, 65, 127, 156, 161, 164, 165, 201
fortune 27, 30, 33, 123, 147, 163, 169, 176
freedom 15, 36, 46, 94, 113, 133, 147, 167, 169, 182-184, 188, 190
geomancy 190
ghost 183, 184
Godly Way 74-76, 129
golden light (practice) 180
good and evil 145, 146, 148
Great Dipper 55, (practice) 56, 144, 181
Great Yu 63, 192
habits 15, 178, 190, 200
happiness 20, 94, 96, 129, 147, 186
harmony 10, 17, 49, 56, 93, 111, 121, 123, 126, 148, 175, 182, 197
healers 5, 34, 176
healing 23, 25, 27, 34, 40, 42, 44, 69, 176, 178, 181
Heavenly kingdom 89, 93, 101, 142
heavenly law 63, 181, 200
Heavenly Way 33, 74, 88, 178
herbs 22, 23, 34
honesty 90, 147
host 6, 29, 30, 34, 68, 74, 102, 190, 192, 195
Hun 108, 109, 111-113, 117, 121, 125, 126, 189, 202
Hun and Po 108, 113, 117, 121, 126, 189, 202
I Ching 3, 48, 78, 95, 118, 119, 122
immortal spirits 76, 77, 79, 127, 162, 164, 178, 179, 182, 186, 190, 194
immortality 1, 5, 20, 72, 86, 105-109, 111, 113, 144, 173, 174, 175, 177, 181-183, 188, 193, 194
immortals 1, 154, 177, 179, 181-184, 186, 190
incantation 24, 30, 31, 42, 43, 47, (practice) 54-56, 193
incense 26
infinity 144, 149, 162
inner light 12
inspiration 4, 15, 41, 74, 78, 159, 171, 192

Intake the Godly Golden Energy (practice) 143
Integral Way 8, 51, 53, 54
integration 51, 77, 94, 95, 106, 113, 115, 121,
    126, 145, 154, 166, 169, 171, 202
intuition 1, 30, 78, 88, 95, 114, 117, 130, 131, 134,
    135, 150
jing 144
karma 158-165
Kingdom of God 89, 90, 92, 95, 96, 140, 141, 148,
    153
law of yin and yang 124
leadership 1, 92, 95-97, 151, 162, 183, 196
light body 55, 117
longevity 56, 144, 180
lunar cycle 102
lunar energy 144
magic 19-22, 25, 27-34, 39-43, 58, 67, 68, 72,
    110, 156, 203
mantra 8
market 6, 22, 23, 26, 28, 29, 37-39, 43, 69, 118
Master 48-50, 96-101, 158-161
medicine 5, 34, 47
meditation 4, 52, 54, 55, 103, 126, 143, 159, 163,
    164, 172, 180
messenger(s) 4, 80
mirror 111, 171
moon 22, 102, 103, 105, 109, 119, (practice) 144,
    164, 165, 185, 203
Mu (practice) 54
music 72, 112, 139, 199
mystical mother 48, 49, 56
natural life 2, 12, 90, 121, 127, 138, 153, 161, 169,
    202
Niao 63
north star 144, 181
nothingness 42, 46, 54, 91
octagon 171, 172
organs 24, 25, 39, 40, 88, 106, 125, 134
perineum 55
persistence 51, 73
personality 16, 161, 186
planets 4, 103
po 108, 109, 111-113, 117, 121, 125, 126, 189,
    202
powers 3, 13, 19, 53, 56, 135, 193
prayer 13, 54, 147, 158, 185
prejudice 71, 149, 177, 179, 195, 200
process 15, 16, 33, 50, 65, 77, 92, 136, 177
projection 10, 40, 41, 55, 71, 79, 115-117, 188,
    189, 191
proverb 53
psychology 129
punishment 6, 76, 79, 100, 147, 176, 197, 200
purification 115
purity 47, 136, 141, 147
reason 9, 70, 153, 155, 156, 184
red baby 93-95
reincarnation 153, 161, 186
religions 8, 137, 148, 158-161, 166, 168, 169, 177,
    178, 184

retreat 74, 169
rock 61, 62, 117
school 53, 102, 170, 180
seclusion 64
self-cultivation 55, 58, 138, 178
self-discipline 145, 170, 177, 178, 197
self-healing 34
self-nature 7, 10, 16, 52
sen 56, 109, 137, 144, 188, 190, 191
sensitivity 4, 135, 175, 196
seven-day cycle 102
sex 56, 63, 141, 196
sexual energy 108, 109, 111, 113, 125, 172, 173,
    180
shadow 27, 61
shien 81
shrine 164
shuan 144
Shun 63, 159
simplicity 72, 115, 121, 147, 203
sin 63, 99, 122, 139
sincerity 5, 150, 178, 179
sky energy 94
sleep 21, 70, 115, 116, 171, 172, 174
solar cycle 65, 102, 103
solar energy 103, 143
Song of the Tribal Hero 199
spine 55, 180
spiritual baby 189, 191
spiritual center 44, 108, 138, 169, 174
stars 4, 55, 56, 77, 144, 159, 164, 192
stone head 133
stones 23, 27, 30, 110
subtle law 2, 3, 16, 49-51, 154, 172, 175, 179, 182
subtle light 154
subtle origin 82, 84, 85
sun 4, 9, 22, 61, 102, 103, 109, 118, 119, 143,
    144, 159, 164, 193, 203
sword 25, 149, 200
T'ai Chi 107, 131
Tai Chi 112, 130, 164, 171
talisman 26, 66
tan tien 54, 57
Tao Teh Ching iii, 97, 180
temple 5, 8, 43, 169, 193
thieves 103
tiger 11, 33, 66
tribal woman 199
Tzu 37, 65, 129
unity 49, 51, 110, 111, 149, 153, 189, 202
universal mother 50, 197
universal mystical source (practice) 57
vibration 40, 48, 54, 56, 89, 154
virtue 35, 75, 80, 146, 154, 183, 193
visualization 47
vitality 3, 57, 72, 93, 181
well-being iv, 10, 38, 59, 96
Wu (practice) 54, 56, 65
Yellow Calendar 102
Yi, Shi, Vi (practice) 57-58